Organized Criminal Terrorism

Organized Criminal Terrorism

An International Law and International Relations Perspective

By

Inmaculada Marrero Rocha, Francesco Seatzu and Katerina Akestoridi

BRILL | NIJHOFF

LEIDEN | BOSTON

The Library of Congress Cataloging-in-Publication Data is available online at https://catalog.loc.gov
LC record available at https://lccn.loc.gov/2024944636

Typeface for the Latin, Greek, and Cyrillic scripts: "Brill". See and download: brill.com/brill-typeface.

ISBN 978-90-04-42456-2 (hardback)
ISBN 978-90-04-42457-9 (e-book)
DOI 10.1163/9789004424579

This book is printed on acid-free paper and produced in a sustainable manner.

Contents

Notes on Contributors

Dr. Katerina Akestoridi
is an international lawyer and researcher, specializing in international development, global governance, human rights, and the rule of law. She has held various research and teaching appointments at the law faculties of the Université Catholique de Lille, the Università degli Studi di Cagliari, the University of Zurich, and UCL. Katerina has practiced law in Athens and consulted on human rights issues in the NGO sector.

Dr. Matthew Garrod
is a Senior Lecturer and Researcher at Sussex Law School. His area of research expertise is centred around the intersection between criminal law, international law, terrorism and counter terrorism and organised crime. He the Co-Founder and Director of Sussex Terrorism and Extremism Research Network (STERN) and a Member of the 'Criminal Law Reform Now Network', working in collaboration with experts across the UK and the Law Commission of England and Wales. Since 2017, Matthew has worked as an independent expert advisor on counter-terrorism at the United Nations.

Inmaculada Marrero Rocha
is a Full Professor of International Relations at the University of Granada and the Executive Secretary of the Euro-Arab Foundation for Higher Studies.

Hitoshi Nasu
is a Professor of Law at the United States Military Academy, West Point, and a Senior Faculty Fellow at the Lieber Institute for Law and Warfare. Currently, he also serves as a Senior Fellow at the Stockton Center for International Law, United States Naval War College, and a Principal Visiting Research Fellow at the University of Reading School of Law.

Dr. Francesco Seatzu
is a Full Professor of International Law at the University of Cagliari. He has authored three monographs, edited eight books, and written over 120 articles published in international and national journals, as well as renowned edited volumes.

Mirko Sossai
is associate professor of international law at the Law Department of the Roma Tre University, where he also teaches law of international organisations.

Sofia Tzortzi (*JD, MA, LLB*)
is a qualified lawyer, political scientist, accredited mediator and visiting professor of EU law at the Catholic University of Lille.

Javier Valls-Prieto
is Professor of Criminal Law and Criminology at the University of Granada. He is a member of the European BAG-INTEL project and principal investigator of the GOIA project. His research focuses on the use of artificial intelligence to fight crime and cybercrime.

General Introduction

Francesco Seatzu, Inmaculada Marrero Rocha and Katerina Akestoridi

> The depth of the relationship between organized crime (OC) and terrorism is often dependent on the nature of the geographic region in which any specific nexus operates.
>
> TAMARA MAKARENKO

1 The Nexus between Terrorism and Organized Crime: Current State and Reflections

Over the years, global institutions such as the United Nations and regional organizations like the Council of Europe (CoE) and the Organization of American States (OAS),[1] along with scholars,[2] have consistently alerted their member states to the emergence of a new relationship or 'nexus'[3] between jihadist terrorism and transnational organized crime. This heightened awareness underscores the escalated threat to national and international peace and security[4]

1 The UN Security Council has warned the world about the links between international terrorism and transnational organised crime (2482/2019, 2462/2019, 2347/2017, 2396/2017, 2178/2014) and urged states to implement the most appropriate measures to stifle them.

2 See e.g., Tamara Makarenko, 'The Crime–Terror Continuum: Tracing the Interplay between Transnational Organised Crime and Terrorism', 6(1) Global Crime (2004), 129–145 at pp. 131–133; Chris Dishman, 'The Leaderless Nexus: When Crime and Terror Converge', 28 (3) Studies in Conflict and Terrorism (2005) 237–252; Peng Wang, 'The Crime-Terror Nexus: Transformation, Alliance, Convergence', 6(6) Asian Social Science (2010) 11–20; Steven Hutchinson and Pat O'Malley, 'A Crime–Terror Nexus? Thinking on Some of the Links between Terrorism and Criminality', 30(12) Studies in Conflict and Terrorism (2007) 1095–1107; J de Boer and L Bosetti, ' The Crime-Confl ict " Nexus": State of the Evidence', July 2015, www.collections.unu.edu/eserv/UNU:3134/unu_cpr_crime_confl ict_nexus.pdf; Letizia Paoli, Clare Hall, Jan Wouters (eds.), *The Nexus Between Organized Crime and Terrorism: Types and Response* (London: Edward Elgar, 2022).

3 Noting incidentally, a 'nexus' occurs when both activities coincide in terms of both space and time.

4 Amplius, see Alex P Schmid, 'The Links between Transnational Organized Crime and Terrorist Crimes' (1996) 2 (2) *Transnational Organized Crime* 40 ff.

 | DOI:10.1163/9789004424579_002

posed by the collaboration of these two illegal and violent forces.[5]

Unlike other international institutions, such as the EU Parliament,[6] the UN Security Council has played an exemplary role in raising the alarm, addressing the links between international terrorism and transnational organized crime through a series of resolutions (2482/2019, 2462/2019, 2347/2017, 2396/2017, 2178/2014). In these resolutions, the Security Council not only acknowledged the existence of this nexus but also urged states to implement appropriate measures to suppress these threats.

A crucial moment in recognizing the direct link between terrorism and its funding through transnational organized crime occurred with the UN Security Council's adoption of Resolution 2195 in 2014.[7] This resolution highlighted the challenges posed by terrorists benefiting from organized crime, with a specific focus on regions like Africa, where terrorism has exacted a devastating toll. The thematic debate on 'terrorism and cross-border crime,' led by Chad as the president of the UN Security Council, underscored the urgency of addressing the dangerous and growing linkage between terrorism and cross-border crime.[8]

Moreover, resolution 2195 marked a departure from 15 years of UN Security Council inactivity on the general question of the links between terrorism and organized crime as threats to international security.[9] By recognizing a broad range of criminal activities, including the trafficking of arms, persons, drugs, and illicit trade in natural resources, the resolution expanded the understanding of the links between terrorism and organized crime. Importantly, corruption was identified as a facilitating mechanism for terrorism, organized crime,

---

5 Indeed, the expanding nexus between terrorism and organized crime groups poses a challenge to both international and national security. This challenge manifests in the weakening of democratic institutions, compromise of government institutions, damage to the credibility of financial institutions, and infiltration into the formal economy, ultimately resulting in heightened crime and human security challenges.

6 The 2011 European Parliament report on organized crime in the European Union, Europol's EU Terrorism and Trend Report (TE-SAT 2012), and the Organised Crime Threat Assessment (OCTA) emphasize the diversity of organized crime (OC) and terrorist groups, as well as the multifaceted nature of the threats they present. Additionally, these reports recognize these phenomena as complex, frequently extending across multinational boundaries. While these reports explicitly mention connections between organized crime and terrorism, they do not delve into the specifics of the nature or extent of these ties. For more information about this issue, see EU Parliament, 'Europe's Crime-Terror Nexus: Links between terrorist and organized crime groups in the European Union, available at: https://www.europarl.europa.eu/document/activities/cont/201211/20121127ATT56707/20121127ATT56707EN.pdf.

7 S/RES/2195 (2014). This resolution was adopted under the Security Council's international security enforcement powers in Chapter VII of the UN Charter.

8 See Matthew Garrod, ch. 5.

9 Ibid.

and the links between them.[10] Since the adoption of Resolution 2195, the link between terrorism and organized crime has become a regular thematic topic in the UN Security Council's debates.[11] Bold assertions have been made about terrorists benefiting from organized crime, both domestically and transnationally, as a significant source of funding and logistical support.[12] This shift in policy-making reflects a growing acknowledgment of the evolving nature of threats to international peace and security. The resolution not only emphasized the linkages between terrorism and organized crime but also called for a better understanding of these links through further research, empirical data collection, and the production of new evidence.[13] This imperative resonates with the broader need highlighted in the volume of essays discussed earlier – the need for a more informed discussion based on empirical evidence to formulate appropriate policy and legal responses to the complex nexus between terrorism and organized crime.

In the aftermath of the 9/11 terrorist attacks to the US soil, scholars, policy experts, and security officials have increasingly focused on investigating the crime-terror nexus. The expanding body of literature, albeit curiously paying less attention to the connections between terrorism and organized crime in Africa or the applicability and effectiveness of AU legal instruments in countering the phenomenon,[14] portrays the convergence of these two domains as a prevalent characteristic of the contemporary security landscape. This depiction implies that such convergence heightens the terrorism threat by strengthening the financial foundations of terrorist organizations.[15]

The crime-terror nexus concept introduces a widely accepted connection, distinguishing tactical and organizational relationships among these entities. This, along with poor border security, weak law enforcement, corrupt public officials, and established smuggling networks, has facilitated the potential

---

10 Ibid.

11 See Alessandra Annoni, 'The Relationship between Transnational Organised Crime and Terrorism: An International Law Perspective', in Stefania Carnevale, Serena Forlati, Orsetta Giolo (eds.), *Redefining Organised Crime: A Challenge for the European Union?* (Oxford: Hart publishing, 2017), p. 121 ff.

12 Amplius, see Tamara Makarenko, above n. 2, 129 ff.

13 Amplius, see Mc Keever D. Revisiting Security Council action on terrorism: New threats; (a lot of) new law; same old problems? (2021) 34 *Leiden Journal of International Law*, 441–470.

14 See Matthew Garrod ch. 5.

15 Incidentally, it is worth noting that, in the years following 9/11, research conducted primarily in unstable regions of Central Asia, South America, South, and Southeast Asia revealed that the connections between organized crime (OC) and terrorism had evolved more significantly than initially anticipated.

emergence of hybrid forms of violent actors resulting from the convergence of their motives and activities.[16] Recent perspectives deviate from emphasizing formalized collaboration between criminal and terrorist actors, instead highlighting the existence of "overlapping ecosystems" or similar social environments from which both criminals and terrorists recruit their members.

The initial conceptualizations of the crime-terror nexus focused on the growing similarity in tactics employed by both criminal and terrorist groups.[17] Examples include the involvement of drug trafficking organizations in acts of terrorism or the efforts of terrorist groups to participate in activities such as the drug trade, kidnapping, arms trafficking, and human trafficking. Derived from its conceptual forerunner, "narco-terrorism," this approach concentrates on documenting the tactics adopted by criminal or terrorist actors and assessing the extent to which the borrowed tactics have aided a group in achieving its goals.[18] A surge in research has occurred, documenting the utilization of criminal activities by terrorist and insurgent groups. These activities encompass drug trafficking, human trafficking, oil smuggling, diamond smuggling, trafficking in cultural artifacts and wildlife, extortion rackets, and engagement in cybercrime.

An alternative organizational viewpoint redirects attention from tactics to the methods of collaboration between terrorist and criminal groups. It examines how these organizational linkages contribute to the advancement of the groups' goals. Research on the crime-terror nexus has recorded instances in which criminal and terrorist groups leverage each other's expertise, skills, networks, and institutional structures for mutual advantage.[19] For instance, there is evidence of the Colombia's Revolutionary Armed Forces of Colombia (FARC) and the Tamil Tigers of Sri Lanka providing security support to criminal cartels engaged in drug production and trafficking, all in exchange for monetary compensation.[20] In the 1990s, the leftist National Liberation Army (ELN)

---

16 This was exemplified by the Albanian mafia and the KLA in the mid-1990s, both of which gained advantages from a membership and recruitment base that could be interchanged. Amplius, see Saša Mijalković, 'THE IDEOLOGY OF „GREATER KOSOVO" IN THE VISION OF ALBANIAN NARCO-TERRORIST CLANS' (2020) 25 *NBP – Journal of Criminalistics and Law*, available at: https://aseestant.ceon.rs/index.php/nabepo/article/view/27336.

17 Amplius, see Steven Hutchinson, Pat O'Malley, "A Crime–Terror Nexus? Thinking on Some of the Links between Terrorism and Criminality." (2007) 30 *Studies in Conflict & Terrorism* 1095–1107; Mariva Y. O Melicheva, Lawrence P. Markowitz, 'Rethinking Intersections of Crime and Terrorism: Insights from Political Economies of Violence' (2021) 23 *International Studies Review* 1541–1565.

18 See Matthew Garrod, ch. 5.

19 See Mariva Y. O Melicheva, Lawrence P. Markowitz, above n. 17, 1544.

20 Ibidem.

allowed itself to be hired by Colombian cartels to carry out several car bombings.[21] Hezbollah, a Shiite Muslim group with political and militant facets, has established sophisticated smuggling schemes that involve collaboration with criminal actors.[22] These endeavors are aimed at facilitating its extensive drug trafficking and smuggling activities. Al Qaeda has broadened its associations with criminal organizations in various European countries.[23] Additionally, it has extended its involvement in drug trafficking in regions such as Pakistan and Afghanistan.

Studies on the crime-terror nexus have also delved into the evolution and complete convergence of criminal and terrorist groups.[24] The concept of hybrids suggests that the systematic engagement of a terrorist group in criminal activities or an enduring relationship between terrorist and criminal entities could lead to a shift in the terrorists' ideological agendas towards profit-seeking motivations, and conversely, among organized criminal actors. The crime–terror studies highlight numerous instances of this occurrence.[25] The Abu Sayyaf movement, an extremist separatist Moro Muslim terrorist group in the Philippines that developed connections with Al Qaeda and ISIS, initially participated in kidnapping and drug trafficking as a means of generating revenue.[26] Nevertheless, the group ultimately evolved into a criminal entity, prioritizing profit motivations over its original ideology. Experts have also portrayed the Islamic Movement of Uzbekistan (IMU) similarly, as it shifted from being a jihadist movement to functioning as a drug trafficking ring.[27] At one point, it briefly gained control of two-thirds of the Central Asian opium routes from Afghanistan. On the "organized crime" aspect of the nexus, it is claimed that common criminals have demonstrated the ability to transform into "criminal soldiers." Street gangs and drug cartels in Central America and beyond have reportedly engaged in a conflict with the state, characterized as a form of "criminal insurgency."

---

21 See Juan D. Rojas, Olivier J. Walther, 'Revolutionary Insurgents or Conservative Reactionaries? National Liberation Army's Transnational Expansion in Colombia and Venezuela' (2022) 13 *Journal of Latin American Geography*, also available at: https://muse.jhu.edu/pub/15/article/864717/summary.

22 Amplius, see Krista E. Wiegand, 'Reformation of a Terrorist Group: Hezbollah as a Lebanese Political Party' (2009) 32 *Studies in Conflict & Terrorism*, available at: https://www.tandfonline.com/doi/abs/10.1080/10576100903039320.

23 EU Parliament, above n. 6.

24 See Mariva Y. O Melicheva, Lawrence P. Markowitz, above n. 17, 1544.

25 Ibid.

26 Ibid.

27 Ibid.

Acknowledging the increasing complexity of violent actors and the fluidity of their motivations, scholars studying the crime–terror nexus have aimed to create frameworks that capture the transitions of groups between ideological and profit motives, as well as their engagement in various forms of intergroup cooperation. Tamara Makarenko's analysis represents a significant endeavor thus far in providing a conceptualization of diverse collaborations between terrorism and organized crime. In Tamara Makarenko's revised framework, criminal and terrorist actors, along with their intersections, are illustrated on two planes.[28] The first plane involves the adoption of tactics from the "other," while the second plane accounts for the merging of a criminal and terrorist group. A hybrid entity can simultaneously exhibit both ideological and economic motivations. Scholars, drawing on Tamara Makarenko's spectrum, clarify the shifts of groups toward tactical and operational changes driven by financial pressures on terrorist groups or political pressures on criminal organizations.[29] The rising occurrence of former criminals within terrorist cells in Europe, often referred to as "gangster jihadists", has spurred new perspectives on operational connections within the crime-terror nexus. A recent line of research has integrated the recruitment patterns of criminal and terrorist groups into its analyses, emphasizing their recruitment from shared environments or "melting pots." This research also explores the process of how individuals with a criminal history undergo radicalization. According to this line of thinking, terrorist organizations perceive strategic advantages in recruiting former criminals. Individuals with criminal backgrounds possess qualities deemed valuable by terrorist groups, including experience with violence and clandestine behaviours. Additionally, the connections of offenders to existing criminal networks can be useful for terrorist groups in coordinating, financing, and arming terrorist activities.

Despite significant progress in comprehending the diverse intersections of crime and terrorism, numerous questions persist in the existing literature. First and foremost, who are the actors within the crime–terror nexus, and what motivates them? Indeed, this inquiry remains relevant despite the widely accepted consensus that the increasing interconnection of shared tactics and methods among terrorist and criminal groups shall be attributed to four significant developments: globalization, the Internet-driven communication revolution, the conclusion of the Cold War, and the global "war on terror."[30] The

28 See Tamara Makarenko, above. 2.

29 See Mariva Y. O Melicheva, Lawrence P. Markowitz, above n. 17, 1544.

30 Ibid.

concept of the "crime–terror" nexus and related frameworks frequently blend together terrorist and insurgent groups, often perceiving all activities as transnational, thereby neglecting the links between crime and terrorism and their ties to local dynamics.[31] Even though recent studies have uncovered a complex structure of motives guiding groups' involvement in crime, encompassing simple financial calculations[32] to ideological and strategic purposes, the adoption of criminal tactics by terrorist groups is frequently presumed to be motivated primarily by revenue-generating considerations.

Moreover, the existing crime–terror literature commonly regards the collaboration between terrorist and criminal groups, driven by organizational similarities in methods and tactics, as a prevailing mode of organizational interactions between these two entities. The numerous inhibitors affecting the relationships between terrorist and criminal actors have been overlooked, leading to an inflated assessment of the prevalence of criminal–terrorist partnerships and the ease with which they can be established.

Secondly, the foundational conditions for the development of the crime–terror nexus have typically revolved around two prevailing paradigms, emphasizing the facilitating impact of globalization and the permissive influence of "ungoverned" and "poorly governed" territories conducive to the nexus's emergence.[33] While these studies explored the connections among non-state violent actors, they frequently neglected or obscured the more direct role of the state in the relationship between crime and terrorism. Thirdly, the current explanations for the crime–terror nexus leave a crucial question about the variation in groups' preferences unanswered. For instance, why do some violent groups choose to engage in certain types of criminal activities but not others, if at all? Finally, the outcomes of the criminal–terrorist convergence arguably represent the least developed area of the scholarship on the crime–terror nexus. The impacts of the crime–terror nexus are often inferred from the observed levels of violence rather than systematically tested.

---

31 Ibid.

32 Incidentally, this is generally what occurs in Western democracies, where the nexus is primarily confined to the operational aspect, with a focus on terrorist groups participating in criminal activities as a means of acquiring funds. Contrastingly, in transitional states, the nexus encompasses both the operational and conceptual aspects, with indications of convergent motivations prevailing among groups operating in regions such as the Balkans.

33 See Mariva Y. O Melicheva, Lawrence P. Markowitz, above n. 17, 1544.

2 The Nexus between Terrorism and Organized Crime: An Examination from International Relations and International Legal Perspectives

The present collection of essays aims to address these and other issues, either directly or indirectly, by exploring the transnational criminal phenomenon referred to as 'organized criminal terrorism' from the dual perspective of public international law and international relations. The adoption of this perspective stems from the idea shared by the editors of this edited collection that only such a dual approach, and only an approach that considers all continents, enables an effective addressing of the complex questions and issues posed by this transnational criminal phenomenon, both theoretically and practically. It is essential to note that, while not every paper in the volume embraces this multi-level perspective but only an international legal perspective, the introductory work by Professor Inmaculada Marrero Rocha from the University of Granada (Spain) stands out in doing so.

Contrariwise, it is noteworthy that a predominant focus within the volume leans towards a purely international legal perspective.[34] This emphasis is discernible as numerous contributions delve into the impact of international legal instruments on counter-terrorism concerning the intricate phenomenon of organised criminal terrorism. A case in point is found in the work of Katerina Akestoridi and Sofia Tzortzi, whose paper meticulously examines the United Nations' existing legal approach to terrorism, organised crime, and the amalgamation of the two in 'organized criminal terrorism'. Moreover, Francesco Seatzu directs his efforts towards a thorough examination of the Council of Europe's counterterrorism approach, thereby contributing to the broader international legal perspective. In delving into the Council of Europe's strategies for countering terrorism, Seatzu provides insights that resonate with the overarching global legal framework. His examination not only enriches our comprehension of regional responses within Europe but also provides perspectives for shaping a comprehensive and effective international approach to counterterrorism. In this way, Francesco Seatzu's contribution underscores the interconnected nature of efforts to combat terrorism, emphasizing the importance of a cohesive and coordinated international legal response.

The exploration is extended even further through Sossai's thorough examination of the role that the OAS has played in addressing the threat posed by

---

34 For an examination of this theme from an international legal perspective, see also the excellent work by Ben Saul, 'The Legal Relationship between Terrorism and Transnational Crime' (2017) 17 *International Criminal Law Review*, 417 ff.

terrorist and criminal groups in the Americas,[35] as well as through Hitoshi Nasu's comprehensive examination of the applicability of ASEAN instruments in combating organized criminal terrorism. Nasu's contribution significantly enriches the broader discourse on the global legal framework, offering valuable insights into the regional dynamics within the ASEAN context. By scrutinizing the effectiveness and adaptability of ASEAN instruments in the face of organized criminal terrorism, Nasu not only enhances our understanding of regional responses but also contributes essential perspectives to the overarching global discourse. This examination reinforces the importance of fostering cohesion and collaboration across international legal frameworks to effectively counter the intricate challenges posed by organized criminal terrorism on a global scale.

Furthermore, Matthew Garrod's insightful chapter adeptly navigates the intricate landscape of the African Union's Instruments for Organized Criminal Terrorism. In doing so, it provides valuable insights into the legal mechanisms deployed on the African continent in response to the multifaceted challenge of organized criminal terrorism. By delving into the specific instruments employed by the African Union, Garrod sheds light on the region's legal strategies, emphasizing the need for a nuanced understanding of the measures adopted to combat this complex phenomenon. In essence, this collective dedication to a primarily international legal viewpoint not only enriches our comprehension of the African response but also underscores the broader imperative to understand and address organized criminal terrorism through the lens of global legal frameworks and instruments. This approach becomes paramount in fostering international collaboration and coherence in tackling the evolving threats posed by transnational criminal networks intertwined with terrorist activities.

The rationale behind this specific choice and emphasis becomes readily apparent upon closer examination. The absence of an international legal framework tailored to address the nuances of this criminal phenomenon serves as the driving force. In honing their focus, the authors of the aforementioned chapters and related papers, with the sole exception of Javier Valls-Prieto who focuses on combating terrorism financing through artificial intelligence,[36] meticulously probe the question of whether international terrorism and organized criminality should be perceived as distinct entities or as intertwined facets of a unified criminal phenomenon – aptly termed organized criminal

35 See Mirko Sossai, above n. 7.

36 See Javier Valls-Prieto above n. 4.

terrorism. This theoretical exploration prompts a critical inquiry into the necessity of formulating new international legal tools and provisions expressly designed to combat offenses arising from organized criminal terrorism on a global scale. At present, the prospect of such a comprehensive framework remains visible only in specific instances and is contingent on a case-by-case basis. The ongoing theoretical discourse aims to discern not only the nature of the relationship between terrorism and organized crime but also to envisage a potential trajectory for the development of international legal mechanisms tailored to this intricate intersection of threats.

In this respect a somewhat variegated picture arises from the volume: on the one hand there are papers that recommend the adoption of new international legal instruments and rules to better cope with this not recent but growing phenomenon of transnational criminality.[37] On the other hand, other papers defend the current approach in international law of regulating international terrorism and international organized crime through different international legal tools and provisions regardless of the existence of a 'nexus' between them in practice.

The volume, taken as a whole, suggests that there are strong arguments that may be used for supporting both views. The fact of the separate treatment that has been applied so far to organised criminal activities and terrorism in most domestic legislation together with the different character assumed by the phenomenon of 'organized criminal terrorism' in various countries across the world suggests that no new and uniform rules should be adopted to regulate the latter phenomenon at global level. However, the common characteristics of terrorist groups and criminal organized groups in several countries, such as countries in Latin America and Western Europe, suggest instead their consideration as mere variations of the same criminal phenomenon. The same consideration is also suggested by the lack of a clear distinction between terrorism

37 See also C Dishman, 'The Leaderless Nexus: When Crime and Terror Converge' (2005) 28 Studies in Conflict and Terrorism, 2005, pp. 239 ff, also recalling that during the second half of the 20th century, occasional relationships involving logistical cooperation and strategy exchange were identified between ethno-nationalist terrorist groups, and ones embracing radical political ideologies, and classic organised crime groups, based on ties of nationality, or ethnicity, without this entailing any detriment to the preservation of terrorists groups' political objectives and criminal groups' economic ones. Unlike in past decades, in recent times there has been an increase in the intensity of the relationships between these two types of groups, blurring the political and economic lines separating terrorism from organised crime.

and organized criminality in international law[38] as well as from the enduring differences in the nature of these two criminal phenomena.[39]

In summary, organized criminal terrorism has taken center stage as a disconcerting phenomenon, drawing heightened concern and attention. The pivotal question revolves around whether and when it should be subjected to a distinct legal treatment within the framework of international law. The present book endeavors to serve as a foundational resource, paving the way for a more informed and nuanced discussion of these pressing issues. By delving into the multifaceted dimensions of organized criminal terrorism from both international law and international relations perspectives, the collection of essays strives to offer valuable insights that contribute to a comprehensive understanding of this complex challenge. It is anticipated that the knowledge disseminated through this book will foster a more informed discourse, facilitating the development of effective legal responses to address the evolving landscape of organized criminal terrorism on the global stage.

---

38 See e.g. Alessandra Annoni, 'The Relationship between Transnational Organised Crime and Terrorism: An International Law Perspective', in Stefania Carnevale, Serena Forlati, Orsetta Giolo (eds.), *Redefining Organised Crime: A Challenge for the European Union?* (Oxford: Hart publishing, 2017), p. 121 ff.

39 See e.g. Steven Hutchinson, Pat O'Malley, 'A crime–terror nexus? Thinking on some of the links between terrorism and criminality' (2007) 30 Studies in Conflict & Terrorism, p. 1095 ff. See also James J. Forest, 'Kidnapping by Terrorist Groups, 1970–2010: Is Ideological Orientation Relevant?' (2002) 6 Crime & Delinquency, p. 6 ff. See also Angelina Stanojoska, 'The Connection Between Terrorism and Organized Crime: Narcoterrorism and the Other Hybrids', available at: https://wb-iisg.com/wp-content/uploads/bp-attachments/4745/Angelina-Stanojoska_The_Connection_between_Terrorism_and_Org.pdf.

CHAPTER 1

Defining the Crime-Terrorism Nexus

The Changing Face of International Terrorism and Organized Crime

Inmaculada Marrero Rocha

1 Introduction

In 2014, the United Nations Security Council in its Resolution 2195 began to express its concern regarding the interaction between terrorism and transnational organised crime and its consequences for international peace and security. Following this, in 2016 via Resolution 2322 it called upon all states to enhance their cooperation to prevent terrorists from benefiting from cooperation with organized crime and improve their capacity in this respect. A year later, it adopted Resolution 2370 (2017), in which it urged member states to strengthen, where appropriate, their judicial, law enforcement and border-control capacities, and develop their investigation capabilities of arms trafficking networks to address the link between transnational organised crime and terrorism and their activity on illegal trafficking routes.[1] In July 2019, the UN Security Council adopted Resolution 2482 (2019) regarding the linkages between organised crime and terrorism. This resolution addressed the financial needs of global terrorism as a fundamental element for the development of this relationship, the extortion networks generated by the cooperation between both groups and the increasing number of goods being trafficked, along with the need to investigate this issue further. It concluded by requesting the Secretary-General to submit a joint report by the United Nations Office of Counter-Terrorism (UNOCT) and the United Nations Office of Drugs and Crime (UNODC) to address the issue of linkages between terrorism and organised crime, whether transnational or domestic.[2]

---

1 Resolution 2195 (2014) adopted by the Security Council at its 7351st meeting on 19 December 2014, S/RES/2195 (2014); Resolution 2322 (2016), adopted by the Security Council at its 7831st meeting on 12 December 2016, S/RES/2322 (2016), and Resolution 2370 (2017) adopted by the Security Council at its 8017th meeting on 2 August 2017, S/RES/2370 (2017).

2 Resolution 2482 (2019) adopted by the Security Council at its 8582nd meeting on 19 July 2019, S/RES/2482 (2019).

 | DOI:10.1163/9789004424579_003

The concern expressed by international institutions and organisations and the data offered by many research centres raise the question whether a quantitative and qualitative change is taking place in the relationship between organised crime and terrorism compared to earlier periods of international relations. This chapter will analyse the extent to which the nexus between criminal groups and terrorist groups has been transformed. To do so, firstly it will consider the definitions of both groups and whether their characteristics have evolved in a manner which has shaped their current relations. Secondly, it will consider the changes to the peculiar features shared by organised crime and terrorism and how they have evolved to foster new processes of collaboration between criminal organisations and more globalised terrorist organisations. Thirdly, it will consider the aspects of the relationship between organised crime and terrorists in previous decades in order to subsequently identify which of these aspects have changed. Fourthly, an analysis will be made of the factors that have led to the maintenance and strengthening of relationships between terrorist groups and organised crime from two viewpoints: firstly, examination of the aspects of the international system that favour the establishment of relationships between both groups; and secondly, identification of the difficulties faced by states and cooperation efforts to address the transformation of the organisational parameters of international terrorism and organised crime which has led to their increased collaboration. Finally, an analysis will be made of the cooperation between crime and terrorism, taking into account the geographical and socio-political contexts in which this phenomenon takes place and characterising these relationships to determine the possible situations in which their strategies and activities converge.

The aim of the analysis proposed in each of the sections of this chapter is to serve as a guide to evaluate the political-legal responses that international organisations are implementing at a universal and regional level to address these new dynamics in the relationships between organised crime and terrorism, and what types of actions should be undertaken to ensure we have the most suitable instruments to deal with this phenomenon.

2 Elements for the Definition of Global Terrorism and Transnational Organised Crime

The current relationships between organised crime and global terrorism have been defined using expressions such as links, nexus, alliance, symbiosis and convergence, and depending on their nature and intensity one term or another may be used. Until the late 1990s, the connections between criminals and terrorists were not considered a threat that could transcend the domestic frameworks in which both groups carried out their activities, and the differences between the objectives of both types of organisations were clearly identifiable.[3] However, some authors consider that one of the obstacles preventing analysis of the evolution of the nature of relationships of cooperation between criminal and terrorist groups is the lack of consensus regarding the definition of terrorism and organised crime, given that both are phenomena in constant evolution which manifest themselves in a multitude of forms.[4]

In the case of terrorism, many studies defend the need to adopt a consensus-based definition of terrorism at an international level, but one which considers terrorism as an objective in itself associated with non-state actors and not as a strategy or practice.[5] Based on these premises, we can identify two main lines of research, the former focusing on characterising the causes of terrorism and the latter more concerned with identifying the best strategies and policies to combat the phenomenon of terrorism.[6] After more than 20 years of debate by the Ad Hoc Committee on International Terrorism of the UN General Assembly no agreement has been reached regarding its definition,[7] despite

---

3 Ruggiero, V. "Hybrids: on the Crime–Terror Nexus", *International Journal of Comparative and Applied Criminal Justice*, Vol. 43, 2019, No. 1, pp. 49–60.

4 In the case of terrorism, a definition could be derived from different sources such as academic doctrine, treaties governing different aspects of terrorism, judicial decisions and the legal precedent deriving from international organisations. The Oxford Dictionary defines terrorism as "the unlawful use of violence and intimidation, especially against civilians, in the pursuit of political aims." (Stevenson, A. (ed.). *Oxford Dictionary of English*, Oxford University Press, 2010. Various authors have addressed the issue of the need to reach a definition of terrorism: Cooper, H., "Terrorism: The Problem of Definition Revisited", *American Behavioral Scientist*, 2001, No. 44, pp. 881–893; Gibbs, J., "Conceptualization of Terrorism", *American Sociological Review*, 1989, No. 54, pp. 329–340; Hoffman, B., *Inside Terrorism*, New York, Columbia University Press, 1998 and Ruby, Ch., "The Definition of Terrorism", *Analyses of Social Issues and Public Policy*, 2002, No. 2, pp. 9–14.

5 Stohl, M., "Old Myths, New Fantasies and the Enduring Realities of Terrorism", *Critical Studies on Terrorism*, Vol. 1, 2008, No. 1, pp. 146–148 and Chomsky, N., "International Terrorism: Image and Reality", *Crime and Social Justice*, 1987, No. 27/28, pp. 172–200.

6 Meisels, T., "The Trouble with Terror: The Apologetics of Terrorism. A Refutation", *Terrorism and Political Violence*, Vol. 18, 2006, No. 3, pp. 465–483.

7 The definition of terrorism proposed by the Committee is as follows: "Any person commits an offence within the meaning of the present Convention if that person, by any means, unlawfully and intentionally, causes: (a) Death or serious bodily injury to any person; or (b) Serious damage to public or private property, including a place of public use, a State or government facility, a public transportation system, an infrastructure facility or to the environment; or (c) Damage to property, places, facilities or systems referred to in paragraph 1 (b) of the present article resulting or likely to result in major economic loss, when the purpose of the conduct, by its nature or context, is to intimidate a population, or to

the fact that, paradoxically, the UN Security Council has prepared an extensive list of around 700 individuals and 400 terrorist groups subject to sanctions.[8] There is even divergence of opinion regarding its definition as 'international', although the vast majority of cases refer to the objectives and strategies of terrorist groups as having an international scope, not to mention the extensive geographical reach of their organisational structures and the different networks used to perpetrate acts of violence under these hierarchical units.[9] However, the academic interest in developing a definition of terrorism has not been reciprocated by states, which have failed to agree on a definition despite having adopted treaties to prohibit certain terrorist practices and combat their financing.[10]

If terrorism is understood as being unlawful acts of violence that induce psychic fear within a certain society or sector of society which far exceeds its purely material consequences, then it is not so relevant to consider who the perpetrators of those acts – insurgent groups, national liberation movements, warlords, extremist religious or ecological groups or ultra left-wing or right-wing groups, etc. – may be.[11] However, if we consider terrorism as a

---

compel a Government or an international organization to do or to abstain from doing any act." United Nations Report of the Ad Hoc Committee established by General Assembly resolution 51/210 of 17 December 1996 Sixteenth session (8 to 12 April 2013) General Assembly Official Records, 68th Session Supplement No. 37; Annex I Preamble and articles 1, 2 and 4 to 27 of the draft Comprehensive Convention on International Terrorism prepared by the Bureau. United Nations, New York, 2013, p.6 (A/68/37).

8 UN Security Council Sanctions List, in https://www.un.org/sc/suborg/en/sanctions/un-scconsolidated-list & URL: https://scsanctions.un.org/r/?keywords=car, and European Union Sanctions List in http://top-topics.thefullwiki.org/european_union_designated_terrorist_organizations.

9 Malik, O., *Enough of the Definition of Terrorism*, London, The Royal Institute of International Affairs, 2000; Kennedy, R., "Is One Person's Terrorist Another's Freedom Fighter? Western and Islamic Approaches to "Just War", *Terrorism and Political Violence*, Vol. 11, 1999, No. 1, pp. 1–21 and Sorel, J. M., "Some Questions about the Definition of Terrorism and the Fight against Its Financing", *European Journal of International Law*, Vol. 14, 2003, No. 2, pp. 365–378.

10 Since 1963, the international community has elaborated 19 international legal instruments to prevent terrorist acts, which may be consulted at: http://www.un.org/es/counterterrorism/legal-instruments.shtml.

11 Crenshaw, M., "The Causes of Terrorism", *Terrorism Studies: A Reader*, 2012, pp. 99 and ss. See also the Schmid definition on terrorism: "A 'terrorist group' is a militant, usually non-state, clandestine organisation with political goals which – by definition – engages, in whole or in part of its activities, in terrorism, that is, a communication strategy for psychological (mass) manipulation whereby mainly unarmed civilians (and non-combatants such as prisoners of war) are deliberately victimised in order to impress third parties (e.g. intimidate, coerce or otherwise influence a government or a section of society, or public opinion in general), with the help of portrayals of demonstrative violence

type of violence intended to achieve political objectives and we focus on the political-ideological-moral element present at the heart of terrorist actions, it would need to be analysed as a type of political violence. Political violence is understood as being "violence exerted as a means of political-social struggle, with the aim of maintaining, modifying, substituting or destroying a state or societal model or also with the aim of destroying or repressing an identifiable group of people within society due to their social, political, trade union, ethnic, racial, religious, cultural or ideological affinity, whether or not it is organised."[12] Accordingly, if the use of force for the purpose of triggering social-political change is carried out via a terrorist strategy, it is therefore political violence, regardless of who exerts that violence and the nature of the ideas being defended.[13]

The debate as to what type of political violence may be classified as terrorism has given rise to a specific field of critical research studies known as critical terrorism studies, which adopts a contrary approach to the orthodox theory of the majority of terrorism studies.[14] According to this critical approach, terrorism obeys a rational calculation of advantages-benefits deriving from a political choice. Accordingly, ignoring this fact complicates an analysis of strategic terrorist actions which involve cooperation with transnational organised crime.[15]

---

in front of witnessing audiences and/or by means of induced coverage in mass and social media". In Schmid, A. P., Revisiting the Relationship between International Terrorism and Transnational Organised Crime 22 Years Later. *ICCT Research Paper, The Hague*, 2018, and, Schmid, A. P. "The Definition of Terrorism," in Alex P. Schmid (Ed.), *The Routledge Handbook of Terrorism Research*, Routledge, 2011, pp. 39–157.

12 Cinep–Programa por la Paz. *Marco Conceptual de la Red Nacional de Bancos de Datos*, Impresol Ediciones, 2016, p. 14.

13 Wieviorka, M., Onaindía, M. and Martínez Reverte, J. *El terrorismo: la violencia política en el mundo*, Plaza and Janés, 1991 and Della Porta, D. *Social Movements, Political Violence, and The State: A Comparative Analysis of Italy and Germany*, Cambridge University Press, 2006.

14 The fact that the same armed groups have been labelled revolutionaries, liberators and terrorists, as is the case of Hamas (Gaza), Hezbollah (Lebanon), the Revolutionary Armed Forces of Colombia (FARC) in Colombia, the Kurdistan Workers' Party (Turkey) and the Tamil Tigers (Sri Lanka) has also been highlighted by critical terrorism studies. This critical analysis focuses on the perpetrators of terrorism, but without taking into account so-called "terrorist behaviour". This latter perspective is much more restrained and does not enter into any value judgments of the nature and convictions of those committing acts of terrorism (Lizardo, O., "Defining and Theorizing Terrorism: A Global Actor-Centered Aproach", *Journal of World-Systems Research*, Vol. 14, No. 2, 2015, pp. 91–118).

15 Freddman, L., "Terrorism as a Strategy", *Government and Opposition*, Vol. 43, 2007, No. 3, pp. 314–339; Burke, A., "The End of Terrorism Studies", *Critical Studies on Terrorism*, Vol. 1, 2008, No., 1, pp. 37–49; Booth, K., "Critical Explorations", in Booth, K., (ed.) *Critical Security*

Terrorism originally arose as a state phenomenon, because its actions and objectives were within the legal-political scope of states. For example, the radical left-wing anarchist terrorist groups of the period from the 19th century through to the early 20th century were largely composed of national citizens and involved activities and objectives that were limited to the borders of their respective states.[16] Terrorism has since undergone significant changes, especially following the expansion of its activities from a national context to a more international context and the adoption of objectives with a global dimension. This internationalisation of terrorism began when terrorist organisations begin to cross state borders for operational reasons, basing themselves in other jurisdictions to establish safe havens, provide training for members or obtain military supplies and economic resources, as was done for various reasons by ETA in France, the Red Army Faction (RAF) in former East Germany, or the Kurdistan Workers' Party (PKK) in Iraq.[17]

The internationalisation of terrorism commenced when ethno-nationalist or radical terrorist groups expanded beyond the borders of their respective states with the aim of perpetrating terrorist acts in other states in which they also had interests or with population linked to the objectives and activities of the organisation, or simply because they wished to eliminate dissidents taking refuge in foreign states. Examples include the Popular Front for the Liberation of Palestine and the Armenian Secret Army for the Liberation of Armenia.[18]

Studies and World Politics, London, Lynne Rienner, 2005, pp. 1–18; Gunning, J., "A Case for Critical Terrorism Studies?", *Government and Opposition*, Vol. 42, 2007, No. 3, pp. 363–393 and Jackson, R., "Constructing Enemies": Islamic Terrorism in Political and Academic Discourse", *Government and Opposition*, Vol. 42, 2007, No. 3, pp. 394–426.

16 Jensen, R. B. "Daggers, Rifles and Dynamite: Anarchist Terrorism in Nineteenth Century Europe", *Terrorism and Political Violence*, Vol. 16, 2004, No. 1, pp. 116–153; Jensen, R. B. *The Battle against Anarchist Terrorism: An International History, 1878–1934*, Cambridge University Press, 2013; Malkki, L. "Left-wing Terrorism", *Routledge Handbook of Terrorism and Counterterrorism*, Routledge, 2018, pp. 113–123; Catanzaro, R. *The Red Brigades and Left-Wing Terrorism in Italy*, Bloomsbury Continuum, 1991; and Merkl, P. H. "West German Left-wing Terrorism", *Terrorism in Context*, 1995, pp. 160–210.

17 Gregory, Sh. "France and the War on Terrorism", *Terrorism and Political Violence*, Vol. 15, 2003, No. 1, pp. 124–147; Paredes Badía, I. RAF: "Red Army Faction. Revision of History", *Dirigido*, 2009, No. 387, pp. 44–45; Wunschik, T. and Bravo Basiche, T. "La protección del terrorismo. El apoyo de la Seguridad del Estado de la RDA a la Fracción del Ejército Rojo germano-occidental", *Ayer*, 2011, pp. 137–157; and Casier, M. "Designated Terrorists: The Kurdistan Workers' Party and Its Struggle to (re) Gain Political Legitimacy", *Mediterranean Politics*, Vol. 15, 2010, No. 3, pp. 393–413.

18 Ruiz Durán, F.J. "La internacional terrorista patrocinada por la URSS", *Revista Contribuciones a las Ciencias Sociales*, July-September 2017, http://www.eumed.net/rev/cccss/2017/03/internacional-terrorista-urss.html.

Even state governments themselves have recurred to terrorist strategies to achieve international objectives, such as the cases of terrorism attributed to the Gaddafi government of Libya.[19]

The concept of global terrorism arose in the year 2000, although it also went by other names such as jihadist terrorism, while some decided to continue calling it international terrorism. Global terrorism differs from 'classic' terrorism due to the global scope of its objectives and strategies based on a religious ideology. Its global purposes defy state borders and seek to reconfigure international power relations, create new states or unify others where they can develop a new political and social project based on their political-ideological principles.[20] Unlike classic terrorist groups, the members of global terrorist groups are of a markedly international nature. Despite the different geographical origins of their members, they may be identified on the basis that they profess a violent, extremist version of Islam, neo-Salafism. This new identity seeks to substitute previous identities based on state-national logic,[21] granting these organisations greater autonomy and independence compared to other actors which are conditioned more by national and state elements.[22] Although global terrorism is associated with permanent violence and barbarism as if it were an exercise in irrational and deranged violence, it is still political violence and intentionally depoliticising it only makes its scientific analysis more difficult.[23] This explains why the heightened degree of fanaticism attributed to

---

19 Hoffman, B. "Intelligence and Terrorism: Emerging Threats and New Security Challenges in The Post-Cold War Era", *Intelligence and National Security*, Vol. 11, 1996, No. 2, pp. 207–223.

20 Rougier, B. "Le jihad en Afghanistan et l'emergence du salafisme-jihadisme", en Rougier, B. (dir) *Quèst-ce que le salafisme?*, Puf, 2008, pp. 65–86; Paz, R., "Debates Within the Family: Jihadi-Salafi Debates on Strategy, Takfir, Extremism, Suicide Bombing and the Sense of the Apocalypse", *Salafism. Global Islam's New Religious Movement*, Columbia University Press, 2009, pp. 267–300 and Martini, A., "El terrorismo global como amenaza al orden internacional. El caso del Estado Islámico", *Relaciones Internacionales*, 2016, No. 32, pp. 79–95, (http://www.relacionesinternacionales.info/ojs/article/view/708.html).

21 Hegghammer, Th., "The Rise of Muslim Foreign Fighters: Islam and the Globalization of Jihad", *International Security*, Vol. 35, 2010, No. 3, pp. 53–94 and Van Zuijdewijn, J. and Bakker, E., *Returning Western Foreign Fighters: The Cases of Afghanistan, Bosnia and Somalia, The Hague: International Centre for Counter-Terrorism*, 2014, pp. 2 and ss.

22 Malet, D. *Foreign fighters: Transnational Identity in Civil Conflicts*, Oxford University Press, 2013, p. 277 and ss.

23 Paz, R., "Debates Within the Family: Jihadi-Salafi Debates on Strategy, Takfir, Extremism, Suicide Bombing and the Sense of the Apocalypse", *Salafism, Global. Islam's New Religious Movement*, New York, Columbia University Press, 2009, pp. 267–300.

global terrorism has led to concentration on analysis of religious radicalisation as the main cause giving rise to global terrorism.[24]

Undoubtedly, despite the international concern generated by so-called global terrorism, states have been incapable of agreeing on a definition, even when this phenomenon is increasingly present in the priority locations of national and international security agendas as a consequence of the multiplication of groups acting as derivatives, splinter groups or under the auspices of the organisation Al-Qaeda or the self-proclaimed Islamic State of Iraq and the Levant (ISIL), which pledge allegiance to their ideals and are prepared to commit acts of terrorism in their name in different geographical zones.[25]

As regards organised crime, the definition of this concept and others such as criminal organisation, organised criminal activity, organised delinquency and illicit association is a complicated task, and nor is there any international consensus given the versatility and varied nature of the characteristics of these groups and the plurality of their actions.[26] The term 'organised crime' has become widely used not only in the media but also in the academic world. The Palermo Convention against Transnational Organised Crime in 2000 did not offer a definition of organised crime but rather identified a series of parameters capable of achieving legislative standards for the signatory states, with the aim of reinforcing cooperation in the fight against this phenomenon:[27]

---

24 Moyano, M. and Trujillo, H., *Radicalización islamista y terrorismo, Claves psicosociales*, Universidad de Granada, 2013 and De La Corte, L., Kruglanski, A., De Miguel, J., Sabucedo, J. M., and Díaz, D., "Siete principios psicosociales para explicar el terrorismo", *Psicothema*, Vol. 19, 2007, pp. 367–374.

25 According to the *Global Terrorism Index* 2016, the highest number of fatalities was reached in 2015 and the groups included in this concept of global terrorism were responsible for 74% of those deaths, namely Al Qaeda, Boko Haram, the Talibans and ISIL (*Global Terrorism Index*, Institute for Economic and Peace, 2016, pp. 49–60).

26 Woodiwiss, M., "Transnational Organized Crime: The Strange Career of an American concept" in Beare, M., (Ed.), *Transnational Organized Crime*, Ashgate Publishers, 2013 and Ruíz Díaz, L., *La lucha contra el crimen organizado en la Unión Europea,* doctoral thesis, University of Granada, September 2015, p 21 and pp. 22–57).

27 "a structured group of three or more persons, existing for a period of time and acting in concert with the aim of committing one or more serious crimes or offences" (United Nations Convention against Transnational Organised Crime and Protocols of 15 November 2000, presented as an annex to General Assembly Resolution 55/25 of the same date (https://www.unodc.org/pdf/cld/TOCebook-s.pdf). This definition was also adopted by Council Framework Decision 2008/841/JAI of 24 October 2008, *DO* L 300/42, 11.11.2008. EUROPOL calculates that there are at least 5,000 criminal organisations being investigated in Europe and has established 11 criteria to identify these types of organisations, which must necessarily meet requirements 1, 3, 5 and 11:1. Collaboration of more than two people; 2. Each with own appointed tasks; 3. For a prolonged or indefinite period of time; 4. Using some form of discipline and control; 5. Suspected of the commission of serious

> Organized criminal group' shall mean a structured group of three or more persons, existing for a period of time and acting in concert with the aim of committing one or more serious crimes or offences established pursuant to this Convention, in order to obtain, directly or indirectly, a financial or other material benefit.[28]

States have taken into account the criteria of the Palermo Convention in their criminal legislation to prosecute these groups,[29] and they have also inspired numerous definitions of organised crime in the academic and political ambit.[30] However, as pointed out by Schmid,[31] the Palermo Convention does not include certain important characteristics of organised crime that have been the subject of considerable study, such as the use of extreme violence, an element shared with terrorist groups, corruption of public officials, including members of the legislature and the judiciary, participation in lawful economic activity with the aim of laundering money obtained from illegal activities and finally interference in political processes.[32] Regardless of the definition of

---

criminal offences; 6. Operating on an international level; 7. Using violence or other means suitable for intimidation; 8. Using commercial or businesslike structures; 9. Engaged in money-laundering; 10. Exerting influence on politics, the media, public administration, judicial authorities or the economy; 11. Determined by the pursuit of profit and/or power (Doc. 6204/1/1997, ENFOPOL 35 rev DG).

28 United Nations Convention against Transnational Organized Crime. Art. 2a and2c. New York: UN, 2000 GA 58th Session, Agenda item 105 (A/RES/55/25).

29 For example, in the case of Spain, Article 570 bis of the Spanish Criminal Code defines a criminal organisation as being made up of more than two persons, with a stable nature or for an indefinite period of time, with members sharing functions and tasks in an agreed or coordinated manner for the purpose of committing serious crimes (Spanish Organic Law 10/1995 of 23 November on the Criminal Code (Last amendment: 28 April 2015, No. 281 of 24 November 1995, pp. 166–167). See Auda, G., "Le crime organisé, une perception variable, un concept polémique", *Cahiers de la Securité*, 2009, No. 7 and López Múñoz, J. "EL orden público bajo la amenaza de la criminalidad organizada", *Revista de Derecho de la UNED*, 2013, No. 13, pp. 233–260.

30 Price, E. "Selected Literature on Terrorism and Organized Crime", *Perspectives on Terrorism*, Vol. 4, 2010, No. 6, pp. 44–54. Jongman, A. J. "World Directory of Extremist, Terrorist and Other Organisations Associated with Guerrilla Warfare, Political Violence, Protest, Organised Crime and Cyber-crime." In Alex P. Schmid (Ed.), The Routledge Handbook of Terrorism Research, Routledge, 2011, pp. 355–442 and Wikipedia offers a partial and non-official list of organised crime groups in https://en.wikipedia.org/wiki/List_of_criminal_enterprises,_gangs_and_syndicates .

31 Schmid, A. P. "Revisiting the Relationship Between International Terrorism and Transnational Organised Crime 22 Years Later", note 11, 2018, p. 4.

32 Schmid defines organised crime as "a violence-prone, profit-oriented clandestine organisation that provides, on a black market, illegal services or illegally obtained licit or illicit products for which there is a substantial demand – but one that governments o regular

organised crime, its activities are characterised by their violent nature and the pursuit of economic benefit in principle without political objectives, although they need to corrupt public officials and politicians to ensure they do not interfere with their activities. To give an example of the extent of the corruption generated by organised crime, Schmid highlights the judicial proceedings against the Russian mafia in Spain, revealing the links this criminal organisation had with high-ranking Russian politicians and the network of corrupt government officials that had been established.[33] Finally, one of the features of organised crime is its hierarchical structure and how access to the organisation is restricted, normally to those with an ethnic, family or geographical origin with which its members identify.[34]

In the early 1990s, organised crime began a process of transformation which has allowed it to earn the title of transnational organised crime. Classic criminal groups (the Italian Mafia, the Russian Mafia, the Albanian Mafia, the Japanese Yakuza and the Chinese Mafia, among others) began to exploit the numerous opportunities offered by the liberalisation of markets and obtained advantages due to the difficulty of controlling the financial transactions they were involved in. Organised crime is increasingly more capable of extending beyond geographical restrictions and developing extra-national links with similar groups thanks to advances in communication and information technology. As a consequence, they now have greater capabilities to challenge state authority and operate at a larger scale and do not need to tie significant amounts of power and resources to a single state, preferring to take advantage of migratory flows to distribute their members in different territories.[35]

---

free market operators do not or cannot meet. The group's structure might be family- or clan-based and hierarchical, or consist of networks shaped more by the organisation's type of activities (drug trafficking, prostitution, racketeering, fraud, arms trafficking, migrant smuggling, counterfeiting, money-laundering, gambling, internet-based extortion, contract killing, etc.)" in Schmid, Alex P. "Revisiting the relationship between international terrorism and transnational organised crime 22 years later", note 11, pp. 7–8.

33 Schmid, A. P. note 11, p. 10.

34 Felsen, D. and Kalaitzidis, A. "A Historical Overview of Transnational Crime", in Reichel, P. (Ed.), *Handbook of Transnational Crime and Justice*, Thousand Oaks, SAGE Publications, 2005, pp. 3–19 and Basiouni, C. and Vetere, E. (eds.), *Organized Crime. A Compilation of U.N. Documents*, 1975–1998, New York, Transnational Publishers, Inc., 1998.

35 Andreas, P. "Transnational Crime and Economic Globalization", *Transnational Organized Crime and International Security: Business as Usual*, Boulder, Lynne Rienner, 2002, pp. 37–52; Cockayne; J., *Transnational Organized Crime: Multilateral Responses to a Rising Threat*, International Peace Academy Publications, 2007; Ruggiero, V., "Transnational Crime: Official and Alternative Fears", *International Journal of the Sociology of Law*, Vol. 2000, No. 3, pp. 187–199 and "Criminals and Service Providers: Cross-National Dirty Economies", *Crime, Law and Social Change*, Vol. 28, 1997, No. 1, pp. 27–38.

These circumstances have led to an expansion of the portfolio of illicit goods and their customers, extension of transport routes and establishment of an extensive network of international cooperation ranging from the source zones of these illicit goods and persons through to the transit zones and finally the destination territories.

3 Similarities and Differences between Terrorism and Organised Crime

Regardless of the dissension regarding the definition of terrorism and organised crime, if we take terrorist behaviour and criminal behaviour as a parameter, we can identify the elements that these groups have in common and which have facilitated their relationships of cooperation over the course of history. These relationships, as will be considered in the following section, have adapted and transformed to keep up with international developments and changes in the nature the actors involved.[36]

In both cases, they consist of violent non-state actors emerging on the international scene as a consequence of the progressive privatisation of international relations and the proliferation of private legal and illegal actors. Both types of groups are capable of making rational calculations to identify the advantages of cooperation for the commission of criminal acts. Their actions cause increasingly negative consequences for the national societies in which they operate and international society as a whole. Both groups have gradually developed increasingly independent organisational systems, especially following the Cold War. As a result, they do not follow the orders of any government nor act for their benefit and this very autonomy and independence has become one of their attributes, even though in earlier periods they may have been sponsored by states or acted with the connivance of public officials or members of the ruling elite. The physical or psychological violence they exercise to achieve their objectives places them beyond ethical and legal boundaries, which determines and limits their relations with other state actors and non-state actors who act within the law. As a consequence, many states have classed not only the activities they carry out but also membership of both groups in itself as a criminal offence.[37] They have also been the object of international treaties and the decisions of international bodies to combat their practices, and in the

36 Ruggiero, V. Organised Crime and Terrorist Networks, Routledge, 2019.

37 Sanderson, T. M. "Transnational Terror and Organized Crime: Blurring the Lines", *SAIS Review*, Vol. 24, 2004, No. 1, pp. 53–54.

case of terrorism they have identified groups and imposed sanctions against their members, as mentioned above.[38] Nonetheless, both groups have proven to be capable of adapting well to the new circumstances. They have managed to innovate and represent a complex asymmetrical threat to states. In fact, they have deftly decentralised their activities and developed them in contexts characterised by an absence of state authority on multiple levels, filling the vacuum of services the population expects to obtain from state institutions and on occasions achieving a certain authority which is also assured with the use of violence against dissidents.

From an operational viewpoint, the needs of terrorist groups and organised crime are identical in terms of the resources they require: false identification, travel documents, transport networks, arms and emergency plans, etc.[39] In terms of their tactics, they share the use of extreme violence or the threat of violence and in addition their most common practices include kidnapping, theft, murder and extortion.[40] Finally, member loyalty is expected by both groups, and if they unilaterally leave the organisation they tend to be the object of violent reprisal. However, in recent times the increase in cooperation between both groups due to the demands of developing global strategies has seen individuals with criminal records join the ranks of terrorist organisations related with global terrorism, especially in so-called Western countries. Meanwhile, in zones such as the Sahel, cooperation between criminals and terrorists to assure passage of illicit goods and guarantee the security and expansion of markets is crucial. As a result, transfer or interchange of group members has become commonplace, particularly when the members of both organisations share ethnic, tribal, family or religious backgrounds, thereby distinguishing them from the characteristics of classic terrorist and criminal groups.[41]

However, there continue to be differences in the nature of both phenomena, which in principle justifies their treatment by states and international organisations as separate entities, although more and more attention is being paid to the nexus existing between criminal and terrorist groups. According to Liz Campbell, whether organised crime is interpreted in a structural or substantive way, it appears to be motivated by the accumulation of wealth;[42] it behaves like

---

38 See, for example, Resolutions 1267 (1999), 1989 (2011), 2161 (2014), 2170 (2014) and 2178 (2014) of the UN Security Council.

39 Sanderson, T.M., note 35, pp. 52–54.

40 Sanderson, T.M., note 35, pp. 49–61.

41 Dishman, Ch., "The Leaderless Nexus: When Crime and Terror Converge", *Studies in Conflict and Terrorism*, 2005, No. 28, pp. 239 and ss.

42 Campbell, L., *Organized Crime and Law*, Oxford, Hart Publishing, 2013.

an illegal international corporation, identifying the most appropriate locations for production, the most profitable routes, contacts and human resources and the most adequate infrastructure to increase and diversify the catalogue of goods they offer and their portfolio of customers.[43] Accordingly, their relations with authorities are focused on evading their control and controlling public officials and decision-makers, but without a political purpose.[44] On the contrary, terrorist groups engage in violent activities that aim to induce fear among the population with the aim of changing governmental decisions and actions in line with certain political or religious ideas, and as such they do not tend to enter into relationships of cooperation with public officials or politicians.[45] Moreover, while terrorist groups wish to publicise their ideas and actions to gain a greater number of sympathisers and followers, organised crime requires secrecy to protect its illegal businesses and does not need to gain the approval of the population. Finally, while disputes between classic terrorist organisations have been practically non-existent given that they do not compete in the same territory or to put into practice their political project, global terrorism has undergone changes in this sense, especially with organisations linked to Al-Qaeda which have disputed control of certain territories with ISIL and in contexts where violence or armed conflict prevail.[46] However, in the case of organised crime, struggles between groups to gain control of territories and illicit business opportunities are much more frequent.[47]

The common characteristics and differences between terrorist groups and organised crime have been maintained practically since the end of the 1990s. Although they are both clandestine groups that use violence against objectives that resist their propositions or combat them, many terrorist groups linked to the dynamics of decentralisation of global terrorism no longer maintain

43 Williams, Ph. "Organizing Transnational Crime: Networks, Markets and Hierarchies" in Williams, Ph and Vlassis, D. (Eds.), *Combating Transnational Crime: Concepts, Activities and Responses, Fran Cass*, London, 2001, pp. 58 and ss.

44 Capbell, L., "Organized Crime and National Security: A Dubious Connection?", *New Criminal Law Review,* Vol. 17, 2014, No. 2, pp. 220–251, p. 230.

45 According to Sergei Boeke, Al-Qaeda in the Islamic Magreb worked with drug traffickers in the region to found a caliphate in Mali (Boeke, S., "Al Qaeda in the Islamic Magreb: Terrorism, Insurgency or Organized Crime?", *Small Wars and Insurgency*, Vol. 27, 2016, No. 5, pp. 914–936).

46 Hamming, T. R. "The Al Qaeda–Islamic State Rivalry: Competition Yes, but No Competitive Escalation", *Terrorism and Political Violence*, 2017, p. 1–18.

47 Calderón, G., et al. "The Beheading of Criminal Organizations and the Dynamics of Violence in Mexico", *Journal of Conflict Resolution*, Vol. 59, 2015, No. 8, pp. 1455–1485 and Varese, F. *Mafias on the Move: How Organized Crime Conquers New Territories*, Princeton University Press, 2011.

neither hierarchical structures nor any strict control over the components of the group. The same occurs in the case of smaller, more recently established organised crime groups, the functioning of which is closely linked to technological development combined with classic criminal structures founded on national or ethnic identity. Similarly, the differences in terms of the characteristics of their respective members have begun to blur. Both organised criminals and terrorist groups are now competing when they recruit from among the same types of individuals. In the Western world, they compete for individuals prepared to embark on a criminal career or redeem their past. In regions affected by violence and a lack of state authority at different levels, criminal organisations recruit individuals with similar ethno-cultural characteristics, contributing to make the activities of both types of organisations more compatible.[48]

4 Evolution of the Link between Terrorism and Organised Crime

The common characteristics of both groups has allowed processes of cooperation between terrorist groups and organised crime during periods of recent history, mainly to cover the logistics needs of both organisations in reduced geographical areas. Bearing in mind the common elements and differences of organised crime and terrorism analysed above, we will now consider the characteristics of the relationships between them in the latter decades of the 20th century and how they have evolved as a series of factors have contributed to activate new processes of collaboration and alter traditional models of the relationship between crime and terror.

The links between global terrorism and transnational organised crime have their origins in the latter decades of the 20th century, when classic terrorist groups reached one-off agreements with organised crime groups with national or ethnic backgrounds. Cooperation between political and criminal violence is therefore not a new phenomenon, and certain cases have been documented of participation by ethno-nationalist terrorists and extremist left-wing and right-wing groups in criminal activities. Examples of collaboration between terrorist organisations and criminal organisations due to logistics needs during the 1980s and the 1990s include agreements to exchange arms for drugs between the Irish Republican Army (IRA) and the most criminal version of the

48 Schmid, A. P. Revisiting the Relationship Between International Terrorism and Transnational Organized Crime 22 Years Later, note 11.

Revolutionary Armed Forces of Colombia (FARC); collaboration between the Red Brigades and the Neapolitan Camorra to attack state law enforcement officers posing obstacles to achievement of their objectives;[49] and the provision of information on handling of explosives by Euskadi Ta Askatasuna (ETA) to the FARC in exchange for drugs.[50] Similarly, in the late 1990s and early 2000s joint operations were documented for heroin trafficking between and the Albanian mafia and the Kosovo Liberation Army, considered at that time to be a terrorist group by certain states, which needed supplies to fight the Serbian government.[51] In this case, both these violent organisations managed to increase their resources to achieve their different purposes. These types of one-off collaborations due to logistics reasons continue to take place, for example, between urban jihadist cells in need of sources of self-financing and criminal organisations which preserve the characteristics of classic criminal activity, with strict internal hierarchy and common national identity of their members. Examples include the exchange of drugs for arms between criminal organisations such as the Ndrangheta and the Neapolitan Mafia and Islamist terrorist cells based in Italian territory which have connections with other terrorist organisations in border countries of Europe.[52]

In past decades, criminals and terrorists also emulated each other's respective strategies. Organised crime groups carried out terrorist acts to intimidate institutions and citizens and thereby achieve political ends. Examples include the assassination of the judges Giovanni Falcone and Paolo Borsellino in 1992 by the Italian mafia in response to the judicial proceedings brought against individuals belonging to these organisations, or the series of terrorist attacks perpetrated by the Medellin drug cartel in response to the policies of the Colombian government regarding the extradition of drug traffickers to the US Similarly, groups considered to be terrorist organisations such as the Kurdistan

---

49 Dishman, Ch. Terrorism, Crime, and Transformation. *Studies in Conflict and Terrorism*, Vol. 24, 2001, No. 1, pp. 43–58.

50 EU Parliament's Committee on Civil Liberties, Justice and Home Affairs Report, 2012. *Europe's Crime-Terror Nexus: Links between Terrorist and Organised Crime Groups in the European Union*, PE 462.503, 2012, http://www.europarl.europa.eu/document/activities/cont/201211/20121127ATT56707/20121127ATT56707EN.pdf., p. 22 and Capbell, L., "Organized Crime and National Security: A Dubious Connection?", *New Criminal Law Review*, Vol. 17, 2014, No. 2, pp. 220–251 and p. 230.

51 Proksik, J. J. "EULEX and the Fight Against Organized Crime in Kosovo: What's the Record?", *Trends in Organized Crime*, 2017, pp. 1–25.

52 Curtis, G. E. and Karacan, T. "The Nexus among Terrorists, Narcotics Traffickers, Weapons Proliferators and Organized Crime Networks in Western Europe", *The Library of Congress, December* 2002, https://www.loc.gov/rr/frd/pdf-files/WestEurope_NEXUS.pdf.

Workers' Party (PKK), the National Liberation Front of Corsica (FLNC), the Irish National Liberation Army (INLA) and Hezbollah among others, have been involved in criminal activities at different levels, including theft, extortion, arms trafficking and drug trafficking to amass financial resources.[53]

Terrorist groups tended to establish a series of limits when collaborating with criminal groups so as not to lose their political identity and the purpose of social and political change which legitimised their use of violence. Accordingly, most of the cooperation processes were established among the terrorist groups themselves, as many of them had support from other states and did not have to resort to collaboration with the mafia. This was the case of the Italian Red Brigades, which paid the Popular Front for the Liberation of Palestine for training in handling of explosives, and the members of ETA who were trained in Palestinian camps in Beirut.[54] Once the leaders of domestic or international terrorist organisations had evaluated the limits of their political ideologies, they then established the limits of their relationship with organised criminals so as not to interfere with their political objectives and detract from the nature of their struggle. They also had to consider to what extent they were prepared to deal with criminal organisations on an equal footing and manage the execution of criminal activity within the limits they had set. Consequently, groups such as ETA had a much more limited relationship with crime, restricting their activities to extortion of Basque businesspeople and collaboration with the FARC to obtain arms. Meanwhile, other organisations such as the IRA had a much closer relationship with criminal activity, because their leaders were capable of managing participation in the illegal arms trafficking market and even bank robberies, acting as if it was yet another criminal organisation and justifying these activities on the basis of the need for significant resources due to the context of ongoing armed conflict.[55] The military wing of Hezbollah

---

53 Curtis, G. E. and Karacan, T. "The Nexus Among Terrorists, Narcotics Traffickers, Weapons Proliferators and Organized Crime Networks in Western Europe", *The Library of Congress, December* 2002, https://www.loc.gov/rr/frd/pdf-files/WestEurope_NEXUS.pdf.

54 According to Ruíz Durán, a clear example of this international cooperation between terrorist groups was the arrest in 1982 by Israeli military forces of around 113 members of ETA, 26 members of the Red Army Faction and two members of the Red Brigades in the Saido camp in Beirut (Ruiz Durán F.J., "La internacional terrorista patrocinada por la URSS", *Contribuciones a las Ciencias Sociales*, 2017, No. 2017–08).

55 Dishman, Ch. Terrorism, Vrime, and Transformation. *Studies in Conflict and Terrorism*, note 49, pp. 43–58. Jupp, J. and Garrod, M. "Legacies of the Troubles: The Links between Organized Crime and Terrorism in Northern Ireland", *Studies in Conflict & Terrorism*, 2019, pp. 1–40.

also acted in a similar way, carrying out criminal activities on a large scale, including drug trafficking, arms trafficking and money laundering.[56]

However, as opposed to what occurred in past decades, the links currently existing between organised crime and terrorist groups have intensified to an extent that the borders traditionally existing between the nature of these two different types of groups have been blurred, with terrorist organisations participating on an ongoing basis in large-scale criminal activities and adopting financial gain as part of their objectives. On the other hand, transnational organised crime frequently relies on terrorist strategies to safeguard its illegal businesses or collaborates permanently with terrorist groups that offer them security on trafficking routes and control the local population and other armed groups located in the zone.[57] These complex, interlinked relationships manifest themselves differently depending on the geographical context and political, social and economic conditions of the space where they take place. In this sense, analysis of the aspects that have favoured an increase in cooperation between organised crime and terrorist groups and their intensity is very useful in order to predict new processes and design instruments to address and prevent them.

5 Factors that Have Fostered the Nexus between Terrorism and Organised Crime

The evolution of international relations towards an increasingly interdependent and complex system has favoured convergence between the needs of terrorist groups and organised crime due to various factors. The first of these is the increasingly active participation of private agents in international relations, which were previously the exclusive domain of nation states. Of the different non-state actors involved together with states in cooperation and conflict processes, organised crime and international terrorism may be categorised as illegal private actors given that their practices and objectives are prohibited by domestic and international law. Even so, they have found a way of exploiting the process of globalisation of international relations initiated as a consequence of the worldwide expansion of the capitalist system, which has ended up extending to other fields such as economics and finance. As a result,

56 Proksik, J. J. "EULEX and the Fight Against Organized Crime in Kosovo: What's The Record?" *Trends in Organized Crime*, 2017, pp. 1–25.

57 Stohl, M., "Old Myths, New Fantasies and the Enduring Realities of Terrorism", *Critical Studies on Terrorism*, Vol. 1, 2008, No. 1, pp. 146–148.

in the post-Cold War era the threats originating from non-state actors have increased and expanded worldwide.[58] The complexity of the globalisation process was perceived initially as being positive due to the development of new technologies and the increase in international trade and the flow of goods and services, in addition to the demand for illicit goods. However, crime has also spiralled out of control, offering ever more lucrative criminal scenarios where participants in the informal economy may become involved in illegal dealings and subject to exploitation. Despite the development of international human rights law, increasing inequality has seen criminal activity jeopardise the rights and security of individuals in many territories in an unhindered manner.[59] In addition, they are occupying a role in armed conflicts which start out as internal but end up being internationalised, partly due to the introduction of the objectives of global terrorism in the struggle of the insurgents and the business opportunities found by organised crime in places beyond the control of state authorities.

Within the global international system, ethno-nationalist and extremist political terrorist groups, which we could call 'classic' terrorist organisations, coexist with new terrorist organisations that are not bound by borders and seek international expansion due to the global nature of their objectives. Meanwhile, 'classic' criminal groups have steadily developed an international focus as the capitalist system expanded at a worldwide level and economic and financial relations acquired an increasingly global nature. In addition, they have designed global operation strategies which go beyond former more localised actions, collaborating with smaller criminal groups which have adapted to the globalisation process by making use of advances in the field of information and communication technologies.[60] Both organisations seek to expand their operations through infiltration of small groups of individuals and groups aligned with their interests across the world, which follow a global strategy in

---

58 Marrero Rocha, I. Global System Dynamics in the Relationships Between Organized Crime and Terrorist Groups, in Vicenzo Ruggiero (Ed.), Organised Crime and Terrorist Networks, Routledege, 2019, pp. 100–1180.

59 Franko, K. *Globalization and Crime*, SAGE Publications Limited, 2019 and Rothe, D. and Friedrichs, D. O. *Crimes of Globalization*, Routledge, 2014.

60 Andreas, P. "Transnational Crime and Economic Globalization", *Transnational Organized Crime and International Security: Business as Usual*, Boulder, Lynne Rienner, 2002, pp. 37–52; Cockayne, J., *Transnational Organized Crime: Multilateral Responses to a Rising Threat*, International Peace Academy Publications, 2007; Ruggiero, V., "Transnational Crime: Official and Alternative Fears", *International Journal of the Sociology of Law*, Vol. 2000, No. 3, pp. 187–199 and "Criminals and Service Providers: Cross-National Dirty Economies", *Crime, Law and Social Change*, Vol. 28, 1997, No.1, pp. 27–38.

their respective local areas. This globalisation-decentralisation pairing offers new possibilities in terms of geographical diversification, multiplication of activities, maximisation of profits and ethnic-cultural-national diversity of their members, while at the same time projecting an image which identifies each criminal or terrorist organisation with certain objectives and a modus operandi.

Accordingly, organised crime has established itself in ever more geographical spaces, operating in the manner of illegal multinationals to increase profits and reduce risks, searching for the most adequate territories for the production of illegal goods, the most convenient and safest transport routes and the most profitable distribution and sales points, while at the same time eluding international and domestic laws which prohibit and prosecute these types of practices.[61] As part of this flexibilisation and adaptation to the socio-economic characteristics of the different locations where they operate, organised crime has been capable of evaluating the possibilities offered by collaboration with other violent groups established in those same territories, even though their objectives are initially of a political nature, as in the case of terrorist groups.[62]

The decentralised approach of global terrorism also differs to the authoritarian centralism of other terrorist groups, characterised by a strict hierarchy and concentration of power in the upper echelons responsible for decision-making. The delocalisation of global terrorism does not prevent the violent activities of their affiliates, splinter groups and derivatives from having a global impact, because they are conceived as part of the same strategy, inspired by a sole ideological programme which grants them a unique identity.[63] The fact they share this same ideology contributes to defend the interests and objectives of this new terrorism in different locations across the world.[64] A good example is Syria, where firstly Al-Qaeda and subsequently ISIL managed to

---

61 Varese, F. *Mafias on the Move: How Organized Crime Conquers New Territories*, Princeton University Press, 2011; Ibáñez Muñoz, J. and Sánchez Avilés, C. *Mercados ilegales y violencia armada: Los vínculos entre la criminalidad organizada y la conflictividad internacional*, Tecnos, 2015, and Albanese, J. S. "The Causes of Organized Crime: Do Criminals Organize Around Opportunities for Crime or Do Criminal Opportunities Create New Offenders?", *Journal of Contemporary Criminal Justice*, Vol. 16, 2000, No. 4, pp. 409–423.

62 Dishman, Ch. "The Leaderless Nexus: When Crime and Terror Converge", note 41, pp. 237–252.

63 Atwan, A. B. *Islamic State: The Digital Caliphate*, University of California Press, 2015.

64 Pearson, F. S., Akbulut, I. and Olson Lounsbery, M., "Group Structure and Intergroup Relations in Global Terror Networks: Further Explorations", *Terrorism and Political Violence*, Vol. 29, 2017, No. 3, pp. 550–572 and Reinares, F., *Terrorismo Global*, Taurus, 2003, pp. 90 and ss.

attract between 25,000 and 30,000 individuals from more than 90 different nationalities and insert them in a new strategy of transnational insurgency.[65] A decentralised structure made up of cells, splinter groups, affiliates and franchise groups has ensured their survival, expansion of their power and dissemination of the ideology of global terrorism, constituting itself as a social movement that promotes jihadism at a worldwide level with its own legends, heroes, symbols, theological foundations and political ideals.[66] The virtual space occupied by these organisations in order to transmit their arguments and objectives and publicise their deeds to attract more individuals has been a crucial element to maintain their ideological-political centralisation in a decentralised worldwide organisational scheme. Decentralisation also grants cells and other types of organisations linked to the central or parent organisation independence to adapt to the political, social, economic, geographical and cultural conditions of the territories where they are established, meaning that at times they are known as franchise groups and they are financed autonomously. They therefore take advantage of the legal or illegal financing sources they have access to depending on their structure, objectives and activities, and above all the context in which they act.[67] Large global terrorism organisations would be incapable of providing resources to all the small organisations with which they are linked across the world, not only because it would be materially impossible but also because international cooperation to combat terrorism financing has made this increasingly difficult.[68]

The fight against terrorism financing since the terrorist attacks of 11 September has been widely supported by more than 165 states, which have developed political and legal instruments capable of preventing persons or groups from accessing funds or receiving funds that other persons or groups wish to transfer to them to carry out terrorist activities. As a result, the informal

---

65 Marrero Rocha, I. and Trujillo Mendoza, H (Eds.). *Jihadism, Foreign Fighters and Radicalization in the EU: Legal, Functional and Psychosocial Responses*, Routledge, 2018; Klausen, J., "Tweeting the jihad: social media networks of Western foreign fighters in Syria and Iraq", *Studies in Conflict and Terrorism*, Vol. 38, 2015, No. 1, pp. 1–22 and Gates, S. and Podder, S., "Social Media, Recruitment, Allegiance and the Islamic State", *Perspectives on Terrorism*, Vol. 9, 2015, No. 4, http://www.terrorismanalysts.com/pt/index.php/pot/article/view/446/html.

66 Mazer, G. "Islamic Radicalization among North Africans in Britain", *The British Journal of Politics and International Relations*, Vol. 10, 2008, No. 4, pp. 550–570.

67 Dishman, Ch. "The Leaderless Nexus: When Crime and Terror Converge", note 41, pp. 237–252.

68 Ruipérez Cnales, J. Terrorism Financing and the Crime-Terror Relationships as a Challenge for Security in Europe, in Vicenzo Ruggiero (Ed.), Organised Crime and Terrorist Networks, Routledege, 2019, pp. 141–154.

remittance system known as Hawala has come under scrutiny and hundreds of millions of dollars from charitable organisations, companies and other organisations have been blocked due to their connection with international terrorism. These circumstances have forced many terrorist organisations to transform themselves into criminal organisations with the justification of achieving their political objectives, such as the Talibans, Hezbollah and the Islamic Movement of Uzbekistan.[69]

As Wang points out, when we refer to classic criminal groups and new criminal groups working together as an incentive for cooperation with groups related with global terrorism by overcoming the reluctance of these more traditional criminal organisations, particularly in stable socio-political contexts, this does not occur in situations of structural violence and conflict:

> However, some newer transnational crime groups, often originating in ungovernable regions, are now establishing their links with terrorist groups; because the criminal groups do not possess long-term and efficient financial strategies and they want nether [*sic*] stability nor strong states who can control them. Another significant reason is that new transnational groups likely take advantages of the chaos of war and dysfunctional state functions and generate huge profits from cooperating with terrorists. Consequently, the new types of transnational crime groups share consistent interests with terrorist [*sic*] and they gradually form terrorist-transnational crime relationship. [*sic*][70]

Some of the factors that have fostered cooperation by transnational organised crime are derived from the limitations faced by states when attempting to address this problem. These including the following: firstly, the absence of international, regional or domestic legislative frameworks that address the existence of these linkages and the most appropriate legal response, as a consequence of the separate treatment that has been applied to criminal activity and terrorism in domestic criminal legislation and the diversity of forms of this phenomenon in different countries; secondly, the intelligence resources continue to be inadequate and many countries have been incapable of adopting measures to prevent recruitment of individuals for participation in criminal or terrorist activities; thirdly, the inability of some states to fight against corruption has granted greater impunity to public officials and politicians,

---

69 Wang, P. "The Crime-Terror Nexus: Transformation, Alliance, Convergence", *Asian Social Science*, Vol. 6, 2010, No. 6, p. 13.

70 Wang, P. Note 69, p. 13.

undermining efforts to halt these new processes of cooperation and granting them a certain degree of political protection;[71] fourthly, the cooperation between the law enforcement agencies of different countries is also inadequate to combat a phenomenon which transcends national boundaries, moves with ease between different jurisdictions and has security implications at a regional and international level;[72] fifthly, international institutions do not possess investigation agencies along the lines of Europol or Interpol and they do not have the necessary resources and skills to adapt and improve investigation processes and thereby reinforce judicial proceedings against persons participating in this criminal terrorism;[73] sixthly, there is no cooperation between states and non-governmental organisations working in the field, which are familiar with the causes and the peculiar features of the proliferation of terrorist groups and the expansion of transnational organised crime in certain contexts,[74] nor is there any cooperation between governmental and non-governmental agencies, which is crucial to design policies adapted to the different spaces in which cooperation between crime and terror takes place; and finally, the international community does not have the resources or the political will to undertake appropriate action in order to empower local governments so that they can build the necessary resilience against organised crime and terrorism and thereby offer the population an alternative means of subsistence.

6 Evolution of the Models of Linkages between Terrorism and Organised Crime

Identifying the linkages between organised crime and terrorism is a complex task, given the constant changes they undergo and the difficulty of obtaining data on clandestine organisations. However, many authors and articles argue

---

71 Harfield, Cl. "The Organization of Organized Crime Policing and Its International Context" *Criminology & Criminal Justice*, Vol. 8, 2008, No. 4, pp. 483–507.

72 Kapucu and Demirhan analysed 305 interviews to study the need for collaboration by public security networks in the fight against terrorism and organised crime, overcoming overly rigid hierarchical structures and establishing the basis for collaboration founded on mutual trust and sharing of information (Kapucu, N. and Demirhan, C. "Managing Collaboration in Public Security Networks in the Fight against Terrorism and Organized Crime", *International Review of Administrative Sciences*, Vol. 85, 2019, No. 1, pp. 154–172).

73 The Hague Good Practices on the Nexus between Transnational Organized Crime and Terrorism, Global Counterterrorism Forum, www.theGCTF.org.

74 Buscaglia, E. "Controlling Organized Crime and Corruption in the Public Sector", in *Forum on Crime and Society*, 2003.

that as organised crime has become increasingly transnational and terrorist groups linked with global terrorism are capable of operating in a greater number of geographical regions, the cooperation between these two groups has also been transformed. More occasional collaboration schemes, justified on the basis of pragmatic logistics needs and invariably driven by the needs of international terrorist groups to obtain arms for their violent activities, have now intensified and become increasingly regular to the extent that it has become a permanent alliance which meets their mutual knowledge, operational and financial support needs. This qualitative leap in their relations is enabled when both types of organisations are able to interchange members and resources and participate jointly in operations, which seems to be an increasingly frequent occurrence. This integration may deepen to the extent that it modifies the very nature of these organised crime and terrorist groups.

Convergence between crime and terror occurs when transnational organised crime develops permanent terrorist strategies, independently associating crime with terror to control the conduct of the population and the weak authorities in places where they engage in illegal activities, or alternately this is done through continued association with groups linked with global terrorism to guarantee the security and profitability of their business. Terrorism allows transnational organised crime to confuse and hamper any type of investigation instigated by the authorities to address this problem and grants them greater impact when countering political initiatives designed to pursue them, as well as demoralising and terrorising law enforcement agencies, politicians, legislators and judges. The use of terrorism by criminal groups without the support of terrorist groups is becoming commonplace in the Colombian and Mexican drug cartels, following the example of the Italian mafia in the 1980s.[75] When criminals engage in acts of terrorism as part of their strategy, they acquire military knowledge which is useful for protection of crops and transit routes. This also makes them capable of destabilising economic and political structures to an even greater extent with the aim of generating a more favourable context in which to carry out their criminal activities.[76] In these types of situations, organisations transform considerably to acquire a hybrid crime/terror status. In other cases, criminal groups develop permanent alliances with terrorist

75 Shelley, J, and Picarelli, T. "Methods and Motives. Exploring Links Between Transnational Organized Crime and International Terrorism", *Trends in Organized Crime*, Vol. 9, 2005, No. 2, pp. 52–66 and Phillips, B. J. "Terrorist Tactics by Criminal Organization: The Mexican Case in Context", *Perspectives on Terrorism*, Vol. 7, 2018, No. 1, pp. 46–63.

76 Schmid, A. P. "Links between Terrorism and other Forms of Crime", *Turkish Policy Quarterly*, Summer 2004, pp. 43–56.

groups which already control the territory and population and can provide them with resources. One example is the Chechen mafia in Chechnya, which offers economic support to Chechen terrorist insurgents in exchange for protection and intelligence information relating to their business.[77]

Similarly, the convergence between terror and crime can also occur independently within terrorist groups that include generation of wealth among their objectives, which involves criminal activity at a larger scale and on a continuous basis, as in the case of the Kurdistan Workers' Party, Hezbollah in Lebanon and the Tamil Tigers in Sri Lanka.[78] This is also the case of the Talibans in Afghanistan through their participation in the cultivation and sale of opium, and Al-Shabaab in Somalia, with a volume of criminal activity that already greatly exceeds its terrorist activities.[79] The convergence between terror and crime provides terrorists with more resources to perpetrate terrorist acts, as well as granting them autonomy from their traditional sponsors. They can obtain arms with greater ease and develop criminal skills which are doubly useful when they are applied for a political purpose. Moreover, if they develop permanent alliances with criminal groups their participation in illegal businesses facilitates the use of trafficking routes for their terrorist activities and also expands the range of potential members by including those who seek to legitimise their criminal activity under a religious umbrella. Evidently, in the case of certain terrorist groups this convergence between terrorist and criminal tactics can also compromise their political credibility.

While this convergence can occur independently, it may also arise as a consequence of the converging collaboration between both groups, with merging of their political and economic objectives and unification of their action strategies. This type of convergence has been documented on the drug trafficking routes in Western Africa, which involve collaboration between cartels from Latin America which introduce drugs from Guinea-Bissau to Senegal, Mali to Libya and from there to Europe, with participation by terrorists linked with Al-Qaeda in the Islamic Magreb and other organised criminals in the region.[80] Nonetheless, it is difficult to document and compare these examples

---

77 Insight on the News. *Russia Hammers Chechnya*, 29 November 1999.

78 Williams, Ph. "Terrorist Financing and Organized Crime: Nexus, Appropriation or Transformation?" in Thomas Biersteker and Susan Eckert (Eds), Countering the Financing of Terrorism, London: Routledge, 2008, pp. 126–149.

79 Makarenko, T. Crime, Terror, and the Central Asian Drug Trade. Harvard Asia Quarterly, Vol. 6, 2002, No. 3, pp. 1–24.

80 Obaji, Ph. JR., "Inside the Networks of Sex Slaves, the Drug Trade, Colombian Cartels and Al Qaeda in Africa," *The Daily Beast*, 3 March 2018.URL: https://www.thedailybeast.com/inside-the-networks-of-sex-slavesthe-drug-trade-colombian-cartels-and-al-qaeda-in-africa.

and determine whether they are effectively examples of convergence between crime and terror. Hübschle believes that convergence between terrorist and criminal organisations is rarely stable, given that the cultural and socio-political reality in these regions and the ideological and operational differences between criminal and terrorist groups make permanent alliances leading to mergers unsustainable.[81] In addition, the state of order in the so-called Sahel, with participation by tribal warlords, militias and government-backed forces among others, makes it difficult to determine whether the merger between crime and terror is due to the action of criminal or terrorist groups or they simply operate in a situation of permanent violence and conflict where it is impossible to distinguish objectives and strategies, creating a 'black hole' in which the type of nexus varies greatly and the nature of these interactions in situations of structural violence and absence of authority cannot be ascertained.[82] In fact, in the case of Nigeria, despite contacts between the Nigerian mafia and Islamist groups in the country, the greatest convergence between terror and crime takes place due to the intense collaboration between Boko Haram and Al-Qaeda in the Islamic Magreb region.[83]

Accordingly, there is no agreement regarding the nature of the nexus, which seems to depend largely on the local context. In countries with stable political systems and a certain degree of democratic quality, most of the connections between crime and terror consist of recruitment by jihadist cells of individuals with a criminal past. Terrorism is especially attractive because it meets the same objectives and needs pursued by criminal activity, given that jihadist cells also engage in robberies, kidnappings, fraud and trafficking of illicit goods, among other activities, in order to achieve resources.[84]

81 Hübschle, A. 'From Theory to Practice: Exploring the Organised Crime-Terror Nexus in Sub-Saharan Africa', *Perspectives on Terrorism*, Vol. 5, 2011, No. 3–4, p. 93, URL: http://www.terrorismanalysts.com/pt/index.php/pot/article/view/157 .

82 Makarenko, T. "The Crime-Terror Continuum: Tracing the Interplay between Transnational Organized Crime and Terrorism", *Global Crime*, Vol. 6, 2004, No. 1, pp. 129–145; Albanese, J. S. The Causes of Organized Crime: Do Criminals Organize Around Opportunities for Crime or Do Criminal Opportunities Create New Offenders?. *Journal of Contemporary Criminal Justice*, Vol. 16, 2000, No. 4, pp. 409–423 and Andrews-Speed, Ph., et al. *Want, Waste or War?: The Global Resource Nexus and the Struggle for Land, Energy, Food, Water and Minerals*, Routledge, 2014.

83 In Pigné, J. *Islamic Extremism in the Sahel*, Institut Thomas More, July 2013.

84 Hasisi, Badi, et al. Crime and Terror: Examining Criminal Risk Factors for Terrorist Recidivism. *Journal of Quantitative Criminology*, 2019, pp. 1–24. Regarding radical offenders with a criminal past, see: Ljujic, Vanja; Van Prooijen, Jan Willem; Weerman, Frank. Beyond the Crime-Terror Nexus: Socio-Economic Status, Violent Crimes and Terrorism. *Journal of Criminological Research, Policy and Practice*, 2017, vol. 3, No.3, pp. 158–172; Rostami, Amir, et al. The Swedish Mujahideen: An Exploratory Study of 41 Swedish

In the case of states in a process of transition after an armed conflict with weak border control, a weak judicial system and high levels of corruption in public administration, it is easy to find terrorist organisations and criminal organisations that have developed a hybrid nature to complement each other's activities. In these post-conflict situations, state authorities find themselves incapable of exercising full, exclusive sovereign authority throughout their territory and over all the population. The confusion between the identities of both organisations is heightened and it is difficult to decipher the nature of the alliances established.[85] The possibilities of convergence between crime and terror are greater in frontier zones with easy access to smuggling routes, where the national economy is complemented by illegal markets, the local population faces significant inequalities and criminals and terrorists offer their financial support. Moreover, if state institutions are weak, corruption is systemic and there are minority groups that do not participate in political, economic and social life to the same extent as the rest of the population because state leadership is divided into different groups, the target population for recruitment by terrorist insurgents and organised crime increases significantly because many individuals see these organisations as the only way out to improve their socio-economic status.[86]

7 Final Remarks

Despite reluctance by classic criminal groups over the course of history to collaborate with terrorist groups because they tended to have control over the territories where they operated, the necessary resources and the necessary

Foreign Fighters Deceased in Iraq and Syria. *Studies in Conflict & Terrorism*, 2018, pp. 1–14; Ilan, Jonathan; Sandberg, Sveinung. How 'Gangsters' become Jihadists: Bourdieu, Criminology and the Crime–Terrorism Nexus. *European Journal of Criminology*, 2019, vol. 16, No. 3, pp. 278–294; Lasoen, Kenneth L. (Plan Bruxellles): Belgian Intelligence and the Terrorist Attacks of 2015–16. *Terrorism and Political Violence*, 2018, pp. 1–19 and Van Leyenhorst, Maarten; Andreas, Ada. Dutch Suspects of Terrorist Activity: A Study of Their Biographical Backgrounds Based on Primary Sources. *Journal for deradicalization*, 2017, no 12, pp. 309–344.

85 Policy Toolkit on The Hague Good Practices on the Nexus between Transnational Organized Crime and Terrorism, United Nations Interregional Crime and Justice Research Institute and Global Counterterrorism Forum, March 2019, pp. 6–9.

86 Policy Toolkit on The Hague Good Practices on the Nexus between Transnational Organized Crime and Terrorism, pp. 9 and ff.

contacts with public officials to guarantee a certain degree of impunity, a series of factors have made it more and more attractive to establish permanent cooperation with terrorist groups or the assumption of terrorist strategies. Firstly, organised crime groups have adapted to exploit the advantages offered by an increasingly globalised international system in order to expand their portfolio of illegal goods, transport routes and profits. Secondly, expansion of their areas of operation has obliged them to cooperate with other actors who also operate in the same territories and with which they have common or opposing interests. The opportunities and at the same time the instability that organised criminals find in other zones of the planet to engage in their dealings has led them to deal with terrorist groups in order to obtain the protection they need and secure their routes. On other occasions, criminal groups have developed terrorist strategies and knowledge in order to deal with hostile contexts without having to depend on other violent groups.

Groups related with global terrorism, as opposed to classic terrorist groups, arose as part of a strategy for worldwide expansion. Right from the outset, they assumed a decentralised organisational structure via networks, in which each of the parts has significant freedom to collaborate and associate with other groups and thereby obtain the resources they need to carry out their activities. The peculiarities of each context have a major influence on the types of alliances with criminal organisations and may even lead to development of a hybrid organisation in which the scope and continuity of participation by the terrorist organisation in criminal activities calls into question their political nature. However, participants in criminal terrorism share a common ideological and religious identity which presents the image of a single planned strategy to international society. Consequently, the global psychological impact of their actions is greater, even though the people and territories that suffer the consequences the most are located on the outskirts of international relations where structural violence prevails, human rights are overlooked and state structures are almost irreversibly fragile.

This nexus between crime and terror has evolved due to changes in the nature and structures of both groups, increasing opportunities in certain territories, loss of prior state control over the objectives and actions of these groups and the series of limitations faced by international cooperation for coordination of resources, cooperation with non-state actors and adaptation to the different state jurisdictions.

CHAPTER 2

The United Nations' Current Legal Approach to Terrorism, Organized Crime and 'Organized Criminal Terrorism'

Katerina Akestoridi and Sofia Tzortzi

1 Introduction

Hardly would someone contend the maxim that both terrorism and organized crime threaten worldwide peace and security.[1] Yet, despite this common assumption, the concepts of organized crime and terrorism remain contested. Definitional problems constitute a recurrent theme in the research of either of the phenomena individually and gain more currency when testing the hypothesis of their interconnectedness and interdependence. The matter is not of theoretic interest only. It has important ramifications for the prevention and repression of the phenomena at the level of policy design and law enforcement by States nationally, regionally and internationally.[2] As the current chapter seeks to elaborate on the latter point, the conceptual discussion about definitions and key aspects of these two crimes will be essential part of the analysis of the United Nations legal framework to combat terrorism and organized crime. Hence, the second section provides an overview of the UN's legal instruments with the view to highlight the critical elements that determine the core of the concepts and the scope of implementation of the international legal framework. It engages in a critique of the instruments vis-à-vis the question on definition given that they fall short of providing one that is legally

1 UN Security Council Resolution 731 (21 January 1992) UN Doc S/RES/731; UNSC Res 1455 (17 January 1993) UN Doc S/RES/1455; UNSC Res 1526 (30 January 2004) UN Doc S/RES/1526; UN General Assembly, '2005 World Summit Outcome' (16 September 2005) UN Doc. A/RES/60/1 para.81; Liz Campbell, 'Organized Crime and National Security: A Dubious Connection?' (2014) 17(2) New Criminal Law Review 220; Anna Sergi, 'National Security vs Criminal Law. Perspectives, Doubts and Concerns on the Criminalization of Organized Crime in England and Wales' (2016) 22 European Journal of Criminal Policy and Research 713.

2 Christina Schori Liang, 'Shadow Networks: The Growing Nexus of Terrorism and Organized Crime', Policy Paper No.20, Geneva Centre for Security Policy (September 2011) <https://dam.gcsp.ch/files/2y10KYWTy5kK2V4ZRXaKUsTujA3CjpNCA5JRiDCk9XNNnIekfgWu> accessed 30 June 2020.

 | DOI:10.1163/9789004424579_004

comprehensive. To this end, the section sheds light to aspects of terrorism and organized crime from a criminological viewpoint that bring to the fore similarities and differences between them and explain the multiple manifestations of interaction between criminal and terrorist groups. With the aforementioned in mind, section three probes the question of effectiveness of the UN legal framework when organized criminal and terrorist groups interact. It assesses gaps and weaknesses, especially with regard to human rights safeguards, and puts forward recommendations for better prevention and enforcement of the law.

2 Terrorism and Organized Crime at the UN: An Overview of the Existing Legal Framework and the Problématique of Definitions

2.1 *Terrorism*

Attempts by the international community to form a generally acceptable, both normatively and politically, definition of terrorism as an international crime are detected as early as 1937 under the auspices of the League of Nations. A Committee of experts was commissioned to draft an international convention that would ensure the 'repression of conspiracies or crimes committed with a political and terrorist purpose.[3] Art.1 classifies as terrorist 'all criminal acts directed against a State and intended or calculated to create a state of terror in the minds of particular persons or a group of persons or the general public'. The said criminal acts were exemplified in Art.2 and included violent acts with an impact on persons (public officials or the public), damage to public property, offenses relating to weapons and auxiliary crimes such as assisting or participating in the acts.[4] The tautology in defining 'acts of terrorism' by recourse to 'a state of terror' is evident, making the text of the Convention quite ambiguous. Yet, the core elements that shaped the understanding of terrorism then can be discerned: a) an intended aim (terror), b) a target (state) and c) the

---

3 *Sixth Meeting of the Eighty-Third Session of the Council* (1934) 15 League of Nations Official Journal 1758–60, 1760.

4 Art.2(1): Causing death or grievous bodily harm or loss of liberty to protected persons and public officials; Art.2(2): destroying or damaging public property of another state; Art.2(3): endangering the lives of the public; Art.2(4) attempting to commit offenses; Art.2(5): manufacturing, obtaining, possessing, or supplying arms, ammunition, explosives or harmful substances with a view to committing an offense in any country; Art.3: conspiracy, incitement, direct public incitement, willful participation, and knowing assistance.

use of prohibited means (method). The Convention never entered into force, however it served as a point of reference for future normative deliberations on terrorism.[5]

Indeed, international lawmaking on terrorism has been marked by several milestones since 1937.[6] With the quest for a generic definition at the background, terrorism could not rise to the rank of international crimes nor be included among the offences tried by the International Criminal Court under the Rome Statute when it came into force. Looking, thus, for a way out of the impasse, the UN adopted a pragmatic approach to the setting of international standards to combat terrorism, following eventually the model of subject-specific treaties that codified various methods used by terrorist (the means of terrorist attacks). Between the 1950s and 1960s, an increasing number of hijacks of civil aircrafts[7] prompted States to take measures focusing on air travel safety. Starting with the *Tokyo Aircraft Convention of 1963*,[8] three other covenants related to civil aviation were concluded by the end of the 1980s.[9] Whereas the 1963 Convention does not create separate offences but only targets criminal offences covered in national legislation of the State of registration of the aircraft[10] committed on board of an aircraft in flight[11] or actions that jeopardize on-board safety,[12] the subsequent agreements establish distinct offences and require adhering States to penalize specific acts affecting in-flight

5 Ben Saul, 'Attempts to Define Terrorism in International Law' (2005) LII Netherlands International Law Review 57, 65–66.

6 Id.

7 Ilias Bantekas, 'The International Law of Terrorist Financing' (2003) 97 The American Journal of International Law 313.

8 UNGA, Convention on Offenses and Certain Other Acts Committed On Board Aircraft (adopted 14 September 1963, entered into force 4 December 1969) 704 UNTS 219 (hereafter Tokyo Convention).

9 UNGA, Convention for the Suppression of Unlawful Seizure of Aircraft (adopted 16 December 1970, entered into force 14 October 1971) 860 UNTS 105; Convention for the Suppression of Unlawful Acts against the Safety of Civil Aviation, 1971 (adopted 23 September 1971, entered into force 26 January 1973) 974 UNTS 177 (hereafter Montreal Convention); Protocol for the Suppression of Unlawful Acts of Violence at Airports Serving International Civil Aviation, supplementary to the Montreal Convention (adopted 24 February 1988, entered into force 6 August 1989) 1589 UNTS 474.

10 Except laws of a political nature or based on racial or religious discrimination. For an illustrative analysis of this exception, Sami Shubber, *Jurisdiction Over Crimes on Board Aircraft* (Martinus Nijhoff 1973).

11 For the purposes of the Tokyo Convention 'in flight' means from take-off until landing.

12 Article 1 Tokyo Convntion.

safety.[13] Several of these acts such as 'the seizure or exercise of the control of a civil aircraft unlawfully, by force or threat thereof, or any other form of intimidation'[14] or the intentional performance of an act of violence against a person on board an aircraft need to become severely punishable criminal offences in all States, which should take offenders into custody under the principle *aut dedere, aut judicare*. During the same time, terrorists favored also the kidnapping of diplomatic agents 'as a very effective method to achieve their objectives'.[15] The issue was viewed as particularly significant considering the special status of diplomatic agents under the Vienna Convention on Diplomatic Relations.[16] Hence, the *Convention on the Prevention and Punishment of Crimes Against Internationally Protected Persons, Including Diplomatic Agents*[17] was 'an important step forward in the battle against worldwide terrorist activities'.[18] Attacks against internationally protected persons such as kidnapping or murder, threats and attempts thereof need be criminalized and punished under this Convention 'by appropriate penalties which take into account their grave nature'.[19] Jurisdiction criteria are extended for the first time further to territoriality on the basis of nationality.[20] Again, States parties must extradite alleged offenders, if not submitted to prosecution.[21]

Proliferation of hostage-taking in the 1970s[22] beyond diplomatic agents resulted in the *International Convention Against the Taking of Hostages* (*the*

---

13 UN Office on Drugs and Crime, 'UN Legislative Guide to the Universal Anti-Terrorism Conventions and Protocols' (2003), 27 para 66 <https://www.unodc.org/pdf/crime/terrorism/explanatory_english2.pdf> accessed 6 April 2020.

14 Montreal Convention (n 9), art 1(a).

15 Louis M. Bloomfield and Gerald F. FitzGerald, 'Crimes Against Internationally Protected Persons: Prevention and Punishment' (1976) 54(1) Canadian Bar Review 197. Kidnapping is actually used mainly by TOC groups, borrowed and favored since the 1970s also by terrorists. As common practice of both criminal groups it is exemplary of the nexus between the two criminal manifestations. See also infra Chapter 1.

16 L.M. Bloomfield and G.F. FitzGerald (n 15).

17 (adopted 28 December 1973, entered into force 20 February 1977) 1035 UNTS 167.

18 L.M. Bloomfield and G.F. FitzGerald (n 15).

19 Convention on the Prevention and Punishment of Crimes Against Internationally Protected Persons (n 17) art 2(2).

20 Id. art 3(1) of the Convention. 'This is the first of the universal anti-terrorism instruments to introduce the requirement that a State party should establish jurisdiction over an alleged offender who is a national of that State': UNODC, 'UN Legislative Guide' (n13).

21 Convention on the Prevention and Punishment of Crimes Against Internationally Protected Persons (n 17) art 3.

22 Ben Saul, 'International Convention Against the Taking of Hostages' (2014) Sydney Law School Research Paper 14/105 <https://papers.ssrn.com/sol3/papers.cfm?abstract_id=2536150> accessed 2 May 2020.

"Hostages Convention") that intended to tackle for the first time hostage-taking in time of peace in circumstances which are 'manifestations of international terrorism'.[23] With similar wording as preceding instruments, the Convention defines the related offences, including the aim 'to compel a State, an international Organization, a natural or juridical person, or a group of persons, to do or abstain from doing an act'[24] as part of them, and obliges parties to make them appropriately punishable given their grave nature.[25] The convention, which is also underpinned by the 'prosecute or extradite' dogma, establishes mandatory jurisdiction over those offences on the basis of territoriality, nationality and passive personality.[26]

'[T]he growing threat to society posed by international terrorism and similar phenomena'[27] was among the motives for the adoption of the 1980 *Convention on the Physical Protection of Nuclear Material*,[28] which criminalizes the unlawful possession, use and transport of nuclear material and requires prosecution under the territoriality or nationality principles, or extradition based on the *aut dedere, aut judicare* axiom. As underlined during the drafting of the convention, preventing the use of nuclear material by terrorists through controls and bringing offenders to justice demanded international cooperation. Hence, alongside the criminalization of certain conduct, the convention imposes several obligations on States parties for the control and the security protection in the transfer of nuclear material.[29] The 1980s saw also the rise of terrorism aboard or against ships. States criminalized the seizure of ships and acts of

---

23 Till then, hostage-taking had been regulated under humanitarian law. UNDOC, 'Terrorism international Framework: International Terrorism-Related Conventions', E4J University Module Series: organized Crime/Counter-Terrorism (March 2019) <https://www.unodc.org/e4j/en/organized-crime/module-16/key-issues/terrorism-international-framework---international-terrorism-related-conventions.html>.

24 UNGA, International Conventions Against the Taking of Hostages (adopted 17 December 1979, entered into force 3 June 1983), 1316 UNTS 205, 206ff (hereafter Hostages Convention).

25 Id., art 2. The translational element is specified in art 13 which provides that the Convention 'shall not apply where the offense is committed within a single State, the hostage and the alleged offender are nationals of that State and the alleged offender is found in the territory of that State'.

26 'For example, one United States court found that article 5 of the Convention supports the optional exercise of extraterritorial jurisdiction on the basis of the passive personality principle' B. Saul, 'International Convention Against the Taking of Hostages' (n 22) referencing United States v. Yunis 924 F.2d 1086 (DC Cir 1991) 1090.

27 Statement by the representative of Austria (31 October 1977) CPNM/7 in International Atomic Energy Agency, *Convention on the Physical Protection of Nuclear Material* Legal Series N.12 (1982), 303.

28 (adopted 3 March 1980, entered into force 8 February 1987) 1456 UNTS 124.

29 Id., art 7.

violence against a ship (e.g. placing destructive devices) and against persons aboard under the *1988 Convention on Suppression of Unlawful Acts against the Safety of Maritime Navigation*, which was negotiated by the International Maritime Organization (IMO). Furthermore, they extended criminalization to acts threatening the safety of offshore platforms (e.g. oil platforms) with the adoption of the *Protocol for the Suppression of Unlawful Acts against the Safety of Fixed Platforms Located on the Continental Shelf* (SUA Protocol).[30] Simultaneously, the 'Lockerbie bombing'[31] brought air travel back to the spotlight and prompted international legal action against plastic explosives, leading to the adoption of the *Convention on the Marking of Plastic Explosives for the Purpose of Detection* in 1991.[32] This agreement has been characterized as "somehow special"[33] because it does not criminalize a certain manifestation of terrorist action but aims to enhance the detectability of plastic explosives to control their use by terrorists and other criminals. Indeed, by this Convention States need to mark plastic explosives manufactured for lawful purposes (e.g. army, police etc.) and only properly marked explosives are allowed. However, the convention also creates obligations to criminalize certain conducts; ergo, manufacturing, possessing, transferring and transporting unmarked explosives is prohibited. Ultimately, in that context it criminalizes these behaviors after all; besides how can States Parties prohibit a certain conduct if not by introducing it as a criminal offense in national legislation?[34]

The mid-1990s witnessed notorious terrorist attacks in public places, such as the poisonous gas attacks in Tokyo's subway[35] and bombings in Sri Lanka,[36]

---

30 (adopted 10 March 1988, entered into force 1 March 1992) 1678 UNTS 221.

31 'Timeline: Lockerbie bombing' *BBC.com* (London, 10 March 2020) <https://www.bbc.com/news/uk-scotland-34541363> accessed 20 May 2020.

32 (adopted 1 March 1991, entered into force 21 June 1998) 2122 UNTS 359; Roderick D van Dam, 'New Convention on the Marking of Plastic Explosives for the Purpose of Detection, A' (1991) 16 Air Law 167.

33 UNDOC, 'Convention on the Marking of Explosives for the Purpose of Detection 1991' <https://www.unodc.org/documents/treaties/terrorism/Commonwealth_Chapter_11.pdf> accessed 16 July 2020. The prohibition and destruction of unmarked explosives is also included [Article IV(2)].

34 Indicative research in national implementing legislation demonstrates that -in fact- offenses are added in national criminal codes and legislation. Conduct prohibited by the Convention is punishable by fines and custodial sentences. See for example, Law and Justice Legislation Amendment (Marking of Plastic Explosives) Act 2007 (AU), Title VI of the Antiterrorism and Effective Death Penalty Act enacted on 24 April 1997 (USAo), Law 19(III)/2002 (CY).

35 The so-called "Tokyo subway sarin attack" on 20 March 1995.

36 The so-called "Colombo Central Bank" bombing happened on 31 January 1996.

Israel[37] and the UK.[38] The tipping point was the lethal bombing on US military personnel in Saudi Arabia in June 1996[39] which prompted the US to address the absence of a multilateral instrument dealing with terrorist attacks in public places[40] and initiate negotiations of the *1997 International Convention for the Suppression of Terrorist Bombings*.[41] Art.5 obliges States to penalize gravely the described criminal acts 'where they are intended or calculated to provoke a state of terror in the general public or in a group of persons or particular persons' since such acts are totally unjustifiable under political, ideological, racial, ethnic or religious considerations. Two years later, the adoption of the *International Convention for the Suppression of the Financing of Terrorism* established as a separate offence the use of funds to carry out any of the offenses prescribed in the sectoral UN anti-terrorist treaties or 'any act intended to cause death or serious bodily injury to a civilian, or to any other person not taking an active part in the hostilities in a situation of armed conflict, when the purpose of such act, by its nature or context, is to intimidate a population or to compel a government or an international organization to do or abstain from doing any act'.[42] Pursuant to Art.8, Parties must take domestic measures to identify, detect, freeze, or seize terrorist-related funds and in accordance with Art.18 to prevent the commission of the targeted offense. Remarkably, this article exemplifies preventive measures to be adopted. A distinct feature is that the convention is directed not only to States but addresses directly private financial institutions.[43]

As shown, terrorist offenses are condemned on the international level, yet States did not opt for direct criminal responsibility of the offenders under international law strictly speaking. Instead, transnational criminal cooperation was effectuated via the mobilization of domestic criminal law systems. Impunity is to be avoided by establishing an increasingly wide range of States' jurisdiction, eventually covering even universality, and always being complemented by the

37 The Jaffa Road bus bombings which took place on 25 February 1996 and the Dizengoff Center suicide bombing which took place on 4 March 1996.

38 The Docklands bombings which took place on 9 February 1996 and the Manchester bombing of 15 June 1996.

39 Samuel M. Witten, 'The International Convention for the Suppression of Terrorist Bombings' (1998) 92 The American Journal of International Law 774.

40 Id.

41 UNGA (adopted 15 December 1997, entered into force 23 May 2001), 2149 UNTS 256 (hereafter Terrorist Bombings Convention).

42 UNGA (adopted 9 December 1999, entered into force 10 April 2002), 2178 UNTS 197, art 2(1) (a) and (b) [hereafter Terrorist Financing Convention].

43 I. Bantekas (n 7) 323.

aut dedere, aut judicare system.[44] Crucially, these instruments also explicitly remove the value of any ideological defensive veil, legally sealing the political adage that 'nothing can justify terrorism – Ever'[45] with provisions which effectively also supersede and nullify (or at least should) any political exception clause of a bilateral extradition treaty.[46] The ramifications for a comprehensive definition of terrorism are also interesting since the 'sectoral approach' did not

44 Five core principles of jurisdiction are recognized in total in international law: nationality, territoriality, passive personality, the protective principle and universality. Various writers report that through the UN counter-terrorism treaties, the covered offenses effectively become international crimes and 'activate the application of the universality principle' as crimes against humanity; 'any State is permitted to arrest, prosecute […] accused offenders on behalf of the international community', see Christopher C. Joyner, 'International Extradition and Global Terrorism: Bringing International Criminals to Justice' (2003) 25 Loyola International & Comparative Law Review 493. Strictly speaking, the term 'universal jurisdiction' (or universality) refers to the rule or principle of international law that confers on 'any nation which has the custody of the perpetrators' the right to prosecute them for 'crimes [that] are so universally condemned that the perpetrators are the enemies of all people', Demjanjuk v. Petrovsky, 1982, 776 F.2d 571, at 582 cited in: Daniel O'Donnel 'International treaties against terrorism and the use of terrorism during armed conflict and by armed forces' (2006) 88 International Review of the Red Cross 853, 856. It is not in the scope of this chapter to analyze the academic debate about the specifics of universal jurisdiction or the connection with *aut dedere, aut judicare* principle which remain unabated (on this question, Matthew Garrod, 'Unraveling the Confused Relationship Between Treaty Obligations to Extradite or Prosecute and "Universal Jurisdiction" in the Light of the Habré Case' (2018) 59 Harvard International Law Journal 125). We use the term of universality generically, in the sense that it allows prosecution of an alleged perpetrator of an offense covered by the sectoral anti-terrorist conventions by more or less any State without other connection with the act or the person(s) involved.

45 UNSC '"Nothing Can Justify Terrorism – Ever", Says Secretary-General, as Security Council Hears from Some 50 Speakers in Day-Long Debate' (Meetings Coverage SC/10882, 15 January 2013) <https://www.un.org/press/en/2013/sc10882.doc.htm> accessed on 31 March 2019.

46 A wide discussion can be raised over that point especially considering the variety of interpretations of a "political" offense as well as on the basis of earlier US case-law such as the *Irish Quinn* case or the *Artukovic* decision, sec Mary V. Mochary, Victoria Toensing, Nigel Sheinwald, Thomas Moseley, Ruth Wedgwood and Torsten Stein, 'Extradition and the Political Offense Exception' 81 (April 8–11, 1987) Proceedings of the Annual Meeting (American Society of International Law), 467–483 and Antje C. Petersen, 'Extradition and the Political Offense Exception in the Suppression of Terrorism' 67 (1992) Indiana Law Journal 767. However, it is our position that any offense covered in one of the UN counter-terrorism treaties cannot be covered by the political offense exception in terms of extradition.

clarify the elements that would make terrorism a separate offense. In fact, the use of the term 'terrorism' was absent but in a few instruments.[47]

The turning point for anti-terrorism law was the terrorist attack to the US on September 11, 2001 in the aftermath of which a number of UN Security Council (SC) Resolutions were issued calling the international community to suppress terrorist activities.[48] While the sectoral treaties adopted pre-9/11 are, of course, in force and amendments/additions to them are still being adopted,[49] the new era of UN counter-terrorism action is dominated by SC Resolutions.[50] Resolutions 1368/2001 and 1373/2001 created the new legal basis for the global

---

47 Hostages Convention (n 24), Terrorist Bombings Convention (n 41), Terrorist financing Convention (n 42).

48 Aniel Caro de Beer qualifies the September 11 attacks as 'a Grotian moment', i.e. a great leap forward in the field of international law or a paradigm-shifting development resulting in new rules of customary international law emerging with less state practice and with unusual rapidity and acceptance, Aniel Caro de Beer, *Peremptory Norms of General International Law (Jus Cogens) and the Prohibition of Terrorism* (Brill Nijhoff 2019).

49 Namely Protocol of 2005 to the Convention for the Suppression of Unlawful Acts against the Safety of Maritime Navigation (adopted 14 October 2005) IMO LEG/CONF.15/21 (1 November 2005); the Protocol of 2005 to the Protocol for the Suppression of Unlawful Acts Against the Safety of Fixed Platforms located on the Continental Shelf (adopted 24 October 2005, entered into force 28 July 2010) IMO LEG/CONF.15/22; the 2005 Amendments to the Convention on the Physical Protection of Nuclear Material (adopted 8 July 2006, entered into force 8 May 2016) INFCIRC/274/Rev.1/Mod.1 (9 May 2016); International Convention for the Suppression of Acts of Nuclear Terrorism (adopted 13 April 2005, entered into force 7 July 2007) 2445 UNTS 89; Convention on the Suppression of Unlawful Acts Relating to International Civil Aviation and the Protocol Supplementary to the Convention for the Suppression of Unlawful Seizure of Aircraft (adopted 10 September 2010, entered into force 1 July 2018); Protocol to Amend the Convention on Offenses and Certain Acts Committed on Board Aircraft (adopted 4 April 2019, entered into force 1 January 2020).

50 Security Council antiterrorism action did not firstly appear as a response to 9/11. It has been witnessed in the past, e.g. SC Res 1127 (28 August 1997) UN Doc S/RES/1127 and SC Res 1173 (12 June 1998) UN Doc S/RES/1173 and Res 1176 (24 June 1998) Un Doc S/RES/1176 introducing the 'smart sanctions' (see, Andrea Bianchi, 'Assessing the Effectiveness of the UN Security Council's Anti-terrorism Measures: The Quest for Legitimacy and Cohesion' (2006) 17 European Journal of International Law 881) and notably SC Res 1267 (15 October 1999) UN Doc S/RES/1267, which introduced the UN sanctions regime, initially only against Osama bin Laden and Al-Qaida. Equally, the sectoral approach is not completely abandoned, despite the prevalence of the SC-led holistic policy. However, the conventions are in the margin of SC resolutions whose extent clearly pinpoints a new era driven by an impetus for speedy action. In addition, previous SC resolutions were based on article 41 of Chapter VII of the UN Charter and not on the articles allowing the use of force.

counter-terrorism system[51] directing antiterrorist action towards the law on armed conflict rather than criminal law.[52] By implying that terrorist acts are 'armed attacks',[53] resolution 1368 '[brought] international terrorism within the ambit of Art.42 UN Charter under which the SC may authorize the use of force and introduced self-defense as a possible justification against terrorist attacks under Art.51. Besides, Resolution 1373 – the first and most far-reaching resolution,[54] due to its 'strong legislative [and binding] nature',[55] imposing on all states obligations to penalize terrorist acts[56] – focused on measures to restrain the movement of 'terrorist persons' and to control funds of 'persons who commit [...] terrorist acts' through banning travel and freezing funds.[57]

In the following years, the SC reaffirmed Res 1373 and 1368 and adopted further resolutions focusing on the financing of terrorist acts,[58] the control of Foreign Terrorist Fighters (FTFs),[59] preventing/countering violent extremism

51 UN SC Res 1368 (12 September 2001) UN Doc S/RES/1368; UN SEC Res 1373 (28 September 2001) UN Doc S/RES/1373; William B. Messmer and Carlos L. Yordán, 'A Partnership to Counter International Terrorism: The UN Security Council and the UN Member States' (2011) 34 Studies in Conflict & Terrorism 843.

52 Cora True-Frost, 'When the UN addresses the "conditions conducive to terrorism" what happens to human rights?' (2017) Michigan State Law Review 805.

53 Resolution 1368 literally 'regards such [terrorist] acts, like any act of international terrorism, as a threat to international peace and security'. If read concurrently with article 51 of the UN Charter, which provides on the right to self-defense 'if an armed attack occurs against a Member of the United Nations', it can be deduced that they are ever since considered "armed attacks". This is further supported by the characterization of the September 11 attacks as "armed conflicts" by relevant decisions of NATO. See on the last point, Carsten Stahn, 'Terrorist Acts as Armed Attack: The Right to Self-Defense, Article 51(1)(2) of the UN Charter, and International Terrorism' (2003) 27 Fletcher F. World Affairs 35.

54 Sebastian von Einsiedel, 'Assessing the UN's Efforts to Counter Terrorism' (12 December 2016) United Nations University Centre for Policy Research, 2 <https://collections.unu.edu/eserv/UNU:6053/AssessingtheUNsEffortstoCounterterrorism.pdf> accessed 10 May 2020.

55 Aniel Caro de Beer (n 48) 26.

56 UNSC Res 1373 (n 51): '2.[...]e. ensure that any person who participates in the financing, planning, preparation or perpetration of terrorist acts or in supporting terrorist acts is brought to justice'.

57 The United Nations Security Council Counter-Terrorism Committee (CTC) was established in article 6 Res 1373 (n 51) and later enhanced by SC Res 1624 (14 September 2005) UN Doc S/RES/1624.

58 UN SC Res 2178 (24 September 2014) UN Doc S/RES/2178, UN SC Res 2396 (21 December 2017) Un Doc S/RES/2396, UN SC Res 2347 (24 March 2017) UN Doc S/RES/2347 and recently UN SC Res 2462 (28 March 2019) UN Doc S/RES/2462.

59 UN SC Res 2396 supra.

(P/CVE)[60] but also undermining respect of human rights in anti-terrorist action.[61] Over and above, the sanctions' list of Res 1267 seq[62] is being regularly updated.

Again, an explicit definition of terrorism is largely missing from SC Resolutions, however Resolution 1566/2004 seems to capture the phenomenon analytically. In the text the SC affirms the many forms and manifestations of terrorism and condemns all such acts regardless of their motivation given the serious threat they pose to peace and security. Paragraph 3 reads: 'criminal acts, including against civilians, committed with the intent to cause death or serious bodily injury, or taking of hostages, with the purpose to provoke a state of terror in the general public or in a group of persons or particular persons, intimidate a population or compel a government or an international organization to do or to abstain from doing any act, which constitute offenses within the scope of and as defined in the international conventions and protocols relating to terrorism, are under no circumstances justifiable by considerations of a political, philosophical, ideological, racial, ethnic, religious or other similar nature'.

Whereas the Resolution did not oblige States to align their legislation with it, it did function as a roadmap for defining terrorism.[63] Nevertheless, the SC confined itself to criminalize conduct that was already classified as terrorist under existing legislative initiatives and further, violent conduct only against people, aiming at intimidation or coercion of population, governments or

60 Triggered by the growing concern of Foreign Terrorist Fighters (FTFs), action to counter violent extremism (CVE) which was initiated by UNSC Res 2178 (n 58) evolved into the UN Plan of Action to Prevent Violent Extremism (P/CVE) addressing conditions conducive to terrorism. UN Secretary-General launched the Plan in January 2016 launching a comprehensive approach beyond 'law enforcement, military or security measures to address development, good governance, human rights and humanitarian concerns', UNGA Res 70/674 (24 December 2015) UN Doc Res A/70/674, para 41.

61 The issue appeared for the first time in UN SC Res 1456 (20 January 2003) UN Doc S/RES/1456, which highlights that 'States must ensure that any measure taken to combat terrorism comply with all their obligations under international law [...] in particular international human rights, refugee, and humanitarian law'.

62 The latest update of the 1267 seq ISIL (Da'esh) & Al-Qaida Sanctions regime initiated by Res1267 (n 50) was with Res 2368 (20 July 2017) UN Doc S/RES/2368.

63 UNCHR, 'Report of the Special Rapporteur on Promotion and Protection of Human Rights and Fundamental Freedoms While Countering Terrorism, Martin Scheinin' (28 September 2005)UN Doc E/CN.4/2006/98 para 26 et seq. discussing the problems arising from the lack of a universal definition of terrorism and the variances in domestic legislation, especially for human rights abuses; OHCHR, 'Report on the protection of human rights and fundamental freedoms while countering terrorism' (2 June 2008) UN Doc A/HRC/8/13 paras 20–23.

international organizations. As such, it did not elaborate on the *other forms and manifestations* of terrorism, excluding thereafter the settlement of controversial issues that had emerged throughout the years in relation to two broad categories of issues: a) state-sponsored terrorism[64] and the relationship between the law on terrorism and international humanitarian law, with particular emphasis on the actions of state armed forces when the exercise of their official duties is governed by or is in conformity with international law and b) the distinction of national liberation movements as an exercise of people's right to self-determination from terrorist acts and the treatment of freedom fighters.[65] With regard to the latter, the specific motivation that has been suggested to be a distinctive (legal) component of the crime of terrorism, namely considerations of political, religious, ethnic and ideological kind, is brought to the foreground.[66]

Notwithstanding continuing disagreement on various issues, the current universal definition of terrorism that is put forward in the Draft Comprehensive Terrorism Convention[67] does not refer to ideological, political or religious objectives and expands the *actus reus* of the offense to include damage to public or private property alongside harm to persons. Art.2 stipulates:

'*Any person* commits an offense within the meaning of the present Convention if that person, by *any means*, unlawfully and intentionally,

---

64 UNGA, 'Declaration on Measures to Eliminate International Terrorism' (17 February 1995) UN Doc A/RES/49/60 focused on the issue, urging States to refrain from instigating, tolerating or facilitating terrorist activities, for example by allowing the use of their territory for training or other preparations and are disallowed to grant international protection to anyone engaged in terrorist acts (paras 4, 5(a) and (f)).

65 Lim, C. 'The question of a generic definition of terrorism under general international law' in Victor V. Ramraj, Michael Hor, Kent Roach and George Williams (Eds.), *Global Anti-Terrorism Law and Policy* (Cambridge University Press 2005). Danja Blöcher, 'Terrorism as an International Crime: The Definitional Problem', (2011) 8 Eyes On the ICC 107. B. Saul, 'Attempts to define Terrorism' (n 5).

66 *Declaration on Measures to Eliminate International Terrorism* (n 64) para 3 stresses the unjustifiability of terrorist acts on ideological grounds. Also, Antonio Cassese, 'The multifaceted criminal notion of terrorism in international law' (2006) 4 Journal of International Criminal Justice 933, 937–43; Reuven Young, 'Defining terrorism: the evolution of terrorism as a legal concept in international law and its influence on definitions in domestic legislation' (2006) 29 Boston College International and Comparative Law Review 23, 58 & 64.

67 An Ad hoc Committee to assist in developing a comprehensive legal framework for international terrorism was first established by UN GA Res 51/210 (17 December 1996), whereas discussions on the conclusion of the Comprehensive Terrorism Convention started in 2000 and are still open. See, <https://legal.un.org/committees/terrorism/> accessed 20 February 2020.

causes: (a) death or serious bodily injury to any person; or (b) serious damage to public or private property, including a place of public use, a State or government facility, a public transportation system, an infrastructure facility or to the environment; or (c) damage to property, places, facilities or systems referred to in paragraph 1(b) of the present article resulting or likely to result in major economic loss, when the purpose of the conduct, by its nature or context, is to intimidate a population, or to compel a Government or an international organization to do or to abstain from doing *any act*'.[68]

The conclusion of the Convention faces a stalemate at present but the provided definition of terrorism is representative of the international community's understanding of it since the generally-agreed upon denominators of terrorism as a crime are identifiable: unlawful use of violence causing physical harm or death to persons or damages to public/private property with the intended purpose to spread fright among a population or to coerce and compel state authorities or an international organization. To this end, any means can qualify as a method of terror. That said, the Draft Convention introduces a 'separate and autonomous regime' in parallel to the sectoral treaties.[69] Consequently, it may provide the foundation for considering terrorism a distinct offense, which is not defined exclusively by the sectoral crimes. Even so, the vagueness of the terms (any person, any means, any act) may be a caveat to the Convention's effectiveness.

2.1.1 Assessing UN Counter-Terrorism Law So Far

A full assessment of the UN's action in the context of terrorism goes beyond the scope of this chapter. Besides, it is an immense task in itself that requires a comprehensive methodological analysis, comprising of theoretic and quantitative research alike in order to ensure the cohesion and legitimacy of the conclusions.[70] As we are confronted with limitations in this regard, we will only raise some points, which should be useful for our analysis here.

---

68 UNGA, 'Measures to Eliminate International Terrorism, Report of the Working Group' (3 November 2010) UN Doc A/C.6/65/L.10, 6.

69 With the Draft Convention, being considered lex specialis. The matter is not resolved. B. Saul (n 5), 82 and footnote 202 therein.

70 As Andrea Bianchi puts it regarding SC's work on antiterrorism, 'To provide an overall assessment of the effective implementation of the UN SC's anti-terrorism measures is a daunting task. Not only are lawyers traditionally little inclined to use quantitative methodology analysis to carry out their research, they also lack adequate parameters to objectively judge the efficacy of states' implementing measures as well as their consistency with other obligations incumbent on them', A. Bianchi, 'Assessing the Effectiveness of the UN Security Council's Anti-terrorism Measures: The Quest for Legitimacy and Cohesion'

Overall, claiming that UN action so far in the framework of countering terrorism is not a total success-story would be no exaggeration.

In practice, statistical analyses show that there has been no significant mitigation of terrorist attacks after the entry into force of counter-terrorist sectoral treaties, indicating they are an insufficient tool.[71] Equally, the switch from sectoral treaties, which define about fifty offenses to be incorporated into national criminal legislation[72] and are punitive in nature,[73] to more repressive action routed in the SC Resolutions, is also doubtful to be effective. As repeatedly observed, since the launch of the 'war on terror' right after 9/11, terrorist attacks worldwide have increased instead of being reduced.[74] It is noteworthy that all action in this context is reactive and suppressive.[75] Maybe with the exceptions of the Terrorist Financing Convention and the PVE/CVE that respectively aim at cutting the "fuel" which powers terrorist action and tackling its root causes, all other forms of antiterrorist action respond each time to a specific terrorist manifestation/attack.

Likewise, the failure to adopt a comprehensive anti-terrorist convention is quite significant. In the first place, symbolically it dents the UN's decisiveness on tackling the problem.[76] Even so, Sebastian von Eisendel notes that in reality its absence is not so significant since sectoral treaties address most manifestations of terrorist action[77] and these treaties enjoy a widespread ratification status.[78] Kimberley Trapp believes the opposite. She underlines that it 'creates real dangers both in terms of the "no impunity" project as in terms of prevention' since it 'risks a lack of attention' to manifestations of terrorism not covered by sectoral agreements. Also, as van der Wilt and Paulussen underline, the shortage of a universally accepted, all-encompassing legal definition of the crime of terrorism creates a 'lingering semantic confusion around the concept

(2006) 17 European Journal of International Law 881. We believe this is applicable to the entire UN action against terrorism and TOC.

71 W. Enders, T. Sandler and J. Cauley, 'UN Conventions, Technology and Retaliation in the Fight Against Terrorism: An Econometric Evaluation' (1990) 2 Terrorism and Political Violence 83 cited in: Sebastian von Einsiedel (n 54).

72 S.von Einsiedel (n54),1; Daniel O'Donnell, 'International treaties against terrorism and the use of terrorism during armed conflict and by armed forces' (2006) 88 International Review of the Red Cross 853.

73 Kimberley N. Trapp, 'Holding States Responsible for Terrorism before the International Court of Justice' (2012) 3 Journal of International Dispute Settlement 279.

74 Especially since the 2015 terrorist attacks in Europe.

75 K. Trapp (n73) 282.

76 S.von Einsiedel (n 54) 1.

77 Id.

78 Aniel Caro de Beer (n 48) 40.

of terrorism [...], [which] affects criminal law enforcement [...]'. Indeed, applying the basic criminal law maxim *nulla poena sine lege*, one may doubt how a defendant can be found guilty of an inexistent offense. Adding on that, the lack of a definition might also hinder the upgrade of terrorism to an international crime, which enjoys universal jurisdiction and may be also tried by the ICC.[79]

Surely though there are other characteristics such as the wide basis of extraterritorial jurisdiction allowed in the sectoral treaties analyzed above which lead to a persuasive argument that the prohibition of terrorism not only does enjoy the status of universality but also is a *jus cogens* norm.[80] Also, despite the lack of a definition of terrorism if one takes only selective elements of UN treaties into account, we could argue that the crime of terrorism comprises of a violent conduct that has an immediate impact on a *civilian* – such as bodily harm or death (*actus reus*),[81] in circumstances that do not amount to armed conflict – and a specific *mens rea*, i.e. the offender's intention to intimidate a population or coerce the government/international organization to (in)action. In our understanding of the crime of terrorism, ideological justifications cannot constitute a defense, as the UN GA has stated in Resolution 49/60.[82]

Although for us this could be a valid reading, it is nonetheless not authoritative; it may conflict with the variety of national/regional definitions[83] and the diverse views regarding the classification of terrorism as a crime and crucially, it doesn't reflect the live debate regarding the confusion about the perpetrators' *dolus specialis* with their motives. For example, Naomi Norberg categorizes the intent of an offender to 'intimidate a population or coerce the government' included in the Terrorist Financing Convention as 'an additional element of a motive', which is not even useful; citing Bennoune's list of causes of Muslim fundamentalist movements, Norberg indicates that terrorist acts are acts of retaliation rather than attempts to terrorize. Whereas taking into

79 Naomi Norberg, 'Terrorism and International Criminal Justice: Dim Prospects for a Future Together' 8 (2010) Santa Clara Journal of International Law 11. See also: Islam A. Attia, 'Do the United Nations Terrorism-Related conventions Prohibit and Suppress Terrorism Acts Committed by Terrorists' (2018) 5 Bristol Law review 171.

80 Aniel Caro de Beer (n 48). 230–231.

81 Including incitement, aiding and abetting as well as threat and attempt of those acts thereto.

82 UNGA, 'Declaration on Measures' (n 64) para.3: '[A]cts intended or calculated to provoke a state of terror in the general public, a group of persons or particular persons for political purposes are in any circumstance unjustifiable, whatever the considerations of a political, philosophical, ideological, racial, ethnic, religious or any other nature that may be invoked to justify them'.

83 For an analysis of regional definitions of the crime of terrorism, Aniel Caro de Beer 32–52.

account motives could assist the design of an effective strategy to counter terrorism and its causes, it also jeopardizes effective law enforcement since an assessment of motives entails subjectivity in the evaluation of terrorists' conduct by the authorities.[84] In the same vein, the assessment of the legitimacy of motives behind liberation movements (mentioned earlier) is a subjective exercise in the absence of clear criteria that would justify the political reasons for such attempts, rendering any tactic to achieve a "just" cause defensible.[85] The risks of such judgment are obvious.

Coming to the preventive rationale and without wishing to undermine the magnitude of countering terrorist financing and PCV/CVE, the multitude of the risks, the facets and the pace by which terrorists adapt to new means of conduct are so overwhelming that effective responses are hard to achieve.[86] On the other side of the spectrum, PCV/CVE has been launched as an ambitious project[87] to curb radical extremism conducive to terrorism. Whether it has been effective in doing so in real-life terms, cannot be answered yet. There are too many diverse practices, ranging from community engagement/outreach to banning veils[88] and reporting signs of students "vulnerable to radicalization"[89] and various diverging opinions.[90] But one thing is sure: certain

---

84 George Fletcher, 'The indefinable concept of terrorism' (2006) Journal of International Criminal Justice, 894, 903. Also, Jacqueline Hodgson and Victor Tadros, 'The impossibility of defining terrorism', (2013) 16 New Criminal Law Review 494, 522; Macello di Filippo, 'The Definition(s) of Terrorism in International Law', 9, 11, 13–15 in B. Saul (ed) *Research Handbook of International Law and Terrorism* (Edward Elgar 2014).

85 Bettina Weißer, 'Transnational Organised Crime and Terrorism' in Pierre Hauck, Sven Peterke (eds), *International Law and Transantional Organised Crime* (OUP 2015) 93 & 96.

86 As observed by the Financial Action Task Force (FATF), '[t]errorists regularly adapt how and where they raise and move funds and other assets in order to circumvent safeguards that jurisdictions have put in place to detect and disrupt this activity" and hence is recognized that "there is no one-size fits all approach when assessing TF risk': FATF, 'Terrorist Financing – Risk Assessment Guidance' (FATF 2019), 3 para1.

87 Peter Romaniuk, 'Does CVE Work? Lessons Learned from the Global Effort to Counter Violent Extremism' (2015) Global Center on Cooperative Security 2.

88 Yonghe Zhang and Li Zhang, 'Academic Review of International Seminar on Counterterrorism, De-radicalisation and Human Rights Protection' (2019) 18 Journal of Human Rights 676.

89 Cora True-Frost (n 52) 809.

90 Georgia Holmer, Peter Bauman, Kateira Aryaeinejad, *Measuring Up – Evaluating the impact of P/CVE programs* (United States Institute of Peace 2018) <https://www.usip.org/sites/default/files/2018-09/preventing-countering-violent-extremism-measuringup.pdf> accessed 20 June 2020; Emmanuel Mauleon, 'It's Time to Put CVE to Bed' (*Just Security*, 2 November 2018) <https://www.justsecurity.org/61332/its-time-put-cve-bed/?fbclid=IwAR0Fz3cUfhIYDKiiTmr4bG3tJ95grr-4HhZCpKU_nOZSMaBs54bE5NsjvCY> accessed 19 June 2020.

measures adopted in the context of PCV/CVE are 'seriously infringing on the enjoyment of human rights'.[91]

Repressive measures are not exempt from human rights violations either. On the contrary, the issue constitutes a fundamental critique against the 'war on terror' and repressive anti-terrorist action. '[T]he promotion and protection of human rights for all and the rule of law is essential to all components of the [UN Counter-Terrorism] Strategy [...] [and are] not conflicting goals, but complementary and mutually reinforcing',[92] is established by extensive literature, reports of bodies of the UN[93] as well as other international organizations, such as the Council of Europe and the European Court of Human Rights (ECtHR).[94] The same was reiterated more forcefully in Resolutions 2462/2019 on Financing Terrorism and SC Res 2482/2019 with the additional statement that human rights, fundamental freedoms and the rule of law 'are an essential part of a successful counter-terrorism effort and [States'] failure to comply with these and other international obligations, including under the UN Charter, is one of the factors contributing to increased radicalization to violence and fosters a sense of impunity'.[95] However, it is widely known that in

---

91 UNGA, 'Report on best practices and lessons learned on how protecting and promoting human rights contribute to preventing and countering violent extremism. Report of the UNHCHR' (21 July 2016) UN Doc A/HRC/33/29.

92 OHCHR, 'Human Rights, Terrorism and Counter-terrorism' Fact Sheet No.32 <https://www.ohchr.org/documents/publications/factsheet32en.pdf> accessed 6 June 2020.

93 *Idem.*

94 The ECtHR has found in various occasions ever since *Ireland v. UK* App No 5310/71 (ECtHR, 13 December 1977) violations of article 3 ECHR prohibiting torture for degrading conditions and ill treatment of detention: *Öcalan v Turkey* App Nos 24069/03, 197/04, 6201/06 and 10464/07 (ECtHR, 18 March 2014); incommunicado in police custody: *Portu Juanenea and Sarasola Yarzabal v Spain* App No1653/13 (ECtHR, 13 February 2018); extradition/deportation of convicted persons or suspects: *Aswat v. UK* App No 62176/14 (ECtHR, 6 January 2015). It has also found breaches of the right to liberty (art 5 ECHR): *Fox, Campbell and Hartley v UK* App Nos 12244/86, 12245/86; 12383/86 (ECtHR, 30 August 1990), *MSS v Belgium & Greece* App No 30696/po (ECtHR, 21 January 2011); of the right to a fair trial (art 6 ECHR): *Otegi Mondragon and Others v Spain* App Nos 4184/15, 4317/15, 4323/15, 5028/15, 5053/15 (ECtHR, 6 February 2019) but also the right to life (art 2 ECHR), respect for private and family life (art 8 ECHR): *Sher and Others v UK* App No 5201/11(ECtHR, 20 October 2015), freedom of religion (art 9 ECHR): *Nasr and Ghali v Italy* App No 44883/09 (ECtHR, 23 February 2016) and freedom of expression (art 10): *Döner and Others v Turkey* App No 29994/02 (ECtHR, 7 March 2017) and *Stomakhin v Russia* App No 52273/07 (ECtHR, 9 May 2018). Overall, the ECtHR has been vocal in that 'States have to reconcile their actions in fighting terrorism with their obligation to respect human rights', ECtHR, 'Terrorism' (*COURTalks* 2016) <https://www.echr.coe.int/Documents/COURTalks_Terr_Talk_ENG.PDF> accessed 14 July 2020.

95 SC Res 2462 (n 58) para 4; UN SC Res 2482 (19 July 2019) UN Doc S/RES/2482 paras 9, 16.

practice counter-terrorism policies especially in the post-9/11 period are often in breach of human rights. Besides, as Antonios Tzanakopoulos notes, 'when the SC "makes law" through the imposition of binding measures in accordance with Art.41 of the UN Charter, it may impact on internationally protected human rights'.[96] In this context, the legitimacy of sanctions of the Res 1267 seq system has been questioned ever since the 1990s as having 'affected a number of basic human rights'[97] and it is recognized by well-established case law ever since the landmark ECtHR ruling in *Soering* that alleged terrorists 'face a greater risk of violations of due process'.[98] The oxymoron of violating human rights to address a plague that inherently undermines human rights, i.e. terrorism, is evident.

2.2 *Transnational Organized Crime*

One would think that a more straightforward approach would be followed with respect to the definition of organized crime given the UN Convention against Transnational Organized Crime (UNTOC or the 'Palermo Convention') that is in force since September 2003.[99] The Convention establishes two specific offenses of intentional participation in criminal organizations that States-parties need to criminalize under domestic law. It is supplemented by three Protocols targeting in further detail individual manifestations of TOC: the Protocol to Prevent, Suppress and Punish Trafficking in Persons, Especially Women and Children; the Protocol against the Smuggling of Migrants by Land, Sea and Air;[100] and the Protocol against the Illicit Manufacturing of and Trafficking in Firearms, their Parts and Components and Ammunition.[101]

Nonetheless, suffices to skim through the Convention's text to see that a definition of 'organized crime' is actually missing. Art.2(a) refers to an '*organized criminal group*, which shall mean a structured group of three or more persons, existing for a period of time and acting in concert with the aim of committing one or more serious crimes or offenses established in accordance with the Convention, in order to obtain, directly or indirectly, a financial or

96 Antonios Tzanakopoulos, 'Collective Security and Human Rights' in: Erika de Wet and Jure Vidmar (eds), *Hierarchy in International law: the place of human rights* (Oxford University Press 2012) <https://ssrn.com/abstract=1677477> accessed 20 June 2020.

97 Id. 2.

98 Harmen van der Wilt and Christophe Paulussen, 'The role of International Criminal Law in Responding to the Crime-terror Nexus' (2019) 16 European Journal of Criminology 315.

99 UNGA (adopted 15 November 2000, entered into force 29 September 2003) 2225 UNTS 209.

100 Both adopted by UNGA Res 55/25 (8 January 2001) UN Doc A/RES/55/25. They entered into force on 25 December 2003 and 28 January 2004 respectively.

101 UNGA Res 55/255 (8 June 2001) UN Doc A/RES/55/255.

other material benefit'. This outcome is somewhat surprising considering that between the 1980s and 2000 when the Convention was concluded, States had acquired valuable experience in cross-border criminal phenomena and had developed bilateral and multilateral cooperation frameworks to dispense criminal justice.[102] It would be expected therefore that it would be easier to delineate terminology matters in a legal instrument which essentially built on that international experience and on countries' own domestic expertise from the study and analysis of criminal activities which demonstrated such features in the way they were carried out that distinguished them from ordinary crime.[103]

Yet, States' common understanding of the contours of organized crime led them to focus on the crime's constituent elements. These were: some kind of organization for the commission of criminal acts; the existence of a group whose members were endowed a specific role and obeyed a hierarchical structure or were personally related to each other, allowing thus the leaders of the group to control it; the use of violence and corruption; the pursuit of profit or control of markets; laundering the proceeds of crime with the purpose to finance other criminal activities or to use them for legitimate economic transactions; the incorporation of new forms of activity on a transnational level and the potential of cooperation between organized criminal groups.[104] Consequently, States defined actually organized crime through a description

---

102 Conclusions and Recommendation of the International Conference on Preventing and Controlling Money-Laundering and the Use of the Proceeds of Crime: a Global Approach (1994: Courmayeur, Italy), E/CONF.88/7; Dae H. Chang, 'Main Issues and Key Conclusion of the Courmayeur Conference: Global Approach to Control of Money-Laundering', (1998) 22(1) International Journal of Comparative and Applied Criminal Justice 1. FATF was also established in 1989, see <https://www.fatf-gafi.org/about/> accessed 27 January 2020. Convention against Illicit Traffic in Narcotic Drugs and Psychotropic Substances (adopted 20 December 1988, entered into force 11 November 1990) 1582 UNTS 95; Berlin Declaration on Increased Cooperation Combatting Drug Crime and Organized Crime in Europe (8 September 1994), EU Commission PRES/94/182 <https://ec.europa.eu/commission/presscorner/detail/en/PRES_94_182> accessed 19 July 2020; SAARC Convention on Narcotic Drugs and Psychotropic Substances (23 November 1990) <http://www.asianlii.org/saarc/other/agrmt/scondaps608/> accessed id.

103 UNGA, 'Report of the World Ministerial Conference on Organized Transnational Crime' (2 December 1994) UN Doc A/49/748; UNGA, Naples Political Declaration and Global Action Plan against Organized Transnational Crime (23 December 1994) UN Doc A/RES/49/159 [Naples Declaration].

104 Dimitri Vlassis, 'The Global Situation of Transnational Organized Crime, the Decision of the International Community to Develop an International Convention and the Negotiation Process', 119th International Training Course Visiting Experts' Papers, Resource Material Series No.59 475, 488 <https://www.unafei.or.jp/publications/pdf/RS_No59/No59_33VE_Vlassis2.pdf> accessed 20 July 2020; Naples Declaration, supra para.12.

of the phenomenon based on analytical concepts such as organized criminal group, serious crime, structured group etc. that required further interpretation and concretization as Art.2 UNTOC shows.[105] Corroborative to the latter point are also the multiple (208) definitions, rather conceptions, of organized crime that have been articulated to date by various scholars and in domestic legal instruments.[106]

Turning back to the UN, the Office on Drugs and Crime subsumes under the term 'organized crime' any serious offense committed by a group of three or more people with the aim of profit, acknowledging the broadness of this conceptualization.[107] Indeed, the breadth of the definition of a 'criminal group' in UNTOC has been criticized as problematic. Naturally, the critique is directed to the analytical concepts used to define organized crime: first, regarding their own comprehensive conceptualization given that how they have been expressed in the UNTOC results from the consolidation of relevant provisions in domestic legal systems, and ultimately, in relation to their instrumentality for tackling organized crime. Art.2, the argument goes, does not underscore the characteristics that make the crime particularly despicable and elevate it to a threat to human security nor does it portray the links with the social and political context in which organized crime generates and evolves.[108] On these grounds, the very construction of 'organized crime' as an offense in the convention is substance-free because it doesn't delineate the boundaries of an organized criminal act that would foster a clear understanding of what that activity entails and assist States in legislating effectively on the criminalization of organized crime. Yet, it is the very same broadness that permits the Convention to capture a wide range of organized criminal groups and continue to be relevant to new manifestations of the crime that, by admittance, emerge over the years.[109] Nonetheless, it seems more likely that in the absence

105 David McClean, *Transnational Organized Crime: A Commentary on the UN Convention and its Protocols*, Oxford Commentaries on International Law (OUP 2017) for an article-by-article interpretation of UNTOC.

106 Klaus von Lampe, 'Definitions of Organized Crime' <http://www.organized-crime.de/organizedcrimedefinitions.htm#references>; Id., 'What's new' <http://www.organized-crime.de/whatsnew.htm> both accessed 27 March 2020.

107 UNODC, (2010) *The Globalization of Crime: A Transnational Organized Crime Threat Assessment*, UN publication, Sale No. E.10.IV.6, 19.

108 Michael Levi, 'Thinking About Organized Crime – Structure and Threat', (2014) 159(1) The RUSI Journal 6; Neil Boister, 'The UN Convention against Transnational Organized Crime 2000', 133 in P. Hauck et al (n 85).

109 N. Boister, id.; Klaus von Lampe, 'Organising the nicotine racket: Patterns of cooperation in the cigarette black market in Germany', 42–3 in P. van Duyne, K. von Lampe, J. Newell (eds.), *Criminal Finances and Organising Crime in Europe* (Wolf Legal Publishers

of a more comprehensive codification of transnational organized crime, the purpose of UNTOC to promote cooperation in order to prevent the phenomenon more effectively is undermined.[110]

Definitions are thus important for criminalization and law enforcement at the national and international level. Neither terrorism nor organized crime has been demarcated in the respective UN instruments as a legally concrete concept. Even if a comparison in strictly legal terms were to be drawn, it would be obstructed by the non-identical form of the corresponding treaties, hence the absence of absolutely equivalent elements in the formulation of the crimes therein. By way of example, the UNTOC speaks about an 'organized criminal group' whereas there is no official mention in the Draft Terrorism Convention or the sectoral treaties of a 'terrorist group', albeit groups or organizations that are considered terrorist are named in the UN sanction list along with certain individuals. Another potentially comparable element, namely the methods for the commission of the crimes seem to be more identifiable in the case of terrorism through the sector-specific treaties (although the Draft Convention's reference to 'any means' expands the net of terrorist methods). Contrariwise, the UNTOC mentions only the organizational/structural crimes and apart from the crimes codified in its Protocols, any other 'serious crime' can be used as a method for organized criminal activity. To what extent could this imply that organized criminals might share some of the characteristics of terrorists in their criminal conduct, especially the violent attacks, or even that terrorism is one of these 'serious crimes'? Finally, both have a particular aim/goal – for terrorism, it is the intimidation/coercion and for organized crime, the material or financial benefit.[111] Interestingly, the existence of an aim is the only steady

---

2003): 'whereas definitions of organized crime have a tendency frantically to focus on one specific constellation of these aspects, namely, complex criminal organizations using violence and corruption to attain control over illegal markets and legal institutions, it seems preferable to place the emphasis on the fluidity and diversity characterizing collective criminal behavior. This entails exploring, in as many social and historical settings as possible, how the phenomena in question vary in time and space and in what combinations they appear', as cited in K. Lampe, 'Definitions' (n 106). Arndt Sinn, 'Transnational Organized Crime: Concepts and Critics' in P. Hauck et al (n 85). Tom Obokata, *Transnational Organized Crime in International Law* (Hart Pubishing 2010), 40 also notes that the advantage of UNTOC is that 'it can be used to prosecute and punish a variety of criminal activities, provided they are serious crimes committed by criminal groups as defined in the Convention.'

110 A. Sinn supra, 25 on the value of definitions.

111 Alex P. Schmid, 'Revisiting the Relationship between International Terrorism and Transnational Organized Crime 22 Years Later', International Centre for Countering

characteristic upon which a demarcation line between the two has been drawn, rendering them conceptually separate phenomena.[112] The distinction is based on the ideological background against which terrorism is committed. Whereas it is not a legal requirement for the classification of an act as terrorist, it does come to play as parameter influencing the *modus operandi* of these groups. Insofar that this holds true, how can the alleged link between the two offenses, the crime-terror nexus, be explained?

2.3 *The Crime-Terror Nexus and the Concept of Organized Criminal Terrorism*

It derives from the foregoing analysis that more factors are necessary to establish a common ground for the comparison of crime-terror phenomena and to unravel their potential linkages. To this end, a more detailed enquiry into the offenses' 'nature' is warranted based on variables that explain the mode of perpetrators' operations in each categorical offense, i.e. the causes and the wider social environment that cultivate the organizing dimensions and necessary structures for these criminal activities.

Concerning organized crime, its root causes are associated with an institutional deficit and social pathologies in a given state, which result in the exclusion of deprived individuals from opportunities to participate in the legitimate society and achieve socially desirable goals (e.g. employment, education etc.).[113] Under circumstances of 'blocked opportunities' and social marginalization, the proliferation of 'delinquent customs' and illicit means as deviant substitutes of legitimate methods for the realization of the said purposes emerge. In turn, they lead to the creation of a sub-culture conducive to criminality. From this perspective criminal conduct is presented as a matter of individuals' choice under conditions of differential association with "the dominant" society.[114] Simultaneously, broader systemic issues such as socioeconomic and

---

Terrorism Research Paper (August 2018), 4–8 <https://icct.nl/wp-content/uploads/2018/08/ICCT-Schmid-International-Terrorism-Organised-Crime-August2018.pdf> accessed 20 April 2020.

112 Wilkinson Paul, *Political Terrorism* (Wiley 1974); A. Schmid, 'The links between transnational organised crime and terrorist crimes' (1996) 2 Transnational Organised Crime 40.

113 Vincenzo Ruggiero and Rodolfo Leyva, *Understand the Dimensions of Organized Crime and Terrorist Networks for Developing Effective and Efficient Security Solutions for First-Line Practitioners and Professionals – Literature exploration and Open Access Bibliography* (2016) TAKEDOWN Horizon 2020, 8 downloaded from Researchgate.net <https://www.researchgate.net/publication/312525743_Organized_Crime_and_Terrorist_Networks_Literature_Exploration_and_Open_Access_Bibliography> accessed 31 January 2019.

114 'Sociology of Crime: Criminology Theories' (*Sociology*) <http://sociology.iresearchnet.com/sociology-of-crime-criminology/#criminology-theories> accessed 20 March 2020.

political attributes of the international system may also prove fruitful conditions for organized criminal activity. The asymmetries caused by neoliberal globalization in relation to human and natural resources, income distribution and institutional capacity for good governance and the observance of the rule of law are listed among the facilitators of organized crime.[115] Besides, increasing migration and refugee flows, the ease of movement worldwide through less border controls and technological developments (e.g. the Internet, encrypted electronic communications, online banking etc.) have become key facilitators of TOC.[116] Yet, in recent years attention has shifted to weak and failing States as well as conflict regions as crime-nurturing environments. In the absence of (strong) government structures, criminal organizations have the opportunity to undertake official state functions substituting the state's role in the provision of services and goods or to utilize corrupted core public institutions in order to penetrate business and government.[117]

Looking at terrorism, the factors that give rise to it and sustain it are not very different. A first set of explanations relates to the individual. Psycho-pathological causes, i.e. a kind of psychological and mental disturbance, complemented by psycho-sociological conditions such as deprivation and inequality stand out but of course, the political, historical and cultural context and how it is perceived by the individual weigh more since they form terrorists' ideologies and beliefs. Terrorism enunciates political violence; hence ideological justifications are determinants par excellence. On these grounds, extremist individuals or groups use terrorism to gain ideological power and supposedly bring about social change and more justice in the state.[118]

The second category of explanations reveals the socio-political qualities of a nation-State that have changed as States entered various stages in their development. Rapid economic growth produces abrupt societal changes if it is detached from existing social norms and structures. Moreover, it might prompt natural resource crises between developed and developing countries, generating violent conflicts over their exploitation in which terrorist groups

---

115 UNODC, 'Causes and Facilitating Factors of Organized Crime', University Module Series (May 2018) <https://www.unodc.org/e4j/en/organized-crime/module-6/index.html> accessed 20 March 2020.

116 A. Schmid. 'Revisiting' (n 111), 9–10.

117 UNOC (n 115), Section: Structural Factors and Organized Crime.

118 Brynjar Lia and Katja Skjølberg, (2005) *Causes of Terrorism: an Expanded and Updated Review of the Literature*, Norwegian Defense Research Establishment (FFI 2005), 7–21 <https://publications.ffi.no/en/item/asset/dspace:3116/04-04307.pdf> accessed 20 March 2020.

also engage when they rely on their export as a source of finance.[119] On the other hand, poverty is another variable for political violence.[120] Regarding institutional factors, the political regime of countries plays a significant role. Again, ideological extremism and insurgencies are encouraged in States transitioning to democratic governance. Finally, as much as technological advancement is a component of development it is also a useful tool for terrorists, who harness it either as a communicative means to promulgate their aims and pass on their political messages or as instruments to manifest violent attacks (e.g. technological innovations for weapons).[121]

At a third level, one has to consider the traits of the international system that shape the international relations of States and the position of non-state actors. Globalization is yet again the predominant force for embedding States' interdependence and integration. Notwithstanding the benefits of this process, it favors the immersion of hegemonic powers both economically and culturally.[122] As a result, counteraction to uneven prosperity in the world as well as resistance to the dispersal of a specific global political culture that does not account of cultural diversity trigger violent rebellions. In fact, this is what Islamic terrorism demonstrates – a cultural and relational gap between the West and the East, combined with inequality, injustice and sentiments of suppression all of which have spurred radicalization.[123] When little space is left for peaceful interaction among States through the avenues of economic development, diplomacy and multilateral cooperation, international terrorism finds an exit akin to 'anti-systemic' movement towards hegemonic powers and their allies. Against this background, armed conflicts, weak and failed States are attractive poles for terrorists. They are hubs for the creation and spread of ideological motives for terrorist acts since they facilitate interaction among like-minded groups and opportunities to substitute state control over the

---

119 Leaders, 'Gas, Guns and Guerillas – Jihadists threaten Mozambique's new Gasfields' *The Economist* (2 April 2020) <https://www.economist.com/leaders/2020/04/02/jihadists-threaten-mozambiques-new-gasfields> accessed 3 April 2020.

120 UNDP, 'Journey of Young Africans into Violent Extremism marked by poverty and Deprivation (7 September 2017) <https://www.undp.org/content/undp/en/home/news-centre/news/2017/09/07/vers-l-extremisme-violent-en-afrique.html#.WqNwky2D3EU.email> accessed 30 March 2020 but also Cf. James A. Piazza, 'Rooted in Poverty?: Terrorism, Poor Economic Development and Social Cleavages,' (2006) 18 Terrorism and Political Violence 159.

121 B. Lia, K. Skjølberg (n 118), 21–50.

122 Id., 50–67.

123 V. Ruggiero and R. Leyva (n 113), 22–25.

territory in order to use those zones as training camps, enabling their influence worldwide.[124]

In light of the above, it is appropriate to argue that TOC and terrorism are replicas of "underworld enterprises" that collide with the legitimate structures of society and oppose the State.[125] They may differ in their understanding of the State as their "enemy" as they may also vary in the way they make themselves "visible" to the society.[126] Nonetheless, they both resonate in social and political hindrances; therefore their members usually belong to marginal strata and make a rational choice to join those groups. They are intrigued by risk-taking, enjoy excitement from confronting socially acceptable norms and interests and share a strong desire for power, although this may not be the most evident motivating factor.[127] Such characteristics shape not only the interpersonal relationships between members but also the fashion in which they operate. Regarded as distinct forms of social organization, criminal and terrorist groups rely on trust among their associates and build their ties upon their common values. A code of loyalty, respect and discipline governs, thus, their behavior.[128] For OC this was for long depicted in the groups' rigid hierarchical arrangement and temporal endurance. A typology of an organized criminal group has been described as a tripartite stratification comprising of 'soldiers', who execute the crime; 'planners', who design the criminal strategy and 'the bosses', who lead the organization and are its actual channel of communication with the legitimate economy, the political system and the State's administration.[129] Such a model allows criminal groups to develop professionalism in the crimes they execute since they benefit from the capabilities of high and low-skilled members.[130] However, the neoliberal economic environment within which these groups now function has transformed the groups' "closed bureaucratic" structure into more flexible network-type organizations, which is characterized by horizontal relationships between offenders of different types of organization and magnitude that may not always be cohesive subculture syndicates.[131]

124 B. Lia, K. Skjølberg (n 118), 67.

125 A. Schmid (n.111), 14.

126 Morgane Ferrari, 'Overlaps between Organized Crime and Terrorism' (2018) 4(2) International Comparative Jurisprudence 90, 91. Ana Prokić, 'The Links Between Organized Crime and Terrorism', (2017) 15(1) Law and Politics 85, 89.

127 Frank Bovenkerk and Bashir Abou Chakra, 'Terrorism and Organized Crime' (2004) 4(1–2) UNDOC Forum on Crime and Society 3.

128 Emmanuela Mylonaki, 'The Manipulation of Organized Crime by Terrorists: Legal and Factual Perspectives', (2002) 2 International Criminal Law Review 213, 228.

129 A. Schmid (n 111), 9.

130 V. Ruggiero and R. Leyva (n 113), 10.

131 Id., 9–10; F. Bovenkerk and B. Chakra (n 127), 8; A. Sinn (n 109), 29–30.

Instead, they are flexible groups of criminals or cells, belonging even to the "upper-world", that have as common ground their involvement in the same type of criminal undertakings, which facilitates joint action. In this way organized criminal groups may maneuver in the official world as they adapt to and exploit to their benefit the respective economic, political, legal developments and the multiplicity of (legal and illegal) actors that participate in this order.[132]

The structure of terrorist groups has followed a similar evolution. How they present themselves has been always context-specific. The dominant structural model has been that of clandestine groups, which when they perceive themselves as social reformists, i.e. akin a social movement, they may comprise of a legitimate layer of activists and a hidden tier of violent warriors.[133] More generally though, terrorist groups possessed a strong organizational structure, high degree of coherence and professionalism due to careful recruitment based on proven ideology, possession of resources, skills and expertise of followers etc. that resembled that of criminal groups, providing a frame for terrorists to build a 'program of action'. In reaction to the international socioeconomic and political climate in the last decades and to more robust law-enforcement strategies, such model has been replaced by 'networks of individual cells', which are linked to a core terrorist organization that has its 'headquarters' in a specific region or territory, yet are spread in the periphery and their link to the principal association is based more on the ideological identification and the symbolism of the hostilities rather than on a formal hierarchical relationship and physical connection. This network-type structure is never static.[134]

Network cooperation is more effective and functional for the promotion of each group's purposes. Not only has the 'sense of belonging' that individual members acquire by joining the groups not eclipsed but it may have even be strengthened since they perceive themselves as equal partners endowed with a duty to cooperate and assist the groups.[135] Furthermore, it enhances

132 V. Ruggiero, R. Levya (n 113), 11–17.

133 Id., 25.

134 Id., 25–28. Chris Dishman, 'The Leaderless Nexus: When Crime and Terror Converge', (2005) 28(3) Studies in Conflict and Terrorism 237, 239 gives a description of networks: they contain dispersed nodes – either cells or individuals – internetted together by similar beliefs, ideolody, doctrine and goals. There is no central command, headquarters or single leader. Cells communicate horizontally and rely extensively on technology to faciliate the execution of operations and individual tasks. Participants may be ultra-committed or cooperate only short-term. Organized criminal networks may still demonstrate some hierarchy but the tendency will be to "flatten", decentralize, their structure too (p.240).

135 M. Ferrari (n 126), 92.

the secrecy and confidentiality in the design of those groups' activities since it is hard to identify the organizers of the wrongdoings, and through the use of technology, operations are executed with minimal disclosure.[136] Most importantly, the network-like arrangement permits the contact of these groups through the individual cells. The latter are not constrained by the commands of the leadership so they have more flexibility in actions whereas they need to survive financially in a decentralized environment, hence they are open to whatever activity would help them sustain themselves. Such factors are crucial facilitators for the groups' interaction and the establishment of a nexus between them. What is though the nature of this connection and which its drivers or facilitators?

The answer to the question is predicated on the qualitative features of relationships that these two groups may form and their categorical classification. The basic hypothesis that depicts the crime-terror nexus detects collaborative partnerships between them that are prompted by either group and serve mainly to facilitate their operations through the provision of each other's services and exploitation of their criminal expertise or the maintenance of favorable conditions for their operations.[137] Nevertheless, the little existing evidence in support of the formation of alliances has given credence to the view that the different aims, motivations and means the groups employ are barriers to any kind of cooperation between them.[138] The groups tend to see each other with mistrust or suspicion and regard their differences between political and financial aims more as jeopardizing a successful coalition due to the unwanted attention by law enforcement agencies it would bring. Therefore, when an alliance is formed it will most likely be tactical, episodic and impermanent rather than strategic that posits an agreement for long-lasting cooperation, involves systematic exchange of operations and is guided by shared expectations for the achievement of a long-term common plan.[139] Quite plausibly, however, it could be contended that this does not reflect the true potential for cooperation between cells of organized criminals and terrorists that the network-like structure offers.[140]

136 A. Prokić (n 126), 88.

137 Tamara Makarenko, 'The Crime-Terror Continuum: Tracing the Interplay between Transnational Organized Crime and Terrorism' (2004) 6(1) Global Crime 129, 131.

138 Chris Dishman, 'Terrorism, Crime and Transformation', (2001) 24(1) Studies in Conflict and Terrorism 43.

139 Williams, P. (2000) 'Criminal cooperation: trends and patterns' (Jane's Conference on Transnational Organized Crime, 20–21 September).

140 C. Dishman 'The Leaderless Nexus' (n 134), 246.

The second proposition treats terrorist and criminal groups as transforming organizations and acknowledges a wide spectrum for the manifestation of such transformation. Cases refer to terrorist organizations using crime to raise funds for their activities and organized criminal groups adopting terror practices as a means to their operational aims. Consequently, they engage in political activity without embracing the ideology behind it; profit-maximization remains their primary motivation and goal. The same applies to terrorist groups, which 'retain paramount political objectives and ill-gotten monies serve only as a means to effectively reach their political ends'.[141] Hence, drug and human trafficking, counterfeiting etc. have been operational motivations for finding resources. While appropriating each other's activities, there is no cooperation between the two groups. Rather each organization develops its capacity to interchange strategies in-house by mutating their structures.[142]

These groups are one stage before the third kind of crime-terror interplay, whereby the two groups acquire the ability to convert alternately to another. Displaying already characteristics of both entities (hybrid organizations), the groups mix their tactics and motivations to the extent that they 'no longer retain the defining points that had made them a political or criminal group' and may transform completely into a single unit of the opposite nature. For instance, criminal groups use terror beyond the purpose of destabilizing the institutional environment in which they operate but with the intent to actually take effective control of it through an influence on the judiciary or monopolizing a State's strategic economic sectors and utilizing their economic power in politics. Likewise, terrorists in this case project their ideological rhetoric to displace and prevail over other criminal groups, to manipulate their network (e.g. use their recruits) for their criminal activities and even distract public authorities by making them examine the group's actions as a political threat instead of a purely criminal matter.[143]

Hybrid organizations seem to pose the most aggravated risk to society because when they find themselves in a troubled context, i.e. in conflict regions, transitional states and conditions of unstable economic and political governance more generally, they thrive due to their structural and operational capacities. In such cases, politically motivated criminal groups or commercial terrorists take advantage of the institutional vacuum to gain economic and political control over the State or region, challenging the legitimacy of official authorities and substituting them in their functions. In this regard, they tend

141 C. Dishman, 'Terrorism, Crime and Transformation (n.138), 47.

142 Id.; T. Makarenko (n 137), 133–135.

143 Id. 135 et seq.

to perpetuate with their conduct the institutional deficit in those areas, which become a safe haven for their endurance.[144]

Considering the above, it could be said that the nexus between terrorism and organized crime generates from their common methods and qualities and is explained by etiologies that attribute to both types of criminality similar causations.[145] Yet, their ideological and motivational divergence seems to be an enduring distinction that has led some scholars to argue that the relationship between the two crime groups is controversial.[146] The economic-ideological duality does not allow the merger of the groups as such but fundamentally of their social networks, environments and skills.[147] That is why fully symbiotic cooperation between the two groups is precluded and their interaction is more likely to take the form of temporary (one-off) or parasitic collaboration as long as ideologies do not conflict.[148] It is also contended that situations of instability (weak, failed states, conflict regions etc.) are the only cases where a true nexus is effectuated, i.e. an actual relationship – not simply an interaction – between terrorists and organized criminals that is sustained over time. In transitional States transnational crime groups and terrorist/revolutionary groups act on mutual opportunities and build trust, collaboration and bonds as they both aspire to profit from the chaos.[149]

It follows thus that the nature of the links between organized crime and terrorism is a combination of shared organizational-operational principles and of the contexts where it takes place. Eventually, various levels of links are encouraged that can be coined as 'organized criminal terrorism.' Whatever classification we adopt and however we choose to name the manifold combinations of crime-terror interplay, it is more than true that a study of their versatile correlations should not be neglected for effective state response, the

144 Id.

145 Louise I. Shelley and John T. Picarelli, 'Methods not Motives: Implications of the Convergence of International Organized Crime and Terrorism' (2002) 3(4) Police, Practice and Research 305; V. Ruggiero, 'Hybrids: on the Crime-Terror Nexus' (2019) 43(1) International Journal of Comparative and Applied Criminal Justice 49.

146 Helena Carrapico, Daniela Irrera, Bill Tupman, 'Transnational Organized crime and terrorism: different peas, same pod? (2014) 15(3–4) Global Crime 213.

147 V. Ruggiero, 'Hybrids' (n 145).

148 J. Picarelli, 'The Turbulent Nexus of Transnational Organized Crime and Terrorism: A Theory of Malevolent International Relations' (2006) 7(1) Global Crime 1.

149 Steven Hutchinson and Pat O'Malley, 'A Crime-Terror Nexus? Thinking on Some of the Links between Terrorism and Criminality' (2007) 30(12) Studies in Conflict Terrorism 1095, 1105.

elimination of gaps in existing legislation and the avoidance of contradictory and fallacious preventive and law enforcement strategies.

How does the UN fare in this respect? The discussion in the next section engages with the legal relationship between organized crime and terrorism.

3 Assessing the Legal Relationship between Terrorism and Organized Crime: Recommendations for a Comprehensive Legislative and Policy Approach

Just like the UN instruments fell short of providing a comprehensive legal definition of terrorism and organized crime, they have equally been relatively silent on the matter of their nexus and by implication, on the legal relationship between the two. The most targeted legislative approach responding to the nexus, even in the post-9/11 era, is the Terrorist Financing Convention. Contrariwise, despite affirmations in the preamble of Res 55/25 whereby the UNTOC was adopted about the 'deep concern [on] the growing links between TOC and terrorism', and a call 'upon all States to recognize the links between transnational organized criminal activities and acts of terrorism' as well as the explicit conviction that the Convention will constitute an effective tool and the necessary legal framework for international cooperation in combating, *inter alia* [...]' the said 'growing links', the interplay was 'consciously omitted' from the operative text of the convention; hence leaving 'loopholes that criminals might exploit' and preventing even 'the Convention from becoming an influential element of the international legal system'.[150] Concurrently, Res 1373 emphasized the 'serious challenge' of the 'connection between international terrorism and transnational organized crime', yet it provided nothing further than for a mere invitation to States to 'enhance cooperation'.[151] The issue reappeared in Res 1456/2003, which underlined, *inter alia,* that 'terrorists must also be prevented from making use of other criminal activities such as transnational organized crime, illicit drugs and drug trafficking, money-laundering and illicit arms trafficking'.

Albeit a steady magnification of international counter-terrorism measures extending the language of penalized and unjustifiable acts to all "criminal acts"

150 See the views expressed by the Turkish and Egyptian representatives in the 'Report of the Ad Hoc Committee on the Elaboration of a Convention against Transnational Organized Crime on its tenth session, held in Vienna from 17 to 28 July 2000' (11 September 2000) UN Doc A/AC.254/34 paras 18 and 28.

151 Res 1373 (51) para 4.

intended to 'provoke a state of terror',[152] nothing more precise or binding is provided for on the apposite nexus. Only recently, the abovementioned 2019 SC Resolutions seem to concretize the nexus. Binding SC Res 2462 grasps the financial interconnectedness between organized crime and terrorism. Building on SC Res 2178/2014, 2396/2017 and 2347/2017 on the matter, it notes new forms of financing terrorism and requires states to ensure that domestic legislation provides effectively for the prosecution and penalization of the provision/collection of funds, resources and services from which terrorists might benefit; stresses the importance of effective investigation and prosecution of terrorist financing cases, the implementation of asset freezing mechanisms and sanction regimes and calls upon states to intensify international collaboration on issues such as financial intelligence and the traceability of transactions.[153] Additionally, Res 2482 addresses the nexus per se, although Member States could not agree on a precise definition of the crime-terror relationship and further research on this matter is encouraged. Nevertheless, the Resolution provides an expansive list of organized crimes that may relate to terrorism and, unlike in the past, it shifts its focus equally to transnational and domestic organized crimes. In recognizing broader links between terrorism and OC, the Resolution 'reads more forcefully as a call to arms to fight crime more than it does to address terrorism' given that it requests from States to strengthen their criminal laws and cooperation in that respect to prosecute and penalize appropriately as criminal offenses the described therein illicit activities.[154] On this account, it could be argued that the Resolution strengthens the legal framework on OC, especially the instrumentality of UNTOC in combating the nexus by closing the 'loopholes' that moderate, as mentioned above, its effectiveness.

In fact, by affording a central role to the tackling of organized crime as a means to counter terrorism, Res 2482 is in line with the academic discussion on the legal relationship between the two crimes. Ben Saul explains how conduct by terrorist groups falls within the scope of UNTOC when terrorist crimes are committed inherently for profit or when terrorist groups commit serious (non-terrorist) crimes for profit, even if their ulterior aim is to pursue a terrorist act. On the contrary, terrorist crimes that are solely committed on the basis of political motivation are outside UNTOC's scope. It appears that the profit-oriented and politically/ideologically-motivated distinction between

152 UN SC Resolution 1566 (8 October 2004) UN Doc S/RES/1566.

153 M. Plachta, 'Security Council Adopts Binding Resolution on Financing of Terrorism', (2019) 35(4) International Enforcement Law Reporter 146.

154 Id., 'Security Council Adopts Resolution on Linkages between Organized Crime and Terrorism, (2019) 35(8) international Enforcement Law Reporter 309, 310 (incl. footnote 5).

organized crime and terrorism is taken into account here as a legal feature. A more complicated relationship is formed on the occasion when the political motive is not legally significant for defining terrorism and the crucial element is the intent to coerce or intimidate. As terrorists may coerce/intimidate in order to obtain financial/material benefit or in pursuit of political/ideological beliefs alike, UNTOC will be applicable only in the former case since the specific aim to obtain financial/material benefit therein has to be satisfied for the Convention to apply given that it forms the *mens rea* of an organized crime.[155] Consistent with our view that terrorism should only be defined by the intent to coerce/intimidate as elements of the crime's *mens rea*, it is indeed correct to determine the relationship between terrorism and organized crime on the offenders' *intent*. However, we would take a step further to argue that the same rule should be applied even where terrorism is defined by a political purpose. For the latter is only a motive and not a feature of *dolus specialis*.

Bringing terrorists under the purview of organized crime has a number of legal implications, some quite problematic:[156]

a) the same group may be prosecuted at times as criminal and others as terrorist group, leading to criminalization of same conduct under different regimes. Because of the different framework, different legal results will be borne regarding repression of the phenomena. The risk of double jeopardy cannot be precluded either, although it is true that subsequent prosecution and trial should concern 'the "same act" in material and legal terms'.[157] Even so, law enforcement in these cases seems to treat terrorist and criminal groups as distinct entities since it purports to classify conduct of one group (i.e. terrorists) under types of organized crime, maintaining the theoretical divergence between the two. Provision for groups with mixed motives is not made. Therefore a holistic approach is not effectuated.
b) This approach presupposes that the legal frameworks on transnational (organized) crimes are comprehensive in their own right and maybe directly provide for (regulate) terrorist groups. Instead, most instruments oblige states to have appropriate legislation in

155 B. Saul, The Legal Relationship between Terrorism and Transnational Crime', (2017) 17(3) International Criminal Law Review 417, 423. Beyond UNTOC, instruments that regulate other transnational crimes such as drug trafficking, illicit trafficking in cultural property, environmental crimes may also be applicable when these crimes are carried out by terrorist groups (id. 435 ff).

156 Id. 423 ff.

157 Van der Wilt and Paulussen (n 98) 321–322.

> effect to address those crimes, whereas in certain instances such as the framework to prevent environmental harms or kidnapping for ransom, there is no one specific instrument that addresses the problem in order to provide for terrorist groups as well. Unavoidably, an ad hoc dealing with terrorist groups committing these crimes is the only way forward.

A third issue one should highlight is the risks to human rights and fundamental freedoms, which are exacerbated in the context of the nexus. UN Special Rapporteur on the promotion and protection of human rights while countering terrorism raises concern over the abuse of organized crime and counter-terrorism legislation. In light of the lack of clear definitions of terrorism and organized crime alike, states may expand terrorism legislation to acts that may not meet an agreed threshold under international law or elevate legislation on serious crime to exceptional law, circumscribing human rights and constitutional guarantees. In other words the greater powers that states enjoy under anti-terrorist laws will be applied to the tackling of organized and "ordinary" crime, and in fact by virtue of a SC Resolution, which is the outcome of closed process of deliberation and international lawmaking since only states which are members of the Council have a say.[158]

If prevention and repression of either of the phenomena individually or their nexus are to be pursued effectively, it is paramount that the legislative gaps and weaknesses are first remedied and policy is better coordinated. To this end, the Hague Good Practices[159] on the Nexus between TOC and Terrorism and the respective Policy Toolkit[160] may bolster the UN Counter-Terrorism Framework. The 25 Good Practices constitute recommendations for states at four levels: a) legal, in order to build an effective institutional framework, b) research and information sharing that will build states' capacity to identify the nexus, c) local engagement so that communities build resilience on terrorism and organized crime and cooperate in a trustworthy manner with authorities and d) enhancement of the law enforcement mechanisms. The underlying

158 Fionnuala Ni Aolain, 'The Massive Perils of the Latest UN Resolution on Terrorism' (*Just Security*, 8 July 2019) <https://www.justsecurity.org/64840/the-massive-perils-of-the-latest-u-n-resolution-on-terrorism/> accessed 17 June 2020 (comment apropos Res 2482 that is not binding under Chapter VII UN Charter).

159 Global Counter-terrorism Forum <https://www.thegctf.org/Portals/1/Documents/Framework%20Documents/2018/GCTF-Good-Practices-on-the-Nexus_ENG.pdf?ver=2018-09-21-122246-363> (September 2018) accessed 20 July 2020.

160 UN Interregional Crime and Justice Research Institute <https://www.thegctf.org/LinkClick.aspx?fileticket=GZAXnYJWfuQ%3d&portalid=1> (March 2019) accessed 20 July 2020.

assumption of the Good Practices is that the nexus is largely context-specific and manifests itself in multiple ways depending on the political environment and policies of State response. They, thus, aspire to be applicable to the special circumstances each country faces and to streamline uniform standards in domestic legislations and international policy. While legal considerations unfold around the coherence of anti-crime and counterterrorism legislation with the relevant regional and international legal conventions, the most crucial recommendation to States is to identify convergent areas in anti-crime and counterterrorism policy rather than opt for blanket solutions devoid of the special circumstances (GP1). Equally fundamental is the appropriate prosecution of those who commit illegal activities related to organized crime and terrorism; in other words, not to prosecute or try perpetrators for terrorist offenses or those relating to organized crime only (GP23).

Having this in mind, if a universal instrument on terrorism is ever to be concluded stipulation of nexus-related crimes (i.e. 'organized criminal terrorism crimes') might be introduced as a new category. Motives should not come to play but criminality should be the common denominator of terrorism and organized crime, raising thus the *actus reus*, the *mens rea* and causation, which are already the backbone of criminal law for determining the commitment of criminal offenses and the alleged perpetrator's criminal responsibility, to key determinants of nexus-related crimes. It is indeed questionable how a consensus on the nexus might be achieved when the definitional problems on terrorism and organized crime are open-ended but the on-going consultations on the new Counter-terrorism Convention may be a fruitful opportunity to address the nexus more effectively as well.

4 Conclusion

This chapter presented how the UN addresses the offenses related to acts of international terrorism and TOC and examined if the organization grapples with their nexus. Going through the international framework, it was demonstrated that the remedies offered by international law hitherto fail to take a holistic approach. OC and terrorism are deemed theoretically divergent; but in practice they are inter-connected and inter-dependent. Despite the UN's ostensive assertions about the linkages and the need for a coordinated approach, these appear only in soft law instruments. The reason for this lacuna lies in various factors, namely: the stalemate for a definition of terrorism and OC, the distinctive elements of the different crimes, the attribution (or not) to States, but also the risk of an 'over-broadness' in criminalizing conduct coupled with the challenge for the delicate equilibrium between countering terrorism and preserving human rights, basic criminal maxims and the right for legitimate struggles against totalitarian regimes or alien occupation. However, this purely responsive legal route has confined anti-terrorist policies to suppression measures. Pre-emptive methods are dominated by a 'pre-crime' approach with alarming effects over the respect of fundamental rights and questionable results. Following an adapted criminological approach, OCT can be averted by gradually blocking its constituent elements. Effective prevention could be, thus, achieved by eradicating the environment favouring its flourishing, ergo controlling the entire operational trail. In the current state of affairs, international law should address the two converging phenomena commonly, through a joint penalization for cases when the two phenomena meet, i.e. not only in their integrative or hybrid forms but also in terms of alliances in the various phases of illegal operations.

CHAPTER 3

The Case against Changing the Council of Europe's Approach to Counter-Terrorism

Francesco Seatzu

> much of today's terrorism cannot be insulated from overseas developments – and implicit in this is the link to wider issues of instability and their association with organized crime.
>
> MARK SHAW and PREM MAHADEVAN

∴

1 Introduction

Both the international and national legal systems have witnessed since September 11's attacks to the US soil, also called 9/11 attacks, a growing tendency to merge the concepts of international terrorism and transnational organized crime.[1] While the concept of terrorism was not generally included

---

1 See e.g. Stefan Goertz, Alexander E. Streitparth, 'Cooperation, Interaction and Fusion of Transnational Organised Crime and Transnational Jihadism: The New Terrorism', in Stefan Goertz, Alexander E. Streitparth (eds.), *The New Terrorism: Actors, Strategies and Tactics* (Amsterdam: Springer, 2019), p. 43 ff; Alex P. Schmid, 'Revisiting the Relationship between International Terrorism and Transnational Organised Crime 22 Years Later' (2018) 22 *ICCT Research paper*, available at: https://icct.nl/wp-content/uploads/2018/08/ICCT-Schmid-International-Terrorism-Organised-Crime-August2018.pdf; Id., *Links Between Terrorist and Organized Crime Networks: Emerging Patterns and Trends* (Milan: ISPAC, 2004); Alessandra Annoni, 'The Relationship between Transnational Organised Crime and Terrorism: An International Law Perspective', in Stefania Carnevale, Serena Forlati, Orsetta Giolo (eds.), *Redefining Organised Crime: A Challenge for the European Union?* (Oxford: Hart publishing, 2017), p. 121 ff; Basra, Rajan and Peter R. Neumann, 'Crime as Jihad: Developments in the Crime-Terror Nexus in Europe (2017) 10 *CTC Sentinel*, p. 9 ff; Basra, Rajan, Peter R. Neumann and Claudia. Brunner, *Criminal Pasts, Terrorist Futures: European Jihadists and the New Crime-Terror Nexus* (London: ICSR, 2016), available at http://icsr.info/wp-content/uploads/2016/10/Criminal-Pasts-Terrorist-Futures.pdf; Sergei Boeke, 'Al Qaeda in the Islamic Maghreb: Terrorism, Insurgency, or Organized Crime?' (2016) 5 *Small Wars & Insurgencies* 27, pp. 914–936; Colin P. Clarke, *Crime and Terror in Europe: Where the Nexus*

 | DOI:10.1163/9789004424579_005

in international legal instruments and policies dealing with organized crime a consensus has gradually emerged calling for substantial modifications in traditional legal approaches to fight terrorism and transnational organized criminality, including the extension of preventive and preparatory legal measures against organized crime to terrorism activities and organizations.[2] Recently, nevertheless, the early enthusiasm for the use of criminal policies against transnational organized crime also in the fight against terrorism has gradually faded away in the wake of several criticisms,[3] primarily directed at the fact that the application of these policies to terrorism leads to measures which are proven to be neither 'proportionate' nor 'necessary' from a criminal law perspective.[4] These criticisms are well expressed and developed by those authors

is Alive and Well (The Hague: International Centre for Counter-Terrorism (ICCT), 2016), available at: https://icct.nl/publication/crime-and-terror-in-europe-where-the-nexus-is-alive-and- well/; Wolfgang Benedek, Christopher Daase, Vojin Dimitrijevic and Petrus van Duyne (eds), *Transnational Terrorism, Organized Crime and Peace-building: Human Security in the Western Balkans* (New York: Palgrave Macmillan, 2010), available at: http://cn4hs.org/wp-content/uploads/Human-Security-in-the-Western-Balkans-Benedek-et-alled.chp12.pdf; Tamara Makarenko, The Crime-Terror Continuum; Tracing the Interplay between Transnational Organised Crime and Terrorism, (2004) 6 *Global Crime*, p. 129 ff; Patricia Bibes, 'Transnational Organized Crime and Terrorism: Colombia, a Case Study' (2001) 17 *Journal of Contemporary Criminal Justice*, pp. 243–258.

2 Amplius, see Davor Derencinovic, Anna-Maria Getos, 'Cooperation of law enforcement and intelligence agencies in prevention and suppression of terrorism European perspective' (2007) 78 *Revue Internationale de Droit Pénal*, pp. 79–112; Tom Schalken, 'On joint investigation teams, Europol and supervision of their joint actions' (2002) 10 *European Journal of Crime, Criminal Law and Criminal Justice*, pp. 70–82. See also UNODC, *Handbook on Criminal Justice Responses to Terrorism*, available at: https://www.unodc.org/documents/terrorism/Handbook_on_Criminal_Justice_Responses_to_Terrorism_en.pdf.

3 Council of Europe: Committee of Ministers, *Recommendation of the Committee of Ministers to member States on "special investigation techniques" in relation to serious crimes including acts of terrorism*, 5 July 2017, CM/Rec (2017) 6, available at: https://rm.coe.int/1680730408. See also Alessandro Lentini, *Selected Issues in Counter-terrorism: special investigative techniques and the international judicial cooperation Focus on the European Union* (Pisa: Pacini editore, 2019), available at: http://www.dirittopenaleglobalizzazione.it/wp-content/uploads/2018/03/Alessandro-Lentini-Selected-Issues-in-Counter-Terrorism.pdf; Clive Walker, Alexander Horne, 'The Terrorism Prevention and Investigation Measures Act 2011: One Thing but Not Much the Other?' (2012) 45 *Criminal Law Review*, 421–438.

4 For these criticisms, see e.g. Henrique Carvalho, *The preventive turn in criminal law* (Oxford: OUP, 2017), p. 51 ff; Lucia Zedner,'Terrorizing criminal law' (2014) 8 *Criminal Law and Philosophy – An International Journal for Philosophy of Crime, Criminal Law and Punishment*, pp. 99–121; Clive Walker, 'The Impact of Contemporary Security Agendas Against Terrorism on the Substantive Criminal Law', in Aniceto Masferrer (ed.), *Post 9/11 and the State of Permanent Legal Emergency – Security and Human Rights in Countering Terrorism* (Dordrecht, Boston, 2012), p. 121 ff; Manuel Cancio Meliá, 'Terrorism and Criminal Law: The Dream of Prevention, the Nightmare of the Rule of Law' (2011) *New Criminal Law Review*, p. 108 ff. See

who denounce the risk, in so doing, of introducing in the international legal order a 'criminal law of the enemy' for terrorist suspects and other organized criminals[5] like the one that already exists in the US for the suspected terrorists.[6] According to these and other authors, it is clear that if terrorism is considered as a criminal phenomenon that justifies the least protective criminal procedure and law, any attempt to link terrorism to other criminal phenomena like human trafficking, drug trafficking, smuggling of alcohol and tobacco leads to the application of a less protective criminal law and procedure even outside the measures that are at the core of the counter-terrorism policies and strategies.[7] Indeed this is a statement that could hardly be controverted and rebutted, at least if one considers that the whole concept of civil liberties and civil human rights is becoming increasingly outmoded globally[8] and also,

also Ilias Bantekas, 'The International Law of Terrorist Financing' (2003) 97 *AJIL*, p. 315, who also stresses that even if organized criminal activities are used to finance terrorist operations, such activities constituted distinct and lesser crimes than the ultimate act of terrorism itself, and hence, should be kept separate.

5 On this point see, in addition to the authors cited in the previous note, Katalin Ligeti, Maxime Lassalle, 'The Organised Crime-Terrorism Nexus: How to Address the Issue of ISIS Benefitting From Lucrative Criminal Activities?', in Marc Engelhart, Sunčana Roksandić Vidlička (eds.), *Dealing with terrorism. Empirical and normative challenges of fighting the Islamic State* (Berlin: Duncker & Humblot, 2018), p. 73 ff; Philippe Duhart, 'Criminalizing peace: anti-terrorism law and its impact on peacemaking in the Basque Country and Northern Ireland' (2019) 10 *Peacebuilding*, p. 25 ff; Mariángeles Catalina Benavente, Teresa Manso Porto, 'Combating the terrorism of ETA with the penal model' (2014) 62 *Crime, Law and Social Change*, pp 269–288.

6 For a succinct, but a satisfactory account of the use of special criminal legislation in the United States, see e.g. John A. E. Vervaele, 'The Anti-Terrorist Legislation in the US: Inter Arma Silent Leges?' (2005) 13 *European Journal of Crime, Criminal Law and Criminal* Justice, pp. 208–210; Roberta Belli, Joshua D. Freilich, Steven M. Chermak, Katharine A. Boyd, 'Exploring the crime-terror nexus in the United States: a social network analysis of a Hezbollah network involved in trade diversion' (2015) 8 *Dynamics of Asymmetric Conflict*, available at: https://www.tandfonline.com/doi/abs/10.1080/17467586.2015.1104420; Stefan Sottiaux, *Terrorism and the limitation of rights: the ECHR and the US Constitution* (Oxford: Hart publishing, 2008), ch. IV.

7 Amplius, see Katalin Ligeti, Maxime Lassalle, above n. 5, p. 73 ff.

8 See *ex multis* Julia L. Ernst, 'The Constitution in Times of National Crisis: Contextualizing Post-September 11 Constitutional Ramifications' (2012) 88 *North Dakota Law Review*, p. 52 ff; Paolo Bonetti, *Terrorismo, emergenza e costituzioni democratiche* (Bologna: Il Mulino, 2006), p. 12 ff; Paul J. A. de Hert, 'Balancing security and liberty within the European human rights framework. A critical reading of the Court's case law in the light of surveillance and criminal law enforcement strategies after 9/11' (2005) 1 *Utrecht Law Review*, pp. 68–96; Richard Briffault, 'Facing the Urban Future After September 11, 2001' (2002) 34 *Urb. Law*, pp. 563, 580; Thomas I. Emerson, 'National Security and Civil Liberties' (1982) 9 *The Yale Journal of World Public Order*, available at: http://digitalcommons.law.yale.edu/cgi/viewcontent.cgi?article=1192&context=yjil.

and more specifically, that the inclusion of the concept of terrorism into international legal instruments dealing with transnational organized crime like the United Nations Convention against Transnational Organized Crime[9] would make these instruments unworkable in practice because of the sharp division of opinion among the signatories and the enduring disagreement on the notion of organized crime.[10] Outcomes aside, both legal and non-legal writers have recently criticized in particular the merger of the concepts of terrorist financing and money laundering because of the generally amorphous nature of the concept of terrorism, the difficulties of determining which transactions are indicative of terrorist financing,[11] and also and in particular because of the so-called 'non-financial profiling' (NFP) which often leads to the identification of the 'usual suspects' (that is, people of Arab descendants or Islamic faith) as engaging in suspicious transactions.[12]

9 UN General Assembly, United Nations Convention against Transnational Organized Crime: resolution / adopted by the General Assembly, 8 January 2001, A/RES/55/25, available at: https://www.refworld.org/docid/3b00f55b0.html For a commentary, see *ex multis* John D. McClean (ed.), *Transnational organized crime: a commentary on the UN Convention and its protocols* (Oxford: OUP, 2007); Jean-Paul Laborde, *État de droit et crime organisé: les apports de la Convention des Nations unies contre la criminalité transnationale organisée* (Paris: Dalloz, 2005); Roger S. Clark, 'The United Nations Convention Against Transnational Organized Crime' (2004) 50 *Wayne Law Review*, p. 161 ff.

10 Amplius, see Stefania Carnevale, Serena Forlati, Orsetta Giolo, 'The Notion of Organised Crime: Why Definitions Matter', in Stefania Carnevale, Serena Forlati, Orsetta Giolo (eds.), *Redefining Organised Crime: A Challenge for the European Union?* (Oxford: Hart publishing, 2017), p. 1 ff; Gioacchino Pollimeni, 'The Notion of Organised Crime in the United Nations Convention against Transnational Organized Crime', in *ibidem*, p. 57 ff; James O. Finckenauer, 'Problems of definition: What is organized crime?' (2005) 8 *Trends in Organized Crime*, pp. 63–83; Matti Joutsen, 'Elaboration of a United Nations convention against transnational organized crime' (1999) 86 *Nordisk tidsskrift for kriminalvidenskab*, p. 220 ff.; Dimitri Vlasssis, 'Drafting the United Nations convention against transnational organized crime' (1998) 4 *Transnational organized crime*, pp. 356–362.

11 See *ex multis* Bruce Zagaris, 'The Merging of Anti-Money Laundering and Counter Terrorism Financial Enforcement Regimes After September 11, 2011' (2004) 22 *Berkelely Journal of International Law*, p. 124 ff; Adam Klein, 'The End of Al Qaeda? Rethinking the Legal End of the War on Terror' (2010) 110 *Columbia Law Review*, p. 1865 ff.

12 On the NFP, see Alexandra V. Orlova, James W. Moore, 'Umbrellas or Building Blocks: Defining International Terrorism and Transnational Organized Crime in International Law' (2005) 27 *Houston Journal of International Law*, p. 301 ff, also stressing that NFP is generally based on categories, such as religion, ethnicity, and the ability to speak the local language. See also Reuven Young, 'Defining terrorism: The evolution of terrorism as a legal concept in international law and its influence on definitions in domestic legislation' (2006) 29 *B. C. Int'l & Comp. L. Rev.*, p. 23.

Nevertheless, influenced both by the adoption of a politically-based rather than a criminological based approach to terrorism[13] and by the need of avoiding the confinement of anti-terrorist policies to suppression measures, several commentators continue to insist that transnational organized crime and terrorism should be seen as a single combined threat rather than two distinct phenomena[14] and that the antidote to the failures in the fight against international terrorism is the adoption of several reforms. Among the various reform proposals are those focusing on the progressive assimilation of terrorism to transnational organized crime.[15] In particular, those commentators who either explicitly or implicitly consider terrorism as a sub-category of transnational crime and who generally believe that terrorism and organized crime have moved from specific collaborations to model of hybridization[16] urge to overcome the current fragmented approach to the international legal regulation of terrorism and organized crime that appear to them not justified, especially because limiting the availability and efficacy of the envisaged anti-terrorist measures and sanctions. And, in fact, according to some of these commentators, the assimilation of terrorism to organized criminality, unlike its non assimilation, offers in particular the advantage of bypassing the problem of defining terrorism, thereby indirectly solving the complex issue of the nexus between terrorist activities and transnational criminal organizations. While the merging of terrorism and organized crime is admittedly far from ideal (so the argument goes), it can still be better than their legal regulation as two distinct self-contained regimes.

---

13 See Andrew Richards, *Constructing the terrorist threat: the merging of the discourses of terrorism, radicalization and extremism in the UK and its consequences Constructions of Terrorism Conference* (Santa Barbara: Orfalea Center for Global & International Studies, University of California, 2015), available at: https://repository.uel.ac.uk/item/853vo.

14 See Tamara Makarenko, 'The Crime-Terror Continuum: Tracing the Interplay between Transnational Organised Crime and Terrorism' (2004) 6 *Global Crime*, p. 131 ff; Id.,'Transnational crime and its evolving links to terrorism and instability' (2001) 5 *Jane's Intelligence Review*, pp. 3–4; Chris Dishman, 'The Leaderless Nexus: When Crime and Terror Converge' (2005) 28 Studies in Conflict and Terrorism, p. 24 6 ff; Mark Shaw, Prem Mahadevan, 'When terrorism and organized crime meet' (2018) 6/7 *Policy Perspectives*, available at: https://ethz.ch/content/dam/ethz/special-interest/gess/cis/center-for-securities-studies/pdfs/PP6-7_2018.pdf.

15 See Tamara Makarenko, above n. 14, p. 131 ff.

16 See e. g. Luis de la Corte Ibáñez, Hristina Hristova Gergova, 'Why Do Links Between Terrorism and Crime Increase?', in Henrik Legind Larsen, José María Blanco, Raquel Pastor, Ronald R. Yager (eds.), *Using Open Data to Detect Organized Crime Threats – Factors Driving Future Crime* (Amsterdam: Springer, 2017), p. 261 ff; Ursula C Schroeder, Fairlie Chappuis, Deniz Kocak, 'Security sector reform and the emergence of hybrid security governance' (2014) 21 *International Peacekeeping*, pp. 133–48.

In addition to what has been observed above, the combination of terrorism and organized crime as a single combined threat encounter various obstacles and inconveniences nevertheless. These are evident and clear if one looks at the so called 'war on terrorism'[17] or alternatively or in addition thereto at the phenomenon of the narcoterrorism.[18] Or again, if one considers that international terrorism is a phenomenon that currently takes not just one, but a multiplicity of specific forms including armed conflict.[19] Plus, and more specifically, if, in relation to the phenomenon of narcoterrorism, one recalls what Katalin Ligeti and Maxime Lasalle have correctly acknowledged, that:

> narcoterrorism constitutes a useful *political* way to legitimize the war on drugs.[20]

Focusing both on the Council of Europe's strategy on counter terrorism and the Council of Europe's treaties and protocols on the prevention of terrorism, the main purpose in this work is to challenge this view. I do not believe that any unified response to international terrorism and organized criminality is either desirable or truly indispensable. In my view, commentators often label too many cases as 'terrorism acts and activities' even when the stated rationale for this qualification is far from clear and evident from a criminological point of view. Moreover, they often fail to recognize that while the lack of a legal definition of international terrorism makes a broad treaty on counter-terrorism hard to be drafted (as the recent history teaches us),[21] this disagreement does make

---

17 On the war on terrorism, see e.g. Andrea Bianchi, 'Terrorism and Armed Conflict: Insights from a Law & Literature Perspective' (2011) 24 *Leiden Journal of International Law*, pp. 1–21; Tung Yin, 'Ending the War on Terrorism One Terrorist at a Time: A Noncriminal Detention Model for Holding and Releasing Guantanamo Bay Detainees' (2006) 29 *Harvard Journal of Law & Public Policy*, p. 182; Hans-Peter Gasser, 'Acts of terror, 'terrorism' and international humanitarian law (2002) 84 *International Review of the Red Cross*, p. 568 ff.

18 On the topic, see e.g. Emma Bjornehed, 'Narco-Terrorism: The Merger of the War on Drugs and the War on Terror' (2004) 6 *Global Crime*, p. 305 ff; Donnie Marshall, 'Narco-Terrorism: The New Discovery of an Old Connection' (2002) 35 *Cornell International Law Journal*, available at: https://scholarship.law.cornell.edu/cgi/viewcontent.cgi?article=1522&context=cilj; Robert M. Kimmitt, 'International Law in the War on Narcotics' (1990) 84 *Proceedings of the Annual Meeting of the American Society of International Law*, p. 302 ff.

19 See Andrea Bianchi, above n. 17, p. 1 ff.

20 See Katalin Ligeti, Maxime Lassalle, above n. 5, p. 73 ff.

21 See Dipanjan Roy Chaudhury, 'SCO endorses India's proposal for UN terror treaty', *The Economic Times*, 11th June 2018, available at: https://economictimes.indiatimes.com/news/defence/sco-endorses-indias-proposal-for-un-terror-treaty/articleshow/64548213.cms; Christian Tomuschat, 'On the possible "added value" of a comprehensive convention on terrorism' (2005) 26 *Human Rights Law Journal*, p. 287 ff.

the situation more conducive to narrower treaties focussing on specific acts and activities that constitute terrorism.[22] Hence, precisely, this is why, thus far, the UN has been very successful at drafting and ratifying international treaties that outlaw and punish particular tactics that terrorists might use, including airplane-hijacking, hostage-taking, bombings, nuclear terrorism, etc – and this is also why the Council of Europe Convention on the Prevention of Terrorism (CECPT) of 2005, currently the Council of Europe's main international legal instrument in the counter-terrorism field, instead of providing a general definition of 'terrorist offence' proceed by defining this term operationally by referring to the nineteen existing UN conventions on terrorism presently in force.[23]

Again, and equally importantly, commentators who advocate the consideration of terrorism as a sub-category of transnational organized crime often also overlooks 'the possibilities to institute lower standard of freedoms and rights for terrorists than granted even to organized criminals'[24] as well as the need of introducing a special protection regime for the victims of terrorism.[25] Finally, where existing counter-terrorism policies do pose insurmountable obstacles to address the nexus between terrorism and organized crime *alias* the 'terrorism-crime continuum', I submit that the case has not yet been made that these policies against terrorism in general and in particular the Council of Europe's counter-terrorist policy should be modified and merged with counter organized and transnational organized crime policies in order to efficaciously deal with this issue.

2 The Reform Proposals

Despite increasing calls for an approach to terrorism based on its complete assimilation to the organized crime, it is perhaps telling that few detailed

22 On the problems in drafting a universal treaty on terrorism, see Claude Emmanuelli, 'Legal Aspects of Aerial Terrorism: The Piecemeal vs. the Comprehensive Approach' (1975) 10 J. *Int'l L. & Econ*, p. 503 ff; Thomas M. Franck and Bert B. Lockwood, Jr., 'Preliminary Thoughts Towards an International Convention on Terrorism' (1974) 68 *AJIL*, p. 69 ff.

23 A list of these conventions as well as of other international and regional legal instruments related to terrorism and co-operation in criminal matters in the OSCE area is available at: https://www.osce.org/atu/17138?%20download=true.

24 See Colin King, Clive Walker, 'Counter Terrorism Financing: A Redundant Fragmentation?' (2015) 6 *New Journal of European Criminal Law*, p. 395.

25 See René Ariel Dotti, 'Terrorism, due process of law, and the protection of victims' (2005) 76 *Revue International de Droit Pénal*, p. 227 ff.

proposals have been advanced so far.[26] In summing up views expressed after 9/11 by observers of the relationship between transnational organized crime and terrorism, Ligeti and Lassalle concluded that though most of these views manifested discomfort at addressing a phenomenon between terrorism, organized crime and lucrative petty crime through separate legal instruments and policies applicable respectively to transnational organized criminality and terrorism activities, no alternative to this solution was proposed that balanced the opposing interests at stake: that of avoiding the justification of the least protective criminal procedure as a result of the assimilation of terrorism and transnational organized crime, on the one hand, and that of avoiding the problem of the legal classification of violent activities either as terrorist activities or as activities of organized crime.[27] Exemplary of this situation is, in our view, the UN Security Council's Presidential Statement on the nexus between international terrorism and transnational organized crime of 2018, which merely states that: 'The Security Council ... encourages Member States, as well as international, regional and sub-regional organizations and fora to continue continuing research to better understand the nature and scope of the links between terrorists and transnational organized criminals'.[28]

Perhaps, the most striking aspect of reform is the lack of direct attention paid both within the United Nations' and Council of Europe's counter terrorism policies to the existing and proven facts of the terror-crime nexus.[29] This issue was raised critically by Professors Ana Salinas de Frias and Peter Neumann in 2018 in their lengthy report to the Council of Europe Committee on Counter Terrorism (CDCT) aimed at reducing the opportunities for misuse of organised crime activities that are likely to provide sources of terrorist financing.[30] Here, amongst other things, Professors Neumann and Salinas argued that international legal instruments and protocols in relation to transnational organized

26 But see Ben Saul, 'Defining Terrorism: A Conceptual Minefield', in Erica Chenoweth, Richard English, Andreas Gofas, Stathis N. Kalyvas (eds), *The Oxford Handbook on Terrorism* (Oxford: OUP, 2017), p. 4 ff; Id., 'The Legal Relationship between Terrorism and Transnational Crime' (2013) 3 *International Criminal Law Review*, pp. 417–452.

27 See Katalin Ligeti, Maxime Lassalle, above n. 5, p. 73 ff.

28 S/PRST/2018/9.

29 On this point, see e.g. Mark Shaw, Prem Mahadevan, 'When terrorism and organized crime meet', available at: https://globalinitiative.net/wp-content/uploads/2018/10/PP6-7_2018-1.pdf, also stressing that: 'In the West, if the crime-terror nexus was recognized and aggressively combated it was at the domestic level, even if with limited resources'.

30 See Peter Neumann, Ana Maria Salinas De Frias, 'Report on the links between terrorism and transnational organised crime', available at: https://rm.coe.int/report-on-the-links-between-terrorism-and-transnational-organised-crim/1680711352.

criminality including the Council of Europe's Convention on Laundering, Search, Seizure and Confiscation of the Proceeds from Crime cannot properly and efficiently address the manifestations of the terror-crime nexus for a number of reasons and, in particular, given that they are not usually correctly enforced in national legal systems.[31]

The lack of direct attention to the terror-crime nexus may undermine efforts by States to address threats of violent extremism by terrorists' groups and individuals in a serious manner.[32] Yet this is clear and evident if one considers that most of the criminal activities involved in the terror-crime nexus are not addressed by the existing sectoral legal instruments on terrorism including the Council of Europe's international legal instruments in the counter-terrorism field.[33]

Aside from the above-described difficulty of addressing criminal activities involved in the nexus, critics cite the obstacles presented when states are requested to cooperate internationally for preventing terrorists from benefiting from transnational organized crime, or when they are requested to investigate and to build the capacity to prosecute such terrorists and transnational organized criminals working with them.[34] The drafters of the Hague Good Practices on the Nexus between Transnational Organized Crime and Terrorism, a non-binding instrument that was adopted at the Ninth GCTF Ministerial Plenary Meeting in New York in September 2018, suggest either a modest change, in which a set of non-binding rules and recommendations guide countries as well as global, regional, national and local organizations as they develop policies and initiatives that target terrorism and transnational organized crime, or a

31 In the same sense, see also the proposal before the UN Security Council for a resolution on the linkages between international terrorism and transnational organized crime. On this topic, see e.g. 'International Terrorism and Transnational Organised Crime: What's in Blue-Insights on the Work of the U.N. Security Council', available at: https://www.whatsinblue.org/2019/07/international-terrorism-and-transnational-organised-crime.php#.

32 Amplius, see UNICRI, 'Breaking the Organized Crime and Counter-Terrorism Nexus: Identifying Programmatic Approaches', available at: http://unicri.it/in_focus/files/NEXUS_REPORT_UNICRI.pdf.

33 See Katalin Ligeti, Maxime Lassalle, above n. 5, p. 73 ff.

34 Amplius, see Fernando Reinares, Carlos Resa, 'Transnational organized crime as an increasing threat to the national security of democratic regimes: assessing political impacts and evaluating state responses', available at: https://www.nato.int/acad/fellow/97-99/reinares.pdf, also stressing that terrorist groups benefiting from transnational organized crime (and transnational organized crime benefitting from the use of terrorist tactics) may contribute to undermining the security and stability of affected States.

more radical change, in which strategic good practices would be used to support States to develop an institutional framework.[35]

Before assessing the merits of these proposals, it is important to examine whether the need for these or other reforms has been overestimated. It is the present author's opinion that the need is considerably less than is sometimes suggested. For instance, there is a pervasive tendency of some legal writers and policy makers to underestimate the fact that notwithstanding the enduring lack of a common definition of terrorism, the existing international legal treaties on terrorism including the Council of Europe's international legal instruments in the counter-terrorism field do contain several elements, indicated as preparatory acts of terrors or ancillary offences, which deal indirectly with some manifestations of the terror-crime nexus.[36] The reference is here in particular to the 2005 Warsaw Convention on the Prevention of Terrorism that, at its Article 4, provides that: 'Parties shall, as appropriate and with due regard to their capabilities, assist and support each other with a view to enhancing their capacity to prevent the commission of terrorist offences, including through exchange of information and best practices, as well as through training and other joint efforts of a preventive character'.[37] Moreover, the reference is also to the Additional Protocol to the Council of Europe Convention on the Prevention of Terrorism of 2005,[38] a legal instrument that primarily aims at

35 GCTF, 'The Hague Good Practices on the Nexus between Transnational Organized Crime and Terrorism', available at: https://www.thegctf.org/Portals/1/Documents/Framework%20Documents/C/GCTF-Good-Practices-on-the-Nexus_ENG.pdf?ver=2018-09-21-122246-363.

36 See Marja Lehto, *Indirect responsibility for terrorist acts: redefinition of the concept of terrorism beyond violent acts* (Leiden; Boston: M. Nijhoff Publishers, 2009), ch. 1; Katalin Ligeti, Maxime Lassalle, above n. 5, p. 73 ff.

37 Council of Europe, Council of Europe Convention on the Prevention of Terrorism, 16 May 2005, ETS No. 196, available at: https://www.refworld.org/docid/47fdfafod.html For a commentary, see e.g. Adrian Hunt, 'The Council of Europe Convention on the Prevention of Terrorism' (2006) 12 *European Public Law*, p. 603 ff.

38 Council of Europe: Committee of Ministers, Additional Protocol to the Council of Europe Convention on the Prevention of Terrorism, 19 May 2015, available at: https://www.refworld.org/docid/55af6cf64.html On the Additional Protocol, see *ex multis* Urlich Garms, 'Preventive Criminal Justice Strategy Against Terrorism', in Manfred Nowak, Anne Charbord (ed), *Using Human Rights to Counter Terrorism* (Cheltenham: Edward Elgar Publishing, 2018), p. 281 ff; Michele Nino, *Terrorismo Internazionale, Privacy e Protezione dei Dati Personali* (Napoli: Editoriale Scientifica, 2008), p. 3 ff; Giuliana Ziccardi Capaldo, *Terrorismo Globale e Diritti Umani: A 'fair balance' tra interesse generale e tutela dei diritti fondamentali individuali,* in AA.VV., *Studi in Onore di Vincenzo Starace,* Napoli, 2008, I, p. 745 ff.

enhancing the efforts of Contracting Parties in preventing terrorist acts and activities and their negative effects on the enjoyment of fundamental rights and freedoms.[39] Furthermore, the reference is also to the new Council of Europe Counter-Terrorism Strategy (2018–2022) that contains a section (2.5) entirely devoted to the relationship between terrorism and organized criminality.[40] Following up on the outcomes of the 2nd Malaga Conference on Terrorism and Organised Crime, section 2.5 of the concluding Report by Professors Salinas and Neumann[41] recommends Council of Europe's member states the establishment of a working group specifically tasked with providing to the relevant and competent national authorities dealing with organized crime and terrorism guidelines on common approaches to investigate and prosecute terrorism and transnational organized crime.[42]

In conclusion, for these and other reasons, the present author feels that there is far more adaptability and flexibility in the existing Council of Europe's rules and strategy in the counter terrorism field than is commonly acknowledged and admitted.

---

39 See e.g. Article 9 of the Additional Protocol which provides that: 'Each Party shall adopt such measures as may be necessary to establish as a criminal offence under its domestic law: a Participating as an accomplice in an offence as set forth in Articles 5 to 7 of this Convention; b Organizing or directing others to commit an offence as set forth in Articles 5 to 7 of this Convention; c Contributing to the commission of one or more offences as set forth in Articles 5 to 7 of this Convention by a group of persons acting with a common purpose. Such contribution shall be intentional and shall either: i be made with the aim of furthering the criminal activity or criminal purpose of the group, where such activity or purpose involves the commission of an offence as set forth in Articles 5 to 7 of this Convention; or ii be made in the knowledge of the intention of the group to commit an offence as set forth in Articles 5 to 7 of this Convention. 2 Each Party shall also adopt such measures as may be necessary to establish as a criminal offence under, and in accordance with, its domestic law the attempt to commit an offence as set forth in Articles 6 and 7 of this Convention.

40 CoE, 'Council of Europe Counter-Terrorism Strategy (2018–2022)', available at: https://rm.coe.int/CoERMPublicCommonSearchServices/DisplayDCTMContent?documentId=0900001680 8afc96.

41 See Peter Neumann, Ana Maria Salinas De Frias, above n. 30.

42 According to Section 2.5 of the Neumann/Salinas Report, the working group should be composed of national experts from the member States and international partners of the Council of Europe in the fight against terrorism and organized crime.

3 The Need to Clarify the Meaning and Scope of the 'Terror-Crime' Nexus

Notwithstanding there are a few but authoritative critics who would contest the existence of special international legal rules for terrorist activities and acts in virtually any case,[43] a wide number of commentators and institutions including the European Parliament[44] still assume that there is a category of terrorist acts and activities, namely the criminal acts and activities involved in the 'nexus', that cannot be adequately handled by the existing rules and instruments on counter-terrorism.[45] Moreover, though few specific rule changes have actually been suggested so far, at least in relation specifically to the Council of Europe's international legal instruments in the counter-terrorism field, the assumption seems to be that whatever is done to effectively address the criminal activities and acts involved in the 'nexus' will only be done in this particular circumstances.

But what is 'the terror-crime nexus', anyway? Unlike what might appear at a quick glance, the 'terror-crime nexus' is, in practice, certainly not a new issue for the international community.[46] And, in fact, as early as 1994, the UNGA Declaration on Measures to Eliminate Terrorism (the UNGA Declaration of 1994)[47] noted with great concern the: 'growing and dangerous links between terrorist groups and drug traffickers' and remained convinced of the: 'desirability for closer coordination and cooperation among States in combatting crimes closely connected with terrorism, including drug trafficking, unlawful arms trade etc'.[48] Moreover, one can also recall the United Nations Convention of 15

---

43 See Rosalyn Higgins, 'The General International Law of Terrorism', in Rosalyn Higgins & Maurice Flory (eds.), *Terrorism and International Law* (London: Routledge, 1997), pp. 13–14.

44 See European Parliament, 'Europe's Crime-Terror Nexus: Links between terrorist and organised crime groups in the European Union', available at: http://www.europarl.europa.eu/RegData/etudes/etudes/join/2012/462503/IPOL-LIBE_ET(2012)462503_EN.pdf.

45 See e.g. Jeffrey H. Norwitz, *Pirates, Terrorists, and Warlords: The History, Influence, and Future of Armed Groups Around the World* (London: Skyhorse Publishing, 2009), p. 15 ff, stressing that: 'The nexus between terrorism and crime has not been fully recognized'. A good resumé of these views is found in David A. Jenks, John Randolph Fuller, *Global Crime and Justice* (Oxford: Routledge, 2017), p. 141 ff.

46 See GCTF, 'The nexus between international terrorism and organized crime', available at: https://www.un.org/sc/ctc/wp-content/uploads/2019/05/Concept-note-final-web.pdf.

47 On the topic, see Rohan Perera, 'Declaration on Measures to Eliminate International Terrorism, 1994, and the 1996 Supplementary Declaration thereto', available at: http://legal.un.org/avl/ha/dot/dot.html.

48 The measures subsequently outlined in the UNGA Declaration of 1994 focused, however, entirely on the fight against international terrorism. On the topic, see e.g. Malvina

November 2000, universally known as the 'Palermo Convention' on organized transnational crime, that in clear terms and explicitly: 'call[ed] upon all States to recognize the links between transnational organized criminal activities and acts of terrorism'.[49] However it is true that the terror-crime nexus became an issue prominent in the legal literature and public debates only since the days after 9/11 of 2001, when counter terrorism measures and policies have been adopted in any corner of the world and a growing body of observers and international political institutions including the UN.[50] and the African Union (AU) have acknowledged that the nexus between terrorism and organized crime groups was a serious threat for international peace and stability.[51]

According to an authoritative commentary, 'the terror-crime nexus' is a term that is currently used and is useful to describe the emergence, whether real or only presumed, of networked criminal organizations at international level.[52] More precisely, as Everard Phillips rightly puts it, is a term that serves to illustrate the characteristic of the transitional or failed state, in which insurgency is an essential characteristic of the social and political landscape.[53]

Stated as such, the 'nexus' is somehow a misleading term, because it might be taken to imply that there is a global alliance between organized crime and terrorist entities which in reality does not appear to exist, at least according to a consolidated line of empirical studies.[54] Indeed there is mounting evidence

---

Halberstam, 'The Evolution of the United Nations Position on Terrorism: From Exempting National Liberation Movements to Criminalizing Terrorism Wherever and by Whomever Committed' (2002–2003) 41 *Colum. J. Transnat'l L.*, p. 573 ff; Leila Nadya Sadat, 'Terrorism and the Rule of Law' (2004) 3 *Wash. U. Global Stud. L. Rev.*, p 135 ff.

49 UN General Assembly, United Nations Convention against Transnational Organized Crime: resolution / adopted by the General Assembly, 8 January 2001, A/RES/55/25, available at: https://www.refworld.org/docid/3b00f55b0.html.

50 The U.N. Security Council has acknowledged, and expressed concern at, the connection between organized crime and terrorism in several of its resolutions, including resolutions 1373 (2001), 2195 (2014), 2322 (2016), 2347 (2017) and 2368 (2017), and more recently in its Presidential Statement S/PRST/2018/9 of 8 May 2018.

51 See African Union Peace and Security, 'The 731st meeting of the AU Peace and Security Council – an Open Session on the theme: "The link between terrorism and transnational organized crime', available at: http://www.peaceau.org/en/article/the-731st-meeting-of-the-au-peace-and-security-council-an-open-session-on-the-theme-the-link-between-terrorism-and-transnational-organized-crime.

52 See Tamara Makarenko, above n. 1, p. 129 ff.

53 Amplius, see Everard Phillips, 'The Business of Kindnapping for Ransom', in David V. Canter (ed), *The Faces of Terrorism: Multidisciplinary Perspectives* (London: John Willey & Sons, 2009), p. 192 ff.

54 Amplius, see e.g. Katalin Ligeti, Maxime Lassalle, above n. 5, p. 75, stating that empirical studies do not support such a general claim but show that links between organised crime and terrorism are facilitated by the transformation of both terrorist groups and

that terrorists commit offences with the purpose of producing profit without, however, being effectively part of any structured organization.[55] And in fact terrorist and criminal organizations, which have fundamentally dissimilar motives for their crimes, generally cooperate by networking or subcontracting on specific tasks when their objectives of interest intersect.[56] A good example in this sense is offered by certain South American kidnapping gangs that frequently sell custody of their victims to wider terrorist groups on what amounts to a 'secondary market'.[57] Nevertheless a part of scholarship, which start from the assumption that the terror-crime nexus has blurred the line between terrorism and organized crime, continues, as said above, to maintain that terrorism and organized crime must be considered as a single combined threat, rather than two distinct criminal phenomena.[58]

Things being such, I really doubt that most supporters of the existence of a 'terror-crime nexus' issue at international universal and regional level would be troubled by these and analogous considerations, like the one, for instance, relating to the lack of an all-encompassing and well-defined legal concept of organized crime[59] and the other one concerning the existence of objective

---

criminal groups into 'networked organizations'. See also Ron Chepesiuk, 'Dangerous Alliance: Terrorism and Organized Crime', available at: http://www.globalpolitician.com/23435-crime.

55 See e.g. David Tucker, 'What's New About the New Terrorism and How Dangerous Is It?' (2001) 13 *Terrorism and Political Violence*, available at: https://www.tandfonline.com/doi/pdf/10.1080/09546550109609688, also stating that characteristic of this transformation is the emergence of networked cells that replace the previously prevalent hierarchical structures and allow for rapid and fluid cooperation between organised criminals and terrorists. See also Ron Chepesiuk, above n. 54; Frank Cillufo, *The threat posed from the convergence of Organized crime, drug trafffiking and terrorism* (Center for Strategic and International Studies, Washington, D.C., 2000), available at: http://csis.org/files/media/csis/congress/ts001213cilluffo.pdf.

56 See e.g. Francis G. Shanty, *Organized Crime: From Trafficking to Terrorism* (Santa Barbara: ACB-CLIO, 2008), p. 36 ff.

57 See James J. Forest, 'Kidnapping by Terrorist Groups, 1970–2010: Is Ideological Orientation Relevant?' (2002) 6 *Crime & Delinquency*, p. 6 ff. See also Angelina Stanojoska, 'The Connection Between Terrorism and Organized Crime: Narcoterrorism and the Other Hybrids', available at: https://wb-iisg.com/wp-content/uploads/bp-attachments/4745/Angelina-Stanojoska_The_Connection_between_Terrorism_and_Org.pdf.

58 Reference is to authors cited above in note 14.

59 The definition of 'organized crime' has been much contested in the literature and has been heavily criticized for its vagueness and extensive reach. On this topic, see e.g. Letizia Paoli and Cyrille Fijnaut, 'Organised Crime and its Control Policies in Europe' (2006) 14 *European Journal of Crime, Criminal Law and Criminal Justice*, p. 313 ff.

and relevant differences between organized crime and terrorism.[60] Unlike other commentators who do not support the view of the existence of a 'nexus' issue, they believe that their suggested reforms should be available in order to cope with the unsatisfactory lack of direct attention paid to the proven facts of the terror-crime nexus by the existing international legal instruments on counter-terrorism.

4 The Adequacy of the Council of Europe's Current Rules and Policy in the Counter-Terrorism Field

Whether in relation to the criminal activities involved in the terror-crime nexus, the Council of Europe's current rules and policy in the field of counter terrorism are not nearly as inadequate as it is often either explicitly or implicitly assumed. Yet, a common sense application of the relevant rules and of the new Council of Europe's counter-terrorism policy can go far to accommodate the request of an efficient regulation for the above-mentioned criminal activities.

4.1 *Countering the Financing of Terrorist Activities and of Other Criminal-Related Activities*

Nothing in the Council of Europe's existing rules in the field of financing of terrorism exclude from their scope of application the fight against the financing of the criminal acts and activities involved in the terror-crime nexus. The Explanatory Report to the Council of Europe Convention on Laundering, Search, Seizure and Confiscation of the Proceeds from Crime and on the Financing of Terrorism of 2005 (the 'Warsaw Convention') leaves no uncertainty on this point, as it explicitly requires that the same tools that are used in the fight against terrorist financing should also be used in the fight against money laundering, and this is regardless of the fact that money laundering appears or not to be directly related to a terrorist act or activity.[61] The rationale behind this statement – that is indirectly confirmed by para. 25 of the Explanatory Report in the part where this states that: '*the Warsaw Convention* has a larger scope as compared to the Convention on laundering, search, seizure and confiscation of the proceeds from crime ('the 1990 Convention'), as

60 On the topic, see e.g. Steven Hutchinson, Pat O'Malley, 'A crime–terror nexus? Thinking on some of the links between terrorism and criminality' (2007) 30 *Studies in Conflict & Terrorism*, p. 1095 ff.

61 Available at the Council of Europe's official website at the address: https://rm.coe.int/16800d3813.

it covers *not only* laundering and confiscation ... but also financing of terrorism' – is clear and understandable: the practical difficulty to de-couple questions relating to the financing of terrorism in the application of the Warsaw Convention that includes also provisions on the role and functioning of the Financial Intelligence Units (FIUS) as detailed explained in the Report.[62] Several competent national authorities dealing with transnational organized crime and terrorism have successfully countered the financing of criminal terrorist-related activities by making use of tools which have already proved their utility and effectiveness in countering the terrorist financing.

It may well be true that this approach 'overlooks the possibilities to institute lower standard of rights for terrorists than granted even to organised criminals',[63] but it seems that this drawback should not be overestimated, considering in particular that all measures taken by States to fight against international terrorism should always respect human freedoms and rights as also clarified by the Council of Europe's counter terrorism strategy.[64]

4.2 *Preventing Terrorist Acts and Terrorist-Related Criminal Activities*

There is also a good deal of adaptability and flexibility of the Warsaw Convention in its provisions concerning the prevention of terrorist acts and activities. Article 3 of the Convention, which deals with national prevention policies, does not itself detail precisely whether the envisaged: 'appropriate measures ... in the field of training of law enforcement authorities and other bodies and in the fields of education, culture, information, media and public awareness raising with a view to preventing ... offences and their negative effects while respecting human rights obligations' should also be adopted in order to prevent terrorist-related criminal activities and acts. Moreover, it is worthy observing that similar questions may also arise in relation to the subsequent Article 4 of the Convention that deals with the international cooperation on prevention.[65]

---

62 Ibidem.

63 See Colin King, Clive Walker, above n. 24, p. 395.

64 CoE, 'Council of Europe Counter-Terrorism Strategy (2018–2022)' above n. 40. See also UN Human Rights Council, *Report of the Special Rapporteur on the promotion and protection of human rights and fundamental freedoms while countering terrorism*, 16 June 2015, A/HRC/29/51, available at: https://www.refworld.org/docid/558982fc4.html.

65 Article 4 of the Warsaw Convention reads as follow: 'Parties shall, as appropriate and with due regard to their capabilities, assist and support each other with a view to enhancing their capacity to prevent the commission of terrorist offences, including through exchange of information and best practices, as well as through training and other joint efforts of a preventive character'.

Yet, there is at least one argument that per se suggests that both Articles 3 and 4 of the Warsaw Convention must be interpreted narrowly and, therefore, that they should not be applied to the criminal acts and activities involved in the terror-crime nexus. This argument lies in the language and wording of these two articles that explicitly and repeatedly refer to terrorism in their texts; but this is an issue that has yet to be squarely addressed.

With that said, it would, nevertheless, be difficult to conclude in favor of such a narrow interpretation of the above-mentioned two articles. And this is so especially if one considers the already described space and visibility that is attributed to the issue of the terror-crime nexus within the new Council of Europe's counter terrorism policy, as well as the fact that such interpretation would clearly conflict with the general purpose of the Warsaw Convention to facilitate effective international co-operation and mutual legal assistance in criminal matters.[66] To these observations, one can add further that the non-application of Articles 3 and 4 of the Warsaw Convention to the various acts associated with international terrorism would also be difficult to explain and justify because, notwithstanding the commitment of playing a key role in the fight against transnational organized crime,[67] the Council of Europe is still developing means to facilitate more effective action against transnational organized crime.

4.3 *The Council of Europe Committee on Counter-Terrorism (CDCT) and the Terror-Crime Nexus*

Designed as the key coordinating body for the Council of Europe activities to contrast international terrorism, the Council of Europe Committee on Counter-Terrorism (CDCT) has the possibility, alone or by cooperating with the Committee of Experts on the Evaluation of Anti-Money Laundering Measures and the Financing of Terrorism (MONEYVAL), to address the nexus between international terrorism and transnational organized crime both efficiently and effectively through recourse to various measures, including through the adoption of special international standards and reports on the subject matter and/

---

66 Article 2 of the Warsaw Convention reads as follow: 'The purpose of the present Convention is to enhance the efforts of Parties in preventing terrorism and its negative effects on the full enjoyment of human rights, in particular the right to life, both by measures to be taken at national level and through international co-operation, with due regard to the existing applicable multilateral or bilateral treaties or agreements between the Parties'.

67 See the Council of Europe's White Paper on Transnational Organised Crime, available at https://rm.coe.int/168070afba.

or through technical cooperation projects and the follow-up of its reports.[68] For instance, it appears that the CDCT could extend the application of the supervised Council of Europe's legal instruments on counter terrorism also to criminal acts and activities directly involved in the terror-crime nexus whenever it finds appropriate, and believes that this would be a measure indispensable or even just useful in helping Contracting States to comply with the Council of Europe rules on counter terrorism.

The statutory powers of the CDCT, namely the powers of overseeing and ensuring the successful enforcement of relevant Council of Europe international instruments on terrorism while at the same time providing a means for international experts to analyze and respond to developments in the counter-terrorism area, clearly confirms that this solution is indeed possible.

5 Concluding Remarks

Legal and non-legal international instruments in the field of counterterrorism are not carved in stone. When it is determined that existing instruments, rules and policies are not effectively responsive to the evolution of international terrorism and transnational organized criminality and to their assumedly changing relationship, then they certainly ought to be modified. Practicing lawyers and legal writers, especially Professors Ben Saul, Ana Maria Salinas and Peter Neumann, have performed a valuable service by subjecting current international conventions and protocols, especially the UN treaties in the fields of counter terrorism and organized crime, to searching criticism in light of their lack of direct consideration of the nexus between international terrorism and transnational organized crime.

In my opinion, however, the proponents of reform have not made the case for modifying the traditional (previous 9/11) approach to counter terrorism that has in the Council of Europe one of its few remaining followers. And yet this is though this approach does not directly address the criminal acts and activities related to international terrorism. Nevertheless, their arguments do strongly suggest a greater need for flexibility and adaptability in the interpretation and

68 As indicated in its official website (https://www.coe.int/en/web/moneyval), MONEYVAL is a permanent supervisory body of the Council of Europe entrusted with the task of assessing compliance with the main international standards to counter money laundering and the financing of terrorism and the effectiveness of their enforcement, as well as with the task of formulating recommendations to national authorities in respect of indispensable improvements to their systems.

application of the relevant Council of Europe's legal rules, instruments and policy than has previously been recognized by legal writers and opinionists.[69]

Regardless whether any particular reforms are effectively adopted, commentators like Professors Ben Saul, Ana Maria Salinas and Peter Neumann deserve our gratitude for bringing up important issues to the attention of international relations and legal scholars, and the same appreciation must go to the drafters of the new Hague Good Practices on the Nexus between Transnational Organized Crime and Terrorism. It is very much to be hoped that the academic debate on the relationship between terror and transnational organized crime will continue and be extended.

---

69 The reference is made in particular to the authors quoted above at note 14 who, each on their own terms, insist on the inadequacy of the current international legal instruments on counter-terrorism to efficaciously and properly address the terror-crime nexus.

CHAPTER 4

Combating Terrorist Financing with Artificial Intelligence Systems

Javier Valls-Prieto

1 Introduction

Terrorism is a phenomenon that changes very quickly with time. One of the key factors to survey and evaluate its success is its flexibility and the ease with which it mutates into new forms that adapt its actions depending on their goals and their facility to get funding. International terrorism uses international corporations' structure and management methods adapted to new technologies to produce a new form of decentralized terrorism that is complicated to fight with only the classical tools of legal enforcement agencies, as at present.

One of the first problems to face is the definition of terrorism, which it is not easy although there are attempts to do so. One of the difficulties is that terrorism changes depending on its political goals, the state where its activities are conducted and the way it is funded.

The European norms have made a considerable effort to define it, but because of the ability of terrorist groups to adapt to new situations, to have a full definition of this concept is complicated. For this reason, we need to look for non-normative definitions (economic, political, criminologist or sociologic ones).

The regulation of money laundering and terrorist financing is different and a good system of money tracking and information sharing has been introduced, hindering the possibilities of financing criminal activities. Although money laundering and terrorist actions have different aims, one being economic and the other to have political impact, the modus operandi is quite similar. In the end the economic benefit of the operation is not personal profit but for the final success of the terrorist attack. The duties implemented by the update of the European norm, Council Framework Decision 2002/475/JHA of 13 June 2002 on combating terrorism, on the transfer of information between the private sector, in particular, the financial and banking system, and the law enforcement agencies is a big step in the fight against terrorism. As we will see later, terrorist organizations need large sums of money to operate, not only for the attack, but for the basic infrastructure. However, as with all criminal activities,

 | DOI:10.1163/9789004424579_006

terrorist groups change their financial methods to avoid establishing institutions to move the money by using new practices based on new technologies.

The new strategy of information-sharing between institutions and the free movement of capital throughout the world creates a new need for states to obtain the economic evidence to fight terrorism. The European investigation order has provided a new criminal prosecuting cooperation system for requesting evidence from other member states based on the trust between them. For our study, the financial and economic information exchange is a key factor in the fight against terrorism.

But this legal change has produced an evolution in the terrorist groups. Islamic terrorism has developed methods similar to international corporations in its use of international financing systems and the use of new technologies that have helped in the proselytism of terrorism and terrorist financing. But this applies not only to Islamic terrorism but also to far right terrorism, as shown in the Christchurch attack which has developed similar tactics with new technologies for proselytism, financing and obtaining material supplies to perpetrate their attacks.

This changing of the place of action to Internet facilitates terrorist activities due to its anonymity and lack of guardians. That is why the development of artificial intelligence to fight terrorism enables legal enforcement agencies to develop new techniques in two key areas: surveillance and money-tracking. But it is not free from other risks. This massive surveillance and tracking of financial transactions can be dangerous for human rights in a democratic society. One of the challenges is the international legitimation system of the use of this computer technology by intelligence service and law enforcement agencies. The balance between citizen's freedom and security is again on the table when we deal with complicated criminality such as terrorism. That is the aim of this work.

2 Definition of Terrorism

For the propose of this paper we define terrorism as "acts of violence that target civilians in the pursuit of political or ideological aims"[1] although the international legal definition, set out by the General Assembly in its resolution 49/60, considers terrorism as criminal acts intended or calculated to provoke a state of terror in the general public, a group of persons or particular persons for

1 OHCHR, "Human Rights, Terrorism and Counter-terrorism", United Nations, 2008, p. 5.

political purposes.[2] After the terrorist attack of 11 September 2001, the Security Council gave a new definition that referred to criminal acts, including against civilians, committed with the intent to cause death or serious bodily injury, or the taking of hostages, with the purpose of provoking a state of terror in the general public or in a group of persons or particular persons, to intimidate a population or compel a Government or an international organization to do or to abstain from doing any act.[3] The most current definition is provided by NATO and it defines terrorism as the unlawful use or threatened use of force or violence, instilling fear and terror, against individuals or property in an attempt to coerce or intimidate governments or societies, or to gain control over a population, to achieve political, religious or ideological objectives.[4]

At the regional level the European Union has defined terrorism setting out a list of crimes that have the aim of causing serious damage to a country or an international organization by intimidating the population or unduly compelling a Government or international organization to perform or abstain from performing any act, or seriously destabilizing or destroying the fundamental political, constitutional, economic or social structures of a country or an international organization. The list of crimes are: attacks upon a person's life which may cause death; attacks upon the physical integrity of a person; kidnapping or hostage taking; causing extensive destruction to a Government or public facility, a transport system, an infrastructure facility, including an information system, a fixed platform located on the continental shelf, a public place or private property likely to endanger human life or result in major economic loss; seizure of aircraft, ships or other means of public or goods transport; manufacture, possession, acquisition, transport, supply or use of weapons, explosives or of nuclear, biological or chemical weapons, as well as research into, and development of, biological and chemical weapons; release of dangerous substances, or causing fires, floods or explosions the effect of which is to endanger human life; interfering with or disrupting the supply of water, power or any other fundamental natural resource the effect of which is to endanger human life; threatening to commit any of the acts listed above.[5] The Framework Decision follows with the definition of a terrorist group as: a structured group of more than two persons, established over a period of time and acting in concert to commit terrorist offences. 'Structured group' shall mean a group that is not

2 General Assembly, "Measures to eliminate international terrorism", United Nations, 1995, p. 4.
3 Security Council, Resolution 1566 (2004) p. 2.
4 NATO, AAP-06. NATO Glossary of Terms and Definitions, 2018.
5 Article 1 of the Council Framework Decision of 13 June 2002 on combating terrorism (2002/475/JHA).

randomly formed for the immediate commission of an offence and that does not need to have formally defined roles for its members, continuity of its membership or a developed structure. Within this definition, terrorist crime can be committed by directing one of them and participating in one of them by suppling information or material, or funding its activities. These last activities as set out in Article 3 of the Framework Decision are aggravated theft, extortion and drawing up false documents, these three activities being linked to the crimes above. In 2008, the Framework Decision 2008/919/JHA of 28 November 2008, which amends the Framework Decision of 2002, adds three new forms of terrorism: public provocation to commit a terrorist offence, recruitment and training for terrorism. The last update of the European definition of terrorism reorganizes both the Framework in the new Directive of 2017 and adds new crimes: receiving training for terrorism, travelling for the purpose of terrorism and organizing or otherwise facilitating travelling for the purpose of terrorism. Finally, there is a development of the crimes related to terrorist financing, punishing providing or collecting funds, directly or indirectly, to commit or to contribute to the commission of a terrorist attack.

Outside the European Union there are other definitions of terrorism. In the 1980s the CIA defined terrorism as "Terrorism is the threat or use of violence for political purposes by individuals or groups, whether acting for or in opposition to established governmental authority, when such actions are intended to shock, stun or intimidate victims. Terrorism, has involved groups seeking to overthrow specific regimes, to rectify perceived national or group grievances, or to undermine international order as an end in itself".[6] It is true that this definition does not involve all possibilities of terrorism and, moreover, some rebel groups could be included in the definition such as the French resistance in the Second World War. A more modern and narrower definition is provided by Fortna, Lotito and Rubin. They consider terrorism as the systematic use of intentionally indiscriminate violence against public civilian targets … to send a political massage to a wider audience.[7]

Regardless of any definition, specifically because the phenomenon is so difficult to define because of its evolution and its subjectivity, Cronin gives some key point of terrorism. For her, terrorism always has a political nature; it tries to bring about political change with its actions to balance an injustice done.

---

6 Ruwantissa Abeyratne, 'Suppression of the financing of terrorism' (2011) J Trans Secur 4 54, 59.

7 Virginia Page Fortna, Nicholas J. Lotito and Michael A. Rubin, 'Don't Bite the Hand that Feeds: Rebels Funding Sources and the Use of Terrorism in Civil Wars' (2018) *International Studies Quarterly* 62 782, 783.

The use of violence has a non-state character, even when it has military support from states. The third key point is that terrorism deliberately targets the innocent. That is the difference from state violence that could kill the innocent as well, but not as a strategic target. Finally, terrorist groups are not under the enforcement of international laws or norm in their activities and that is to maximize the psychological effect of the attack.[8]

For the purpose of this work the definition of cyberterrorism is also important. It can be defined as attacks against computer networks with a political, religious or ideological motivation. Most of the state infrastructure, such as water and energy supply, hospitals, financial markets, emergency services, air/shipping control and similar.[9] Over time, and similar to the classical definition of terrorism, cyberterrorism has evolved with different definitions that can be separated into two broad categories: when terrorists use technology to facilitate their objectives and when terrorists use computer network tools to harm or shut down national infrastructures.[10] The first definition involves encryption communication systems between the members of the organization or the use of DoS attacks against government websites or servers. In the second one will be added a threatened harm to persons, property or essential services. Thus, the first is not linked with civilian victims, but the second one is closer to the classical concept that we are using and is, in my opinion, the right approach.

The idea of introducing this concept will be explained in greater detail later, but to start understanding terrorism in the twenty-first century we need to see that nowadays the modus operandi of terrorist groups is the use of computer networks to facilitate their activities or to target them. In the first set of tools, we will focus on the virtual funding of terrorism.

In the European Union Terrorist Situations and Trends Report (TESAT)[11] of 2018 the Reporters speak of the current role of the new technologies. Internet plays a key role in the radicalization of some perpetrators. Online propaganda and networking via social media are still essential to terrorist attempts to reach out to EU audiences for recruitment, radicalization and fundraising, particular with Islamic terrorism. But, as the report highlights, not only does religious terrorism use this tool for its aims, so do right and left-wing terrorists. The case of

8 Audrey Kurth Cronin, "Behind the curve: globalization and international terrorism", (2002–2003) *International Security* 27 3 30, 33.

9 Jonathan Clough, *Principles of Cybercrime* (Cambridge University Press 2012), 11.

10 Ibid., 12.

11 European Union Terrorism Situation and Trend Report 2018 (TESAT)https://www.europol.europa.eu/activities-services/main-reports/european-union-terrorism-situation-and-trend-report-2018-tesat-2018 accessed 9 November 2019.

the right-wing attack in Christchurch shows how the internet can be exploited to this end. The attack on two mosques in New Zealand was broadcast through livestreaming video and the gunman's manifesto went viral.

There are three important areas -proselytism, information and funding- in which internet plays an important role in terrorist acts. Encrypted social networks, such as Telegram, WhatsApp and Facebook are used to recruit new terrorists, make contact between different hubs and to deliver propaganda, making all these viral with very little effort.[12] Another possibility is to get bomb-making instructions from internet or file-sharing both from the surface web and from Darknet. The trend is to use fundraising campaigns by crowd-funding and by economic crime. Bitcoin payments gained popularity due to their key characteristics that include ease of access, anonymity, safe transactions, low cost and high speed for international transfers.

We are going to focus on this last point in this chapter. As we will see, one key factor in the fight against terrorism is how these groups get the resources to make their operations a reality. Such groups need to finance two activities: terrorist attacks (operational resources) and the infrastructure of the group (broad organizational requirements).[13] Both are important for their activities, but the second is more expensive than the first. In the next section we will see how European Law pursue these activities.

3 Financing Terrorism

The first international legal act against financing terrorism was the International Convention for Suppression of Financing of Terrorism of 1999 but it was not a success.[14] We had to wait until the terrorist attack of 9/11 to see a real attempt to regulate and fight terrorist finance. In 2001, in an Extraordinary Plenary Session, UNO created the FATS 8 Special Recommendations against Terrorist Financing. This was the start of signed resolutions that had been waited for from 1999, a process that ended with Security Council Resolution 1373, which includes eight Recommendations, one month later they were taken.

12 European Union Internet Organized Crime Threat Assessment 2019 (IOCTA) p. 9. https://www.europol.europa.eu/activities-services/main-reports/internet-organised-crime-threat-assessment-iocta-2019 accessed 9 November 2019.

13 Hamed Tofangsaz, "Rethinking terrorist financing; where does all this lead?" (2015) JMLC, 18, 1, 113–114.

14 Nicholas Ridley and Dean C. Alexander "Combating terrorist financing in the first decade of the twenty-first decade" (2012) JMLC 15, 1, 40.

This extremely quick reaction was not only taken in UNO, but in the European Union as well. The European Council started a battery of actions in the extraordinary European Council meeting on 21 September 2001, setting out a list of terrorist organizations and a plan against terrorist funding.[15] As a result of this plan the Framework Decision 2002/475/JHA was adopted to tackle terrorism. This norm tries to give a general definition of terrorist groups based on what kind of crime it commits, as we have seen above, but it also focuses on liability of legal persons, taking into account victims of terrorism attacks and, what it is important for our work, two offences linked to funding terrorist activities: aggravated theft and extortion. These changes give an idea of the financial structure of terrorist activities, the need for money for the activities that not only come from illegal activities such as theft and extortion, but from legal resources, as we will see, and the necessity for legal persons to manage this money to pay for the needs of the group.

Parallel to this normative develop, the money laundering regulation of 2005 introduced the scope of terrorist financing, defined as the "provision or collection of funds, by any means, directly or indirectly, with the intention that they should be used or in the knowledge that they are to be used, in full or in part, in order to carry out any of the offences" established in the Framework Decision 2002/475/JHA. Basically, this regulation enforces a system of due diligence and tracking of money transfer information, allowing the authorities to follow the transactions of money, with the help of people, financing institutions, casinos and money transfers. This Framework Decision had an update in 2015 in the Directive (EU) 2015/849 particularly, adapting the amount of money and some institutions such as gambling services like casinos. During these twelve years money involved in games of chance have moved to other platforms such as online betting web sites. Thus, these new gambling systems must be included and taken as possible targets. The concept of terrorist financing has no changes. Something new is the risk assessment (Article 7 of the Directive (UE) 2015/849) that the states should implement in their money control systems, which will be important later in this work. The final version of the European normative on financing terrorism is the last update that deals with electronic transfer of money (virtual currencies, wallet providers and electronic money updates) and promotes the criminalization of terrorist financing.

As a summary of this regulation the exchange of data is the key factor to combat terrorist financing and the collaboration between institutions. All

15 Miryam Rodríguez Izquierdo Serrano, 'El terrorismo en la evolución del espacio de libertad, seguridad y justicia' (2010) 36 RDCE 531, p. 541.

this information provides new ways of controlling and fighting against terrorism. The efforts made by the legislative institutions of the European Union to combat terrorist financing by new methods have been really strong in the last decade, but Europol, in its Terrorism Situation and Trend Report of 2018, states that the use of virtual currencies remains very low.[16] On the other hand, Europol in its report on Internet Organized Crime Threat Assessment of 2019, highlights the convergence of cyber and terrorism, how terrorist groups adopt the new technologies for their strategy in online propaganda and recruitment operations, but the adoptions of these new technologies could also include cryptocurrencies[17] in their plan to use the new technologies with the idea of expanding and diversifying their methods to reach their goals more easily and safely.

4 Economic Evidence

The new instrument for cooperation in criminal matters, implemented by the Directive 2014/41/EU of the European Parliament and of the Council of 3 April 2014 regarding the European Investigation Order in criminal matters, goes a step furthe in the fight against terrorist financing.

The European investigation order (EIO) is a great change from the original criminal judicial cooperation system, based on the Council Framework Decision 2003/577/JHA of 22 July 2003 on the execution in the European Union of orders freezing property or evidence and the Council Framework Decision 2008/978/JHA of 18 December 2008 on the European evidence warrant for the purpose of obtaining objects, documents and data for use in proceedings in criminal matters. The new legal instrument tries to speed up the process of requesting evidence in some crimes with an order that all involved member States will facilitate the evidence requested by one partner.

Of all the types of evidence included in this norm, transfer of suspects, hearing by teleconference or by telephone, gathering of evidence in real time, covert investigation, interception of communications and provisional measures, the one that we are interested in for this work is the request for bank

16 European Union Terrorism Situation and Trend Report 2018 (TESAT) https://www.europol.europa.eu/activities-services/main-reports/european-union-terrorism-situation-and-trend-report-2018-tesat-2018 accessed 2 January 2020.

17 European Union Internet Organized Crime Threat Assessment 2019 (IOCTA) p. 48. https://www.europol.europa.eu/activities-services/main-reports/internet-organised-crime-threat-assessment-iocta-2019 accessed 2 January 2020.

or financial accounts and banking and financial information. Whereas under numbers 27, 28 and 29 an EIO may be issued in order to obtain evidence concerning the accounts, of whatever nature, held in any bank or any non-banking financial institution by a person subject to it, this possibility is to be understood broadly as comprising not only suspected or accused persons but also any other person in respect of whom such information is found necessary by the competent authorities in the course of criminal proceedings, according to Article 3 of the Directive 2005/60/EC on money laundering and financing terrorism. The details requested by an EIO should be understood as the name and address of the account holder, details of any powers of attorney held over the account and any other details and documents linked to the account.

5 Reality

From the legal point of view, we have legal instruments for the fight against terrorist financing, but we can see in reality that some difficulties appear. After 9/11 the investigation focused on Islamic banks and financial systems, but the answer from these institutions were weak. Either they had no information or they did not want to collaborate.[18] Although there are some irregularities and some lack of control that enables illicit money to move through Islamic bank institutions, this action from USA and EU legal enforcement agencies was found to be an intrusion from Western countries.[19] This interest in classical banking and financial systems was based on how Al-Qaeda was financed by Osama Bin Laden through different accounts under fake names since he lived in Sudan.[20] But this first attempt to control terrorist financing just made a change of the financing system to an informal money exchange, such as Hawala in Islamic societies, Hundi in India o Fie chi'ien in China.[21] The second way to transfer money is by physical movement of funds, but this imposes a limit on the quantity of money that can be transferred and does not work for large sums of money. The third one is by trade. Trade allows the possibility of transferring valuables and goods through trade flows, giving terrorist groups access to materials and goods that they need for their operations.[22]

18 Nicholas Ridley and Dean C. Alexander (n 9), 49.

19 Ibid.

20 Hamed Tofangsaz, 'Rethinking terrorist financing; where does all this lead?' (2015) JMLC 18 1 112, 117.

21 Steve Kiser, *Financing Terror. An Analysis and Simulation for Affecting Al Qaeda's Financial Infrastructure* (Rand Corporation 2005), 90.

22 Hamed Tofangsaz (n 15), 117–118.

Islamic terrorism is not the only one that needs funding. The empirical study of Fortna, Lotito and Rubin, focused on terrorist and rebels groups from different countries, found a terrorist group is more likely to be created when they have access to natural sources and external financing than the groups based on civilian support.[23] This is important because their financial strengths depend on the geographical situation of the terrorist group activities, basically drug trafficking,[24] but also on other criminal activities. To give an idea on how popular drug trafficking was to financing terrorist groups we have these examples: Kosovo Liberation Army, Basque Homeland and Liberty or ETA in Spain, and the Islamic Movement of Uzbekistan, all well-known as drug traffickers. Groups like FARC obtained weapons and communications technology by trafficking cocaine. In Australia, an investigation found money laundering operations in that country linked to Hezbollah. Producer countries are often the least profitable part of the process; the lion's share of earnings is garnered by those who refine and market the drugs.[25]

The second key point is the external financing that was a major factor in some cases of national terrorism, particularly in those regions with geostrategic interests such as Central America and near East. But not all national terrorism has this influx of money from external actors. The reality of new forms of terrorism such as international Islamic terrorism and far right actions show that the external actor has a considerable influence by encouraging their attacks and by financing them as we have seen before.

The fact is terrorist groups need money for operational activities, basically, for the terrorist attack, which include the cost of the attack, the salary of the terrorist, communications, training, travel and logistics. But large groups also need broad organizational requirements to create, maintain and develop the infrastructure.[26] In this second case the need for money is considerable; while a terrorist attack by a lone wolf is not extremely expensive, to have an infrastructure needing many people and resources is. In some cases, the members pay with their own money, particularly, when the terrorist acts as a lone wolf.[27]

We have already seen how geographical factors can facilitate the terrorist group, but it is also true that the financing method can change the way that

---

23 Virginia Page Fortna, Nicholas J. Lotito and Michael A. Rubin, (n 7), 789.

24 Colin P. Clarke, 'Drugs & Thugs: Funding Terrorism through Narcotics Trafficking.' (2016) Journal of Strategic Security 9 3 15, 9.

25 Ibid, 3.

26 Hamed Tofangsaz (n 15), 113–114.

27 Inmaculada Marrero Rocha, 'Nuevas dinámicas en las relaciones entre crimen organizado y grupos terroristas' (2017) REDI 69 2 145, 154.

terrorist attacks are produced. Thus, there are illegal and legal sources of funding. The first are motivated by the decrease of state-sponsored terrorism, to some extent because of the development of legal controls on money transfers, as we have seen. This factor has created new ways of financing through criminal acts such as drug trafficking, extortion, economic crimes, organized crime and kidnap-for-ransom.[28] The latest development is cybercrime since organized crime is changing the modus operandi on the Internet as well.[29] The use of new ways of financing such as cryptocurrency transactions is a reality.[30] As Vittori has highlighted, globalization of international monetary systems has opened up new ways of financing on a global scale anytime and anywhere.[31]

Legal forms of financing have multiple faces. There are donations and charities, non-governmental organization can help terrorist activities and investment in legitimate business[32] can be sources from legal money that ends in terrorist groups' hands.

This point is important because, depending on the financial source, the type of terrorism can change. Thus, we can classify terrorist groups into six different kinds depending on how they get their money supplies. The first one is a state-sponsored group, which receives money from a State that has the same political objectives.[33] A second possibility is a shell States, an area where the terrorist group exercises its power inside a national state. In this case funding comes from natural resources or criminal acts inside its territory. This is the case of terrorist group linked to narcotrafficking.[34] The third group is a franchise category. It is an evolution from the first one. The resources come from a state, but part also from individual sponsors. These two sources allow the terrorist group to make a survey in case one of the sources ends its funding.[35] A more sophisticated way is the bundled support, in which the number of supporters is bigger than in the franchise category, the majority being small private donors with a national or ethnicity link to the group.[36] The problem is to find a way where all these small contributions can reach the terrorist group and here is where the

28 Ibid, 115.
29 IOCTA (n 12) 48.
30 Angela S.M. Irwin and George Milad, 'The use of cryptocurrencies in funding violent jihad' (2016) JMLC 19 4 407, 410.
31 Jodi Vittory, *Terrorist Financing and Resourcing* (Palgrade Macmillan 2011) 25.
32 Hamed Tofangsaz (n 15) 115–116.
33 Jodi Vittory (n 25) 8.
34 Hamed Tofangsaz (n 15) 118.
35 Jodi Vittory (n 25) 8.
36 HamedTofangsaz (n 15) 118.

legislation about money transfers is strong, but technology has left a door open via cryptocurrencies.

In this increase of structural and financing dimensions of a terrorist group, the latest evolution is the transnational corporation model.[37] This is the structure that Al Qaeda used by implanting a transnational corporation business model into a terrorist group by using technology, sources, and methods. Once this model was destroyed by the international legislation the next standardization has been the lone wolf.[38] This is low-cost terrorism where the need for supplies of money and resources are very modest.

The international regulation on money laundry and terrorist financing can be evaluated as a good legal instrument. It was a step forward and, working with other regulations that we have seen, gives instruments to fight terrorism. It is because of this success that terrorist groups and organized crime are evolving to cybercrime ways of funding.

Technology-adapted terrorism makes administrative tasks in transnational organizations easy and with enhanced efficiency, as well as coordination of operations, recruitment of potential members, and communication with adherents, attraction of sympathizers[39] and transfer of money. The reason for that change is easily explained by cybercrime.

There are six key factors for cybercrime. The first one is Scale. That means Internet allows user to reach many people cheaply and easily. This makes it possible to get more people to sponsor terrorism attacks, but at the same time to communicate with many potential supporters. The second one is Accessibility, the technology has developed so fast and so cheaply that nearly everyone has access to a device connected to Internet at any time or anywhere, not only with a computer but with a smartphone. The third one, Anonymity, is one of the most important for terrorist goals. It is an advantage for the terrorist and for sponsors to make the transfer of money nearly untraceable. Proxy servers, fake emails or IP addresses or anonymous emailers can obtain this anonymity. The fourth, Encryption technologies are easy to get and use so that money transmissions are untraceable. The network enables money to go through different legislations so that it is easy for funding terrorism to pass through an offshore country. Digital technologies have the advantage of easy portability and transferability. One of the possibilities is to store enormous amounts of data in a small space and replicate that data with no appreciable diminution of quality. But not only that, digitalization has the ability to change tangible things

37 Audrey KurthCronin(n 8).
38 Hamed Tofangsaz (n 15) 118.
39 Audrey Kurth Cronin (n 31) 47.

into intangible things, in our case the movement of money that is not physical but electronic. The fifth key is Global reach. As we shall see later the global reach of the networks has facilitated the latest update of a terrorist group to an international terrorist organization. Finally, the sixth point, an important one, is the Absence of capable guardians to enable these new ways of financing to be detected and prosecuted. Electronic data need complicated forensic techniques to ensure they can be used as evidence in a trial. But surveillance is extremely complicated as well. The fact that the infrastructure belongs to the private sector and the communication is routered in different jurisdictions makes the need for interchange of information a big challenge.[40]

6 The Use of Artificial Intelligent to Combat Terrorism

As Internet is the space where many terrorist activities are committed and the need to find electronic evidence and intelligence information to combat it, the only way to fight it properly is with new technologies. Here is where artificial intelligent gives important tools to scrutinize the network to intercept communication, find evidence, detect recruitment of members, make propaganda and exchange of money for funding.

To use artificial intelligence, we must first understand that, in this case, it will be a process of acquisition and use of information about events, trends and relationships in a particular environment to support decision making and planning.[41] To use it against terrorism it is necessary to identify indicators and facilitators of present and future development of these criminal activities. There are signals that anticipate the possible development of the scenarios and these signals should be related with some statistical indicator of some events. With the statistical models the artificial intelligent "learns" where to look and what kind of evidence is relevant or not.[42]

Artificial intelligence applied to combat crime can be formulated in five steps. The first is data acquisition. This task is done by trawling the Internet, Deepweb and Darknet looking for specific information about terrorism chats, webs and forums where information for activities can be found as well as open

40 Jonathan Clough (n 9), 5–9.

41 Chun Wei Choo,'The art of scanning the environment'(1999) *Bulletin of the American Society for Information Science and Technology*, 25 3 21, 21.

42 Javier Valls-Prieto and Juan Gómez-Romero, 'Use of Big Data and the Prediction of Organized Crime' in Joan Balcells Padullés, et al. (eds.), Building a European Digital Space (Huygens 2016), 369.

data sources that could be linked to the case. For that task it is necessary to process natural language in order to extract information that can be processed by a machine.

Once the data are stored, an intelligent extraction of the right information must be made and it must be enriched. Thus, if we find a terrorist chat with conversation it is possible to understand the messages now if the source is good enough. With the additional information from users, geographical connections, time where the chat users connect, we can have data that with an enrichment process from open information can make connections with other online activities and give full information from the subjects, the particular object, money accounts and transfers, etc. If we have information of automatics guns sold in the dark markets, we can enrich this information with the kind of bullets they will need, how they can be developed to a more powerful machine, what other guns should be used and with registers of gun shops if they have potentials clients.

This kind of extra investigation work is crucial and takes us to the next step. Discovery of information that is on Internet but is not connected to the particular case is one of the possibilities that this kind of tool provides. Thus, the nicknames of terrorist chats' members can be tracked on the web to discover where they have other activities. This discovery phase allows legal enforcement agencies to find information that in other situations will be hidden and lets us break one of the key points, as we have seen above, of the cybercrime activity, anonymization. Of course, this is not the end of the process. In this phase the work is concentrated; particular data that are separate from the normal ones can be found with no statistical significance but that may be interesting in the investigation.[43]

An assessment phase should be opened to analyze the information given by the artificial intelligence tool and should be carried out by an analyst with the intention of avoiding false information. To facilitate this work, artificial intelligence presents this knowledge in a convenient way, normally, by a customized human machine interface.

The last action is forecasting. Intelligence tools give the possibility to forecast future terrorist acts by analyzing information and previous cases. This last phase has a strong power to prevent future actions in two ways: firstly, by looking at past situation to avoid new cases and secondly, by creating the need to create new ways to commit terrorist attacks that lowers the possibilities of terrorist attacks.

---

43 Ibid., 370–371.

7 Cryptocurrencies

Cryptocurrencies allow money to be transferred over the Internet with little control. One of the problems we have observed in the different finance systems of terrorism is that small donations by private individuals and cash transfers, such as the Hawala, create problems to restrict the money to international terrorist groups and to finance terrorist cells outside the geographical control of the groups. Hawala, for example, works through trusted traders because the money does not really change hands. It is a system where the person in charge gives the money from his/her resources and has a credit with the other trader in the country where the transfer order comes from. This means you need a person whom you can trust and who will not inform authorities about the transaction. Cryptocurrencies let the terrorist organizations manage funds in the world with more opacity and fewer risks, giving terrorist groups more flexibility and operability. To operate with cryptocurrencies a person has first to open a wallet, that is, the holder of the wallet authorizes a third party to receive and store cryptocurrencies on their behalf. The identity of the holder remains anonymous. The transfer of money goes in packets, secured by blockchain technology managed by miners that can be tracked from point to point. Finally, the money ends in another wallet. All this process secures anonymity but the process can be traced and followed by the currency's address.[44] The weak point is when the subject wants to change the cryptocurrency into real money, needing to give a bank account or a credit card number to receive the money because this information about the real money is under the control of the bank and the financial system and is under the scope of the European regulation explained above. To avoid this control the terrorist can use a cryptocurrency ATM that automatically changes cryptocurrencies to cash without any record. In reverse, it also changes cash into cryptocurrencies.[45] Fortunately, these transactions work only for limited amounts and not with large sums of money or cryptocurrencies.

To avoid this there are three ways to sell crypto currencies: direct-trade with another individual with an intermediary facilitating the connection in an offshore country; online exchange, where the trade is with the exchange rather than an individual; and in a trading marketplace where the sale of products is direct, shipping the purchase to the customer without any intermediary. This

44 Angela S.M. Irwin and George Millad (n 24) 412.
45 Ibid, 414.

third form is the most popular as the terrorists can buy many of their supplies in the Darkmarket to commit a terrorist attack without risks.

These three situations are good examples of where the classical fight against terrorism fails because of the amount of information and the lack of links between this information. Artificial intelligence offers tools to manage all this information and the connections between them in a short time. This time could be crucial to avoid a terrorist attack. As we have said before the automatic decision making should be controlled by humans, but it is true that the help given by these machines could be crucial in terrorist fighting.

8 How to Combat Terrorism and Its Funding

Being aware of the difficulties to combat a phenomenon that is changing and transforming itself very quickly, the experts have provided different solutions to fight terrorism. From an American point of view Ridley and Alexander affirm that more manpower, financial resources, and attention are needed, but also greater collaboration, information-sharing and fewer turf wars. The government needs to focus on the fact that terrorist groups also need to live in the real world to fund their activities. This means that much financial information must be exchanged between law enforcement and financial institutions as well as collaboration with the private sector.[46] In a similar approach Abeyratne asks for the adoption of practical measures to discourage the commission of terrorist acts. They are a) the improvement of the intelligence system which will inform the state concerned about the risk of a terrorist attack, b) establishment of counter-terrorism mechanisms focusing on collection of arms, ammunition and weaponry, c) the adoption of such practical measures of self-help and attack in case of a terrorist attack, d) the existence of the necessary machinery to retain the confidence and sympathy of the public at all times, and e) persuasion to convince the public that terrorism of any kind is evil and should not be condoned.[47]

From an economic point of view financing terrorism can be fought by taxing some products needed for this financing, e.g. instruments needed for narcotics production and export.[48] Moreover, from an economic perspective Hausken proposes terrorism can be avoided by the increase of terrorists' costs

46 Nicholas Ridley and Dean C. Alexander (n 9) 52.

47 Ruwantissa Abeyratne (n 6), 67.

48 Peter Berck and Jonathan Lipow, 'Trade, tariffs and terrorism' (2012) Applied Economics Letters 19 1847, 1849.

and decrease in government costs. The cost of terrorism could be increased through law, surveillance, detection, prosecution, etc., making criminal efforts less lucrative, preventing large efficient organizations from financing it and by encouraging benefactors not to fund terrorists engaged in crime. To increase the cost of terrorism Governments can make crime costly, encourage benefactors to punish crime, decrease terrorist resources, and confiscate, freeze, and prevent the accumulation of resources, block benefactors' funding of terrorism, block funding, criminalize terrorist funding, inhibit crime production and prevent effective crime production.[49]

It is true that terrorism is a multifactorial problem and there is not only one solution, but what is also true is that the classical solutions will not work anymore and we need new proposals to solve the problem. In fact, continuing with old attitudes could be dangerous.[50]

One example of the use of new techniques to fight terrorism funding is the MIDAS project developed by IBM. This machine has capabilities to extract information from fines adopted by the control bodies in the USA in money laundering cases and terrorist financing.[51] This information can be reused with artificial intelligence tools to improve tracking of companies involved and provide a methodology about how to find financial information.

As we have seen before, one of the key factors of terrorist fighting is surveillance and for this to be effective the balance of cost between government actions and terrorist attacks should be lower for the government institutions than for terrorists. This means effective surveillance must be as cheap as possible. Here is where the use of artificial intelligence has its place. Surveillance of the Internet is admittedly complicated and human resources expensive. If we can develop strong surveillance systems, the odds to win the fight against terrorism without the latest technology is really low. Particularly, because as we have seen before, Internet allows anonymity and escape from police control and the only way to fight in this space is with these kinds of tools.

49 Kjell-Hausken, 'Government Protection against Terrorists Funded by Benefactor and Crime: An Economical Model' (2017) 11 5 1, 24.

50 Audrey Kurth Cronin (n 31) 31.

51 Vassilis Plachouras and Jochen L. Leidner, 'Information Extraction of Regulatory Enforcement Actions: From Anti-Money Laundering Compliance to Countering Terrorism Finance' (2015) ASONAM 950, 951.

9 Problems Related to the Use of Artificial Intelligence Fighting Terrorism

Artificial intelligence is not free from doubts. There are both positive and negative impacts in its use to fight terrorist funding. On the positive side, as we have seen, is the possibility of tracking money transfers and cryptocurrencies through financial systems, and the possibility of surveillance of terrorist information on the internet. All this will have a positive impact on people's safety. But we must think of the rights of privacy, the presumption of innocence and freedom from discrimination. As Raso et al. have demonstrated, the access of artificial intelligence in criminal justice has a negative impact on the right of privacy, of being considered innocent and the public hearing.[52] At the same time its use has a positive impact in safety rights, as we have seen before, because dealing with such a complicated mass of information and finding evidence on the Internet can be really difficult for humans. In the middle term, it could have an impact on rights such as nondiscrimination; the machine may have a bias but at the same time it can avoid human bias, thus it can be positive or negative, and this may happen with the right of freedom from arbitrary arrest, detention and exile.[53]

As a new technology, and one that has not been tried out over a long period of time, we have to take care to avoid risks linked to its use. That is the fundamental idea of the ethics guidelines for trustworthy artificial intelligence.[54] These guidelines have seven main points for the use of artificial intelligence, in general, but as well as for it use in security matters. The first one is human agency and oversight. With that the idea is that artificial intelligence should help and empower humans but not replace them. The systems must be technically robust and safe, that means the system needs to be resilient and secure, ensure a fallback plan in case something goes wrong. It should respect privacy and must work with data of integrity and of good quality. The system should be built thinking of diversity and nondiscrimination. They must be sustainable and environmentally friendly, thinking of future generations. Finally,

---

52 Filippo Raso, Hannah Hilligoss, Vivekkrishnamurthy, Cristopher Baviz and Levin Kim, 'Artificial Intelligence & Human Rights: Opportunities and Risks' (2018) Berkman Klein Center for Internet & Society Research Publication <http://nrs.harvard.edu/urn-3:HUL.InstRepos:38021439> accessed 9 January 2020.

53 Ibid.

54 Ethics Guidelines for Trustworthy Artificial Intelligence, (2019) <https://ec.europa.eu/digital-single-market/en/news/ethics-guidelines-trustworthy-ai> accessed 9 January 2020.

there have to be mechanisms to ensure responsibility and accountability of the outcomes.

To deal with this configuration it is necessary to make a human rights assessment. This is important because the possibility of bias against particular groups of population is all too easy. Virginia Eubanks describes a good example in the city of Los Angeles where poor people (the majority black) were targeted as dangerous when artificial intelligence used social services data e.g. post code, general income of the neighborhood, education level or psychological illness in Skid Row.[55] There are not too many works in the field of security. One possibility is to start with the baseline of the surveillance assessment done by Wright et al. In an attempt to legitimize surveillance by state institutions that creates an assessment by actors: state institutions, private sector, citizens, ONGs and society. First, they put a list of generic questions that all sector workers should ask themselves before using these surveillance tools. It is a total of 15 questions that are as follows:

1. What is the purpose of the system?
2. Is it really necessary? Is it lawful? Is it proportionate to the envisaged purpose?
3. What less intrusive alternatives are available?
4. Who will develop, operate and authorize it?
5. Who will have access to the data collected by it?
6. How long will the collected data be stored? When will the data be deleted? What measures will be put in place to store or transmit the data securely?
7. To what extent will stakeholders, including the public, be consulted about it and its effects?
8. What external oversight is in place, including a regular, independent, third-party, publicly available audit?
9. How will system operators be trained so that they are sensitive to any harmful consequences?
10. Does the system enable individuals to be identified? If so, is that necessary? Does it provide individuals with a means to opt out?
11. Does the system process "sensitive" personal data? If so, is that necessary?
12. Whose interests does the system serve?
13. Does the system create identifiable harms, e.g., social, environmental, economic or human rights-related harms?

55 Virginia Eubanks, Automating inequality. How high-tech tools profile, police, and punish the poor (St. Martin's Press 2018), 84.

14. If surveillance cannot be avoided or its effects mitigated, how can society be empowered to build capacities to deal with its consequences?
15. Have the possible negative impacts and risks of the implementation or continuation of the particular surveillance system been considered? How do these relate to the benefits?;[56]

These questions must be answered, not with a simple yes or no; the aim is to think how technological surveillance will have an impact on the society. This works for legal enforcement agencies, intelligence services but also for technology developers in the private sector.

Extra questions have to be answered by policy-makers and regulators:

1. Is the surveillance necessary, legitimate, transparent and proportionate? How are these judgments made? Are there any less intrusive alternatives?
2. How has the decision to use surveillance weighed up the costs, benefits and risks, including the consequences of surveillance for human rights, freedoms and democracy? Is the decision-making process publicly documented?
3. What deliberations have taken place concerning the necessity and proportionality of the intrusion into individuals' private lives by means of the surveillance measure or policy? Is the decision-making process publicly documented?
4. How have the views of different stakeholders, especially the public, been taken into account?
5. Have policy-makers identified potential harms e who is harmed by and who benefits from surveillance, what are potential knock-on effects, what are the social consequences? After trying to identify all of the consequences, have policy-makers thought about what they can reasonably do to combat the harms?
6. What systems are in place for adequate supervision, review and oversight of surveillance practices?
7. Have the targets of surveillance (which may be the general public) been informed of the existence of the surveillance system and its general purpose? How can they find out more about the scope of the system? How can they seek personal redress for harm? How can they question, or fundamentally challenge the surveillance system?
8. How can the political and policy-making process best control the proliferation of surveillance?

56 David Wright, Rowena Rodrigues, Charles Raab, Richard Jones, Iván Székely, Kirstie Ball, Rocco Bellanova and Stine Bergersen, 'Questioning surveillance' (2015) Computer Law & Security Review 31 280, 283.

9. If surveillance cannot be avoided, how can society be empowered to build capacities to deal with its consequences?
10. How are the effects of surveillance to be continuously assessed or monitored?
11. How can international regulatory co-operation and standardisation best meet the challenge of the global flow of personal information?
12. How can the political and policy-making process best control the proliferation of surveillance?[57]

These authors also propose six political and regulatory measures. Although it is a general approach to other technologies than artificial intelligence, many of them can be extended or adapted to this computing system. The first one is accountability and oversight that should be introduced through political processes. Accountability requires procedures and rules reporting publicly and engaging in possible challenges to the accounts given. The oversight should be done by independent agencies with public service in mind. Consent, in this investigation process, obviously cannot be given by individuals. In this case it must be a societal agreement between state and society. The third point is to make stronger legal protection of privacy. The Directive (EU) 2016/680 of the European Parliament and of the Council of 27 April 2016 on the protection of natural persons with regard to the processing of personal data by competent authorities for the purposes of the prevention, investigation, detection or prosecution of criminal offences or the execution of criminal penalties, and on the free movement of persons is a good way of protecting and legitimating the use of artificial intelligence in financing terrorism investigations. Unfortunately, it has not had as much success as the data protection Regulatory from the same year, but it is true that the impact assessment is included in it and, if it is done as we have said before, it could be a strong legitimating system as well as a baseline for an international standard as is the data protection regulatory. But what is certain, as we have seen in this work, is that the combat against terrorist financing without the use of new technologies, as the terrorists are doing, is a chimera nowadays.

10 Conclusion

As we have seen in this work, the new forms of terrorism are challenging not only national states but the international community. The ways in which

57 Ibid, 284.

terrorist groups change their modus operandi is the key point of their actions, particularly because law enforcement agencies do not have this same ability.

As we have found in the solutions from the terrorist experts there are two points in which it is possible to make advances: changing citizens' perception of terrorism, and financial supporters, and controlling the money. Both are being developed in Internet because the network is cheap, offers great flexibility, global access and anonymity.

To face the new forms of terrorism and, particularly, to fight on Internet, we need to use artificial intelligence to be, at least, at the same level as terrorists. Otherwise, the possibilities of avoiding police control and increasing the risks for society will be easy for any person who wants to have a political impact in a society.

In our opinion, the use of these tools is necessary. But it is true that we could go from fear of terrorism to a fear of state control.[58] That is the reason we need a legitimate system to use these kinds of tools between civil society, the private sector and the state.[59] In this work we suggest the first step for this new social contract: the impact assessment. As we have seen, the work of Wright et al. put on the table some questions that should be on the mind of all people involved in the development and use of these machines. They can be strongly powerful in the fight against terrorism, but in the wrong hands could put democracy at risk. The first step is their ethical use. The second is the rethinking of privacy protection, in particular, and human rights, in general, from the administrative and criminal points of view.[60] Finally, from international law, an international agreement is needed to deal with online surveillance and financial tracking.

Here there are some clues about how to start regulating the use of artificial intelligence in the sector of security. The advances from the European Union to regulate the field could have a major impact in international society and in the private sector. The Ethics Guidelines for Trustworthy Artificial Intelligent prepared by the High-Level Expert Group on Artificial Intelligence focuses on a human development in this field, based on respect for human rights. This is a challenge for lawyers. Knowing how to translate the principles from the ethic analysis into new rights for the citizens probably requires a rethinking of the whole legal system. The impact of this technology in life is huge, for good and for bad. If normal life is to be ruled by it in many spheres, its use in security, intelligence and crime will have a strong impact on citizens' rights.

---

58 Bruce Sheneier, *Data and Goliath* (W. W. Norton and Company 2015).

59 Ibid. 259.

60 Javier Valls Prieto, *Problemas jurídico penales asociados a las nuevas técnicas de prevención y persecución del crimen mediante inteligencia artificial* (Dikynson, 2018).

We need to open a debate about this. We must react soon about the impact that all this could have because there are two important risks: on one hand, not to use these tools would mean that terrorism and organized crime will have a space of impunity and, in the other hand, it use without any limit will destroy citizens' trust in state institutions. And this, in democracy, is exactly on what our system is based.

Working together, citizens, private sector and state, can produce a new social contract in which respect for human rights will be at the top of the priorities, which will produce new forms of security in our societies, and will base trust on the institutions for an "intelligent democracy". It is in our hands to fight the terrorist with the rule of law, but human rights should be our first and guiding priority.

CHAPTER 5

The Applicability and Effectiveness of the AU's Instruments to Organized Criminal Terrorism

Matthew Garrod

1 Introduction*

In 2014 the UN Security Council took the momentous step of convening a thematic debate on 'terrorism and cross-border crime', in the context of threats to international peace and security, in order to consider the challenges posed by terrorists benefitting from organized crime.[1] During this meeting, the Council unanimously adopted resolution 2195 which recognized that there is a direct link between terrorism and the funding of terrorism through transnational organized crime in different regions globally, particularly in Africa, and called on states to better understand, prevent and suppress the links between these phenomena.[2] The devastating effects of the spread of terrorism in Africa, which is home to some of the world's most lethal terrorist groups who successfully engage in a variety of criminal activities, was a driving reason for the adoption of this resolution.

Resolution 2195 was an important and innovative change in the policymaking of the UN Security Council. It marked the end of Security Council inactivity for some 15 years on the general question of the links between terrorism and organized crime as a threat to international security.[3] It was the first time that

* The author would like to give special thanks to Mthabisi Mayo for assistance in the organization and facilitation of interviews, as well as to Chris Henderson and Paul Eden for valuable feedback on earlier drafts. The usual disclaimer applies.

1 UN Security Council, 69th Year, 7351st Meeting, UN Doc. S/PV.7351 (19 December 2014).

2 S/RES/2195 (2014).

3 S/RES1373 (2001), para. 4. The Council had previously addressed the relationships between some types of organized crime and terrorist activities, such as trafficking in persons (resolutions 2331 (2016) and 2388 (2017)), illicit trafficking in firearms (resolution 2370 (2017)), kidnapping for ransom (resolution 2133 (2014)), illicit trafficking in cultural property (resolution 2347 (2017)), illicit trafficking in oil (resolution 2199 (2015)), illicit trafficking in charcoal by Al-Shabaab (resolution 2498 (2019)) and illicit drug trafficking (presidential statements S/PRST/2010/4, S/PRST/2012/16 and S/PRST/2013/22). Further, the Council had expressed its concern regarding the connection between terrorism and organized crime in Africa (S/PRST/2013/5).

 | DOI:10.1163/9789004424579_007

a diverse range of criminal activities, including the trafficking of arms, persons, drugs and artefacts and the illicit trade in a range of natural resources was linked to terrorist funding, the destructive force of terrorism and the prolongation of armed conflict. The resolution also recognized, for the first time, the centrality of corruption as a facilitating mechanism of terrorism, organized crime and the links between them.[4] Since that time, the link between terrorism and organized crime has featured as a regular thematic topic in the Council's debates, and the Council has made progressively bolder assertions about terrorists benefitting from organized crime, 'whether domestic or transnational', as a source of funding and logistical support.[5]

During the last two decades and especially in the last few years, much has been written on various aspects of the links between terrorism and crime.[6] In that period, scholarly and policy debates have largely evolved from the extent to which links between terrorism and organized crime may exist (and even outright denial in some instances based on the unfounded assumption that a terrorist group's involvement in organized crime would be antithetical to the group's religion or ideology) to include, inter alia, understanding the nature, dynamics, scope and impact of these links in qualitative and (more infrequently) quantitative terms; why the links occur in certain contexts and how they are facilitated; and the relevance and utility of understanding the links for developing policy and operational measures to disrupt and counter both terrorism and organized crime. Particular attention has also been given to certain types of organized crime as a source of terrorist financing.[7]

---

4 See also S/RES/2482 (2019).

5 E.g., Letter dated 11 August 2020 from the President of the Security Council addressed to the Secretary-General and the Permanent Representatives of the members of the Security Council, UN Doc. S/2020/791 (11 August 2020); UNSC, 74th Year, 8569th Meeting, UN Doc. S/PV.8569 (9 July 2019); UNSC, 73rd Year, 8364th Meeting, UN Doc. S/PV.8364 (3 October 2018); SC/RES/2482 (2019); SC/RES/2462 (2019).

6 E.g., J.A. Piazza and S. Piazza, 'Crime Pays: Terrorist Group Engagement in Crime and Survival', 32 *Terrorism and Political Violence* 701 (2020); A. Perliger and M. Palmieri, 'Mapping Connections and Cooperation between Terrorist and Criminal Entities', Studies in Conflict and Terrorism (2019); A.P. Schmid, 'Revisiting the Relationship between International Terrorism and Transnational Organised Crime 22 Years Later', ICCT Research Paper (2018); S. Hutchinson and P. O'Malley, 'A Crime-Terror Nexus? Thinking on Some of the Links Between Terrorism and Criminality', 30 Studies in Conflict & Terrorism 1095 (2007).

7 E.g., M. Koseli et al., 'Use of Kidnapping and Extortion as a Tool for Financing Terrorism: The Case of the PKK', 13 Behavioural Sciences of Terrorism and Political Aggression 215 (2021); Y. Zabyelina, 'The "Capone Discovery": Extortion as a Method of Terrorism Financing', Studies in Conflict & Terrorism (2019); Y.M. Dutton, 'Kidnap and Terrorism Financing', in C. King et al. (eds.), *The Palgrave Handbook of Criminal and Terrorism Financing Law* (2018).

However, considerably less attention has been devoted to examining the links between terrorism and organized crime in Africa or the applicability and effectiveness of AU legal instruments for combatting the phenomenon.[8] For instance, the African Union (AU) has been 'aware of the growing linkages between terrorism and organized crime, including the illicit traffic of arms, drugs and money laundering' since at least 1999.[9] Yet, the African Centre for the Study and Research on Terrorism (ACSRT)—which was established as part of the 2002 AU 'Plan of Action on the Prevention and Combating of Terrorism' (AU Plan of Action)[10] to serve as a structure of the AU for centralizing information, studies and analyses on terrorism and publishes research twice a year—has yet to publish a single study dedicated to examining such questions. Moreover, the vast majority of writing on the subject suffers from a serious lack of empirical evidence to affirmatively establish what links exist in practice.[11] Indeed, up until now most studies examining the links (including in Africa)

8 E.g., J.J. Forest, 'Crime-Terror Interactions in Sub-Saharan Africa', Studies in Conflict & Terrorism (2019); K. Petrich, 'Cows, Charcoal, and Cocaine: Al-Shabaab's Criminal Activities in the Horn of Africa', Studies in Conflict & Terrorism (2019); E. Alda and J.L. Sala, 'Links Between Terrorism, Organized Crime and Crime: The Case of the Sahel Region', 3 Stability: International Journal of Security and Development 1 (2014); A. Hübschle, 'From Theory to Practice: Exploring the Organised Crime-Terror Nexus in Sub-Saharan Africa', 5 Perspectives on Terrorism 81 (2011). On the ineffectiveness of the AU's legal instruments in combating African terrorist groups generally, see H. Solomon, 'Responding to Terror: An Assessment of African Union Counter-Terrorism Strategies', in H. Solomon, *Terrorism and Counter-Terrorism in Africa: Fighting Insurgency from Al Shabaab, Ansar Dine and Boko Haram* (2015), Ch. 6.

9 Organized of African Unity, Convention on the Prevention and Combating of Terrorism 1999, 2219 UNTS 179 (hereafter 'OAU Convention'), preambular para. 11. See also the Organisation of the Islamic Conference Convention on Combatting International Terrorism (OIC Convention) 1999, preambular para. 11.

10 Plan of Action of the AU High-Level Inter-Governmental Meeting on the Prevention and Combating of Terrorism in Africa, High-Level Inter-Governmental Meeting on the Prevention and Combating of Terrorism in Africa, Algiers, Mtg/HLIG/Conv.Terror/Plan.(I) (September 2002).

11 E.g., C.D. Smith, 'Challenging the so-called trafficking–terror finance nexus', 64 Forced Migration Review 56 (2020); Views of the UN Special Rapporteur on the Promotion and Protection of Human Rights and Fundamental Freedoms While Countering Terrorism to the Secretary-General's Pending Report Pursuant to UNSC Resolution 2482 (2019) Addressing the Issue of the Linkage Between Terrorism and Organized Criminal Groups (OCG) (2019); B. Saul, 'The Legal Relationship between Terrorism and Transnational Crime', 17 Int'l Crim. L. Rev. 417 (2017), at 419; FATF-GIABA-GABAC, 'Terrorist Financing in West and Central Africa' (2016), at 1; UN Secretary-General Report on the threat of terrorists benefiting from transnational organized crime, UN Doc. S/2015/366 (21 May 2015), para. 5.

have been mainly conducted from a qualitative perspective and an overreliance on secondary data sources and the associated predominance of the literature review method.[12] This trend appears to reflect a larger problem within contemporary terrorism research.[13] Additionally, existing analyses tend to generalize from a few prominent and idiosyncratic examples, which are repeated many times over, to across the-board conclusions between the two phenomena, potentially resulting in unwarranted exaggeration or inaccuracy.[14] Research commissioned by the UN is not immune from such criticism.[15] Studies utilizing interviews as a data collection technique are few and far between.[16] Even then, such studies typically employ a case study method to examine a specific terrorist group and rarely include sufficient methodological content detailing the research process. As a result, knowledge of both the empirical links between terrorism and organized crime in Africa, which are potentially many and varied, and how research is conducted remains severely limited and far from satisfactory for evaluating and informing appropriate legal, policy and operational responses. It is precisely for these reasons that various UN entities, the European Union (EU) and Interpol have recognized the need to conduct further research, collect empirical data and produce new evidence to better understand the nature and scope of the potential links between terrorism and organized crime across different contexts and to develop responses informed by evidence.[17]

---

12 The secondary sources of data, which provide indirect and second-hand information include, most notably, books, journal articles and media reports.

13 B. Schurman, 'Research on Terrorism, 2007–2016: A Review of Data, Methods, and Authorship', 32 Terrorism and Political Violence 1011 (2020).

14 L. Achilli, and A. Tinti, A., 'Debunking the Smuggler-Terrorist Nexus: Human Smuggling and the Islamic State in the Middle East', Studies in Conflict and Terrorism (2019); P. Williams, 'The Organized Crime and Terrorist Nexus: Overhyping the Relationship', STRATFOR (2018); V. Felbab-Brown, 'Wildlife and Drug Trafficking, Terrorism and Human Security', Brookings Institute (2018); W. Lacher, 'Challenging the Myth of the Drug-Terror Nexus in the Sahel', West Africa Commission on Drugs (2013), at 3–7.

15 Smith, *supra* note 11, at 56–57; UN Special Rapporteur, *supra* note 11, at 1, 11.

16 E.g., T. Keatinge and K. Danner, 'Assessing Innovation in Terrorist Financing', 44 Studies in Conflict & Terrorism 455 (2021); K.D. Maza et al., 'Challenges of Combating Terrorist Financing in the Lake Chad Region: A Case of Boko Haram', 10 Sage Open 1 (2020); Achilli and Tinti, *supra* note 14; J. Jupp and M. Garrod, 'Legacies of the Troubles: The Links between Organized Crime and Terrorism in Northern Ireland', Studies in Conflict and Terrorism (2019); I. Levy and A. Yusuf, 'How Do Terrorist Organizations Make Money? Terrorist Funding and Innovation in the Case of al-Shabaab', Studies in Conflict and Terrorism (2019); Petrich, *supra* note 8.

17 Interview (EU Counter-Terrorism Coordinator representative); Interview (European External Action Service representative); Interview (Interpol representative). See also Council of Europe Committee of Ministers, Guidelines on the links between terrorism and

In order to fill part of the gap in scholarship and policy, the overarching aims of this study are twofold: to provide, based on qualitative interviews, the first empirical study of (1) how terrorist groups in Africa may benefit from nine types of organized crime financially, logistically and operationally; and (2) assess the applicability and effectiveness of relevant AU legal instruments, in particular the 1999 Organisation of African Unity Convention on the Prevention and Combating of Terrorism (OAU Convention), for combatting the phenomenon.[18] Accurately and reliably measuring the effects of treaties is a matter of some debate.[19] In the present context, 'effectiveness' is measured based on the domestic implementation of relevant AU legal instruments, in parituclar the extent to which such instruments provide a legal basis to facilitate coordinated practice with regard to (1) the harmonized criminalization of activity relating to the links between terrorism and organized crime and (2) the operation of the law 'on the ground' in terms of law enforcement cooperation in the investigation, prosecution and extradition of suspects. Relevant AU policy organs regard AU legal instruments, in particular the OAU Convention, as a 'watershed' in Africa's efforts to address the threat of terrorism,[20] and have underscored that such instruments provide a 'sound legal and institutional basis' to

---

transnational organised crime, **CM(2021)12-final**, para. 47 (31 March 2021); UN Secretary-General Report, Action taken by Member States and United Nations entities to address the issue of linkages between terrorism and organized crime, UN Doc. S/2020/754, para. 108 (29 July 2020); UN Special Rapporteur, *supra* note 11, at 1; UNICRI, 'POLICY TOOLKIT on The Hague Good Practices on the Nexus between Transnational Organized Crime and Terrorism', Good Practice 3 (2019); S/RES/2462 (2019), para. 32; S/RES/2482 (2019), paras. 2, 23; Counter-Terrorism Executive Directorate, 'Identifying and Exploring the Nexus Between Human Trafficking, Terrorism and, Terrorism Financing' (2019), at 4; Letter dated 28 December 2018 from the Chair of the Security Council Committee established pursuant to resolution 1373 (2001) concerning counter-terrorism addressed to the President of the Security Council, UN Doc. S/2018/1177, Annex (28 December 2018); T. Reitano, C. Clarke and L. Adal, 'Examining the Nexus between Organised Crime and Terrorism and its implications for EU Programming', Counter-Terrorism Monitoring, Reporting, and Support Mechanism (2017).

18 These nine types of organized crime are as follows: illicit sourcing, manufacture and traffic of weapons and ammunition (including military grade materiel and improvised explosive device components; KFR; illegal taxation; illicit traffic of drugs and humans; migrant smuggling; natural resource exploitation; public and private corruption; and money laundering.

19 See, e.g., R. Goodman, and D. Jinks, 'Measuring the Effects of Human Rights Treaties', 14 EJIL 171 (2003).

20 Report of the Chairperson of the Commission on Terrorism and Violent Extremism in Africa, Peace and Security Council, PSC/AHG/2(CDLV), 455th Meeting, Kenya (2014), para. 34.

facilitate and promote coordinated and effective action against terrorism and its links with organized crime.[21] As such, AU member states have been repeatedly urged to ratify, without delay, these instruments. The primary focus of this study is East and West Africa and the Sahel—sub-regions which are seriously affected both by terrorism and organized crime.[22]

The above aims are empirical in character. To achieve them, this study employs a novel mixed research approach in the collection of empirical data. These methods combine semi-structured interviews with 44 key informants—including representatives of various government agencies, EU, Interpol and UN Office on Drugs and Crime (UNODC) and civil society organizations—who are subject-matter experts in understanding and combatting both terrorism and its links with organized crime in Africa and can provide on the ground insights, with the analysis of data gathered using unstructured interviews with 53 participants (representatives of UN entities, Global Counterterrorism Task Force, civil society and academia) as part of the completion of two major studies at the UN as an independent expert examining the links between terrorism and organized crime from a global perspective with a particular focus on Africa.[23] The above data are triangulated with a comprehensive review of primary and secondary data published in open sources utilizing the literature review method. In addressing the research aims, it is intended that a more accurate and informed understanding of the links will contribute to the current evidence base in order to formulate appropriate policy and legal responses. Additionally, this study aims to shed new light on some of the methodological challenges in the process of researching the links between terrorism an organized crime in Africa and gathering reliable data, including the interview method with 'elite' participants as a data collection technique, when the norm appears to be to exclude such details.

---

21 Peace and Security Council, *Communiqué*, PSC/MIN/COMM.1040(2021), 1040th Meeting, Ethiopia (22 October 2021), para. 12; Peace and Security Council, *Communiqué*, PSC/PR/COMM.1 (DCCCXLV), 845th Meeting, Ethiopia, paras. 3, 9 (25 April 2019); Peace and Security Council, *Communiqué*, PSC/PR/COMM. (DCCCXII), 812th Meeting, Ethiopia, *paras.* 5, 13 (23 November 2018); Peace and Security Council, *Communiqué*, PSC/AHG/COMM.(CDLV), 455th Meeting, Kenya, (2 September 2014), paras. *8, 16;* Report of the Chairperson of the Commission on Terrorism and Violent Extremism in Africa, *ibid.*, paras. 30–36, 67–68, 71–72.

22 *Communiqué (2014), ibid.*, para. 5; Report of the Chairperson of the Commission on Terrorism and Violent Extremism in Africa, *ibid.*, paras. 1, 4, 7, 10–16, 19–24, 67; UN Secretary-General Report on the work of the United Nations to help States and subregional and regional entities in Africa in fighting terrorism, UN Doc. S/2014/9, para. 12 (9 January 2014); S/PRST/2013/5 (13 May 2013).

23 Part 2.

This study empirically demonstrates that, in Africa, terrorism and organized crime are intertwined.[24] All of the more prominent and resilient terrorist groups and individuals who are affiliated with them exploit all seven types of organized crime to varying degrees, both directly and indirectly, in order to generate funds or for logistical or operational purposes.[25] Yet, after more than two decades since the adoption of the OAU Convention, AU legal instruments remain largely inapplicable and ineffective in combatting terrorist groups that exploit organized crime. As a matter of substantive law, the instruments are not designed to address organized crime or its links with terrorism, or public and private corruption as an enabling mechanism of the links between terrorism and organized crime.[26] Moreover, the instruments embrace the conventional and somewhat outdated assumption in scholarship and policymaking that terrorism and organized crime are distinct phenomena and, thus, should be regulated by different legal regimes. Therefore, the instruments require, as a core focus, proof of a special terrorist intent in the definition of acts of terrorism. The specific intent requirement reduces overbreadth and makes terrorism distinctive from ordinary crime; but it also means that the instruments only capture organized crime benefitting an individual terrorist or a terrorist group where it can be established that a specific act of terrorism is involved.

Additionally, the AU instruments grant states with discretion to identify and legislate for themselves the substantive crimes that are included as acts of terrorism, while at the same time requiring states to incorporate into national legislation various international legal instruments relating to terrorist acts (none of which define 'terrorism').[27] In this regard, the instruments lack guidance on how they should be implemented or address the relationship between potentially conflicting norms arising from the respective international and continental legal regimes. While Hübschle suggests that the definition of 'terrorist act' contained in the OAU Convention 'has been employed as a blueprint for domestic anti-terror laws on the continent',[28] the empirical

---

24 See also *Communiqué (2014), supra note 21, paras. 5, 16;* Report of the Chairperson of the Commission on Terrorism and Violent Extremism in Africa, *supra* note 20, paras. 5–6, 17–24, 67; Peace and Security Council Report on Mali and the Sahel and the Activities of the African Union Mission for Mali and the Sahel, Peace and Security Council, PSC/PR/2.(CDXLIX), 449th Meeting, Ethiopia (11 August 2014).

25

26 For discussion of how corruption enables terrorist financing by exploiting links with organized crime, see K. Izenman and T. Keatinge, 'Exploring Connections Corruption, Terrorism and Terrorist Financing', Occasional Paper, Royal United Services Institute for Defence and Security Studies (2020); Solomon, *supra* note 8, at 112.

27 OAU Convention, *supra* note 9, Art. 2; Plan of Action, *supra* note 10, Art. 12.

28 Hübschle, *supra* note 8, at 82.

findings of the present study suggest that legislative practice is diverse. AU member states have incorporated international and AU legal instruments into domestic legislation in different ways, resulting in a wide range of broadly and vaguely defined offences.[29] The lack of harmonization in national legislation is compounded by binding UN Security Council resolutions requiring all states to criminalize 'terrorist acts' and related precursor offences.[30] Therefore, AU legal instruments are not necessarily the main driver of counterterrorism laws in Africa and they are ineffective, it would appear, in coordinating legislative action in response to terrorism and its links with organized crime.

Insofar as the operation of the law 'on the ground' is concerned, the empirical findings suggest that the relative few states who have the willingness and ability to engage in law enforcement activities to investigate and prosecute the links between terrorism and organized crime place weighty reliance on a variety of general criminal offences (including inchoate offences such as attempt, conspiracy and criminal association) and preparatory and accessory acts relating to different forms of support, membership or participation in a terrorist group or enterprise—none of which are established in AU legal instruments. Such offences are broadly defined and criminalize behaviour that requires no connection to future terrorist acts and, therefore, remove the burden of proving a special terrorist intent.[31] More concerning, the instruments are failing to

29 Interview (Human Rights Watch representative); Interview (Global Initiative against Transnational Organized Crime representative); Interviews (3 Institute for Security Studies representatives); Interview (International Crisis Group representative). See also Terrorism (Prevention) Amendment Act 2013 (Nigeria); Law No. 044-2019/AN amending Law No. 025-2018/AN (Burkina Faso); Law N.040-2017/AN modifying Order No. 68-7 of 21 February 1968 establishing the Code of Criminal Procedure (Burkina Faso); Law No.016-2016/AN of May 2016 Relating to the Fight Against Money Laundering Terrorist Financing in Burkina Faso (Burkina Faso); Burkinabe Penal Code, Law No. 025-2018/AN, Book III, Title VI, Chapter 1 ('offenses relating to terrorism'); Law 084-2015/CNT of 17 December 2015, amending Law No. 060/2009/AN of 17 December 2009 on the repression of acts of terrorism in Burkina Faso; Penal Code, as amended by Law No. 2008-18, Title VI (Niger); Terrorist Entities Law No. 8 of 2015 (Egypt); Law No. 95 of 2015 for Countering Terrorism (Egypt); Prevention and Suppression of Terrorism Crimes Proclamation No. 1176/2020 (Ethiopia); Law No. 2014/028 of 23 December 2014 on the Suppression of Acts of Terrorism in Cameroon (Cameroon).

30 As the OAU Convention only entered into force in 2002, UN Security Council resolutions, in paritucular resolution 1373, have had a significant influence on national legislation, Interviews (3 Institute for Security Studies representatives).

31 *Ibid.* Such offences include membership of a terrorist group, the provision of financial, material or other support to a terrorist group, participation in a terrorist enterprise, planning or preparation of a terrorist act, criminal association, criminal conspiracy and rebellion or threats to the internal or external security of the state. See also J. Nozawa and

promote human rights compliant counterterrorism law and practice.[32] Some states evade the law enforcement provisions required by AU legal instruments and, instead, employ various executive powers and practices that violate the protection norms of human rights law in combating the growing links between terrorism and organized crime, such as extrajudicial killing, mass arbitrary arrests and detention without trial, the use of confessional evidence extracted under torture and the trial of alleged members or supporters of terrorist groups absent procedural safeguards.[33] The empirical findings further suggest that AU legal instruments are not facilitating coordinated law enforcement operations in the investigation, prosecution and extradition of suspects whose activities span multiple countries across the continent and beyond. The absence of a clear and commonly accepted understanding of the links between terrorism and organized crime, combined with the divergence between national practice and the lack of capacity and/or willingness among national agencies to share information and intelligence, are some of the important factors impairing inter-state cooperation.[34] An increase in the rate of ratification will not remedy the shortcomings in substantive law or its operation on the ground.

A more fundamental finding of the present study is that the AU has been slow to react at the policy, legal and operational level to understand and combat the links between terrorism and organized crime. Elite individuals in the AU and many of its member states lack the willingness to gather and share information on the links including with the present author. Yet, the policy of the UN in countering these links is underpinned by the presumption that regional organizations and government agencies are willing to cooperate and share information. The main concern here is that both future policies adopted by the AU and its member states in combatting the links and the field of terrorism studies will continue to be uninformed by evidence-based research.

M. Lefas, 'When the Dust Settles: Judicial Responses to Terrorism in the Sahel', Global Centre on Cooperative Security (2018).

32 See also M. Josua, 'What Drives Diffusion? Anti-Terrorism Legislation in the Arab Middle East and North Africa', 6 Journal of Global Security Studies 1 (2021).

33 Interview (Human Rights Watch participant). See also Nozawa and Lefas, *supra* note 31; A. Ngari and A. Olojo, 'Besieged but not relenting: Ensuring fair trials for Nigeria's terrorism suspects', Institute of Security Studies (2020).

34 Solomon, *supra* note 8, has similarly found that many AU member states are unwilling and/or lack the ability to implement AU legal instruments and take legislative and law enforcement action against terrorism including cooperation and sharing information with each other. There is a clear tension between the AU and its member states, which undermines the development, implementation and effectiveness of the AU's legal instruments to combat terrorism.

The study concludes that the AU Commission and the ACSRT need to adopt a policy addressing the links, to update the AU Plan of Action and to revise the OAU Convention (including the legal definition of 'terrorist act') to prevent its potential misuse and encourage member states to comply with their international law obligations, on the one hand, and to capture domestic and transnational organized crime activities that benefit individual terrorists and terrorist groups, on the other. The implementation of the OAU Convention also requires the introduction of a more effective and transparent continental treaty monitoring body.

Addressing this study's aims at the present moment could not be more important. Terrorist groups and attacks are growing in number, geographical scope and intensity, such that Africa is ranked the worst region globally for terrorist violence.[35] Organized crime is contributing to the spread of terrorism.[36] Terrorist groups benefitting from organized crime enables them to acquire sophisticated weapons and ammunition, purchase advanced communication systems, develop greater resilience against counterterrorism campaigns by regular military forces and multinational peacekeeping missions, and expand geographical spheres of control and influence.[37] The ability of terrorist groups to exploit organized crime is growing or at least becoming more clear.[38] The result is that Africa has established itself as not only a 'terrorist

35 Global Terrorism Index 2020: Measuring the Impact of Terrorism, Institute for Economics and Peace (2021).

36 Interviews (2 Global Counterterrorism Forum Capacity-Building in the East Africa Region Working Group representatives); Interviews (3 Global Counterterrorism Forum Capacity-building in the West Africa Region Working Group representatives); Report of the Chairperson of the Commission on Terrorism and Violent Extremism in Africa, *supra* note 20, paras. 17–19.

37 Interview (1 Global Initiative against Transnational Organized Crime representative); Interviews (2 Institute for Security Studies representatives); Interview (Mali Specialized Judicial Unit to Combat Terrorism and Transnational Organized Crime representative); Interview (Nigeria National Counter Terrorism Centre representative); Interview (UNODC Regional Office for West and Central Africa representative).

38 Interview (EU Counter-Terrorism Coordinator representative); Interviews (2 Global Counterterrorism Forum Capacity-Building in the East Africa Region Working Group representatives); Interviews (3 Global Counterterrorism Forum Capacity-building in the West Africa Region Working Group representatives); Interview (Institute for Security Studies representative); Interview (Interpol representative); Interview (Kenya National Counter-Terrorism Centre); Interview (Mali Specialized Judicial Unit to Combat Terrorism and Transnational Organized Crime representative); Interview (Nigeria National Counter Terrorism Centre representative); Interview (UNODC Regional Office for East Africa); Interview (UNODC Regional Office for West and Central Africa representative); *Communiqué (2019), supra* note 21, paras. 1–2; *Communiqué (2018), supra note 21,* para. 4;

breeding ground and source of recruitment and financing' but also the epicentre of the links between terrorism and organized crime globally.[39] Further, both terrorism and organized crime are international in their reach and effect, impacting numerous states beyond the continent.[40] In the words of the delegate of France before the UN Security Council, the growing terrorist threat in the Sahel, which 'knows no borders' and is increasingly linked with organized crime, has a 'direct impact' on the national security of France and of Europe.[41] It is precisely for this reason that several states, including France, the UK and the US as well as the EU, have deployed military operations or invested huge resources in funding, equipping and training national armed forces and law enforcement agencies and sub-regional organizations in Africa to counter the links between terrorism and organized crime.[42]

A. Defining 'Terrorism', 'Organized Crime' and 'Terrorism-Organized Crime Links'

Deepening understanding of some of the links between terrorism and organized crime in Africa and evaluating the applicability and effectiveness of AU instruments to the phenomenon poses a number of challenges, one of which is defining 'terrorism' and 'organized crime'. Schmid rightly observes that not much of the growing literature discussing the relationship between terrorism and organized crime 'has bothered to clearly define these concepts', both of which are contested.[43] There is presently no agreement among states, and certainly no internationally codified definition in a multilateral treaty, of a legal definition of 'terrorism' or 'organized crime'. However, the international community was able to reach agreement on a broad definition of transnational 'organized criminal group' in Article 2 of the UN Convention against Transnational Organized Crime (UNTOC) and its three supplementary protocols relating to the trafficking in persons, the smuggling of migrants and the

---

Report of the Chairperson of the Commission on Terrorism and Violent Extremism in Africa, *supra* note 20, para. 19.

39 Report of the Chairperson of the Commission on Terrorism and Violent Extremism in Africa, *ibid.*, para. 6.

40 Interview (EU Counter-Terrorism Coordinator representative); Interview (European External Action Service representative); Interviews (2 Institute for Security Studies representatives).

41 UNSC, 72nd Year, 7979th Meeting, UN Doc. S/PV.7979, at 2 (21 June 2017).

42 Interview (European External Action Service representative); Interview (UNODC Regional Office for East Africa); Interview (UNODC Regional Office for West and Central Africa representative).

43 Schmid, *supra* note 6, at 2.

illicit manufacture and trafficking of firearms.[44] The discord in defining these phenomena (and the potential links between them) can be seen in recent UN Security Council meetings and resolutions on the links between terrorism and organized crime. Therefore, the Council has given effective carte blanche to states to define 'terrorism' and 'organized crime' (if at all) as they choose at the domestic level, with no transparent oversight as to whether those definitions comport with international law or internationally recognized best practices.[45]

The definition of terrorism and organized crime are equally problematic in the African context. At least some African states are parties to three instruments adopted by relevant regional organizations that require national criminalization of terrorism and terrorist acts.[46] The OAU Convention, which is the principal AU legal instrument for countering terrorism, is the focus of the present study. The Convention glosses over potential divergences in how AU member states understand or define 'terrorism' by avoiding the term in its operative provisions. Instead, the Convention provides a broad outline of the constituent elements of a 'terrorist act' while giving states party discretion to determine what harmful activities constitute a 'terrorist act' in accordance with national law.[47] In the analysis of the links between terrorism and organized crime, the present study utilizes the same definition of 'terrorist act' as the OAU Convention. The absence of a generally accepted definition of 'terrorism' or 'terrorist group' in Africa means that an investigation into the links must also take into account a host of non-state actors including armed groups, militias, insurgents, rebel movements and criminal groups, all of whom are capable of terrorist acts under the OAU Convention.

Similarly, the AU has not defined 'organized crime' in any legal instrument or policy document.[48] An AU Peace and Security Council Communiqué, adopted in 2019, on transnational organized crime expresses 'deep concern' over the

---

44 UN Convention against Transnational Organized Crime 2000, 2225 UNTS 209; Protocol to Prevent, Suppress and Punish Trafficking in Persons, Especially Women and Children 2000, 2237 UNTS 319; Protocol Against the Smuggling of Migrants by Land, Sea and Air 2000, 2241 UNTS 507; and Protocol Against the Illicit Manufacturing of and Trafficking in Firearms, their Parts and Components and Ammunition 2001, 2326 208.

45 UN Secretary-General Report, Action taken by Member States and United Nations entities to address the issue of linkages between terrorism and organized crime, *supra* note 17, para. 117; UN Special Rapporteur, *supra* note 11, at 6.

46 OAU Convention, *supra* note 9; OIC Convention, *supra* note 9; Arab Convention on the Suppression of Terrorism 1998 (Arab Convention).

47 OAU Convention, *ibid.*, Art. 1(3).

48 See also S.W. Khaemba, 'Implications of the African Continental Free Trade Area (AFCFTA) Treaty on the African Union's Policies on Transnational Organized Crime and Terrorism', 9 African Journal on Terrorism 71 (2020), at 77.

growing threat posed by transnational organized crime to peace and security in Africa, 'particularly its increasingly direct linkages and collusion with terrorism' and 'the ability of terrorist organizations and other armed groups to finance their activities through criminal activities'; and urges AU member states to ensure that necessary steps are taken to domesticate the UNTOC in the fight against transnational organized crime including when such crime is committed by terrorist groups.[49] Therefore, the preference of the AU has been to give its member states discretion in how organized crime is defined (if at all) and to utilize the UNTOC as a legal basis for combatting terrorist groups who exploit organized crime.

The UN Security Council has identified the following types of organized crime, 'whether domestic or transnational'—and irrespective of whether such crimes fall within the ambit of the UNTOC regime—from which terrorist groups are able to benefit either directly or indirectly (including in Africa): trafficking of arms, persons, drugs and cultural property; the illicit trade in natural resources, including gold and other precious metals and stones, minerals, wildlife, charcoal and oil; kidnapping for ransom (KFR); extortion; bank robbery; and piracy and armed robbery at sea.[50] As a starting point, the present study adopts the same thematic approach as the UN and examines the following types of organized crime rather than define 'organized crime' as such; namely: the illicit sourcing, manufacture and traffic of weapons and ammunition (including military grade materiel and improvised explosive device (IED) components); KFR; illegal taxation; illicit traffic of drugs and humans; and migrant smuggling; and natural resource exploitation. Additionally, two further types of organized crime are considered, both of which are enablers and facilitators of organized crime: namely, public and private corruption and money laundering. These types of organized crime are selected because an evidence-led approach is adopted. In this regard, they have been identified by the AU and by Mutual Evaluation Reports published by Financial Action Task Force Style Regional Bodies, and they emerged as themes during interviews.[51] Accordingly, other types of organized crime from which terrorist groups may benefit, such as trafficking of cultural property, illicit trade in oil and cigarettes, bank robbery, piracy at sea and cybercrime, are excluded due to insufficient evidence of general trends and the need for further research.

49 *Communiqué* (*2019*), *supra note 21*, para. 3.

50 S/RES/2482 (2019), preambular para. 5; S/RES/2195 (2014), preambular para. 7. See also UN Secretary-General Report on the threat of terrorists benefiting from transnational organized crime, *supra* note 11, paras. 17–44.

51 See also *Communiqué* (*2018*), *supra note 21*, para. 4.

Additionally, the study takes as a point of departure UNTOC's definition of 'organized criminal group' for two main reasons. First, the UNTOC definition is problematic as it misses loose criminal networks (including complex familial, ethnic, tribal and clan-based structures) and individuals who provide services ad hoc (such as the procurement of weapons, counterfeit of identity documents or access to informal smuggling routes) but who are not formally part of a 'structured group', sharing the group's aims, for a 'period of time'.[52] Second, the UNTOC definition requires that an offence committed by an organized criminal group is in some way 'transnational'.[53] Yet, terrorism can benefit from purely domestic organized crime.

Equally problematic is the definition of 'links' between terrorism and organized crime. The links can take a number of different meanings in scholarship—from criminals and terrorists operating in unison, to simply the use of criminal tactics by terrorist actors. Despite various UN entities and regional organizations including the AU, the EU and the Council of Europe (CoE) recognizing the existence of 'links', 'linkages' or a 'nexus' between terrorism and organized crime, conspicuously absent is a definition of these terms. For instance, the EU's Counter-Terrorism Monitoring, Reporting and Support Mechanism suggests that the concept of a 'nexus' should not be applied globally as there is no 'one size fits all' approach.[54] Similarly, the 'Hague Good Practices on the Nexus between Transnational Organized Crime and Terrorism' (Hague Good Practices), which have been endorsed by the UN Security Council, manoeuvre around this thorny issue by suggesting that the 'nexus' comes 'in many forms and manifestations'.[55] Yet, one of the good practices identified is 'research and information sharing' in order to facilitate, at least regionally, the capacity of states to identify the nexus and develop responses based on evidence-based research. The inclusion of this good practice arose out of a concern about the lack accurate and reliable data and analysis and information sharing between states. It remains unclear how, exactly, accurate and reliable data can be collected and shared in the absence of even a basic definition of the term 'nexus'. The CoE's 'guidelines', which are designed as a practical tool for national

52 The UNTOC, *supra* note 44, defines 'organized criminal group' as a 'structured group of three or more persons, existing for a period of time and acting in concert with the aim of committing one or more serious crimes or offences ... in order to obtain, directly or indirectly, a financial or other material benefit'.

53 *Ibid.*, Art. 3.

54 Reitano *et al.*, *supra* note 17.

55 Global Counterterrorism Forum, 'The Hague Good Practices on the Nexus between Transnational Organized Crime and Terrorism' (2019), at 1.

legislative entities and judicial and law enforcement authorities, simply refer to 'links' between terrorism and transnational organized crime without defining what these links comprise other than alluding to some of the same categories of organized crime as the UN Security Council and suggesting that the nature of the links 'depends on the local context' and that understanding them should be a priority for states in order to adequately target the phenomenon.[56] At the time of writing, the AU has not defined what it understands by the meaning of 'linkages'.

In the context of the present study, the term 'links' refers to a terrorist group (including a cell or individual) who fulfils the constituent elements of a terrorist act and benefits from organized crime as a source of financing and/or for logistical or operational purposes. A link may include a terrorist group that engages in criminal activities directly, as well as those that benefit indirectly without necessarily being involved in such criminal activities. A terrorist group may indirectly benefit from criminal activity in various ways including by acquiring logistical and operational materials (for instance, weapons or vehicles) from criminal networks; by imposing taxes on convoys of goods transiting through an area under their control; and by providing escort, protection or transportation services. Corruption is taken into account when considering the links, to the extent that it emerged as a theme in the interview data.[57] Of course, organized crime is just one of the ways that terrorists generate funding. This study does not consider the great variety of potential sources of terrorist financing, ranging from state sponsorship and licit business to petty theft, from crowdfunding and charitable donations to private individuals using their personal wealth to fund a group.[58] In the present context, excluded from the meaning of links is the potential 'convergence' of or 'alliance' or 'organizational' links between distinct terrorist and organized crime groups in the pursuit of common ventures.[59] Also excluded is the extent to which terrorism may have an impact on the presence or expansion of organized crime groups.[60]

---

56 Council of Europe Committee of Ministers, Guidelines on the links between terrorism and transnational organised crime, *supra* note 17.

57 In this context, corruption is defined as the abuse of entrusted power for private gain. This includes actors in both the public and private sectors. See further Izenman and Keatinge, *supra* note 26.

58 M. Freeman, 'The Sources of Terrorist Financing: Theory and Typology', 34 Studies in Conflict & Terrorism 461 (2011).

59 See, e.g., Schmid, *supra* note 6, at 14–15; UN Special Rapporteur, *supra* note 11, at 7–8.

60 G. Kreiman and M.C. Espadafor, 'Unexpected Allies: The Impact of Terrorism on Organised Crime in Sub-Saharan Africa and South-East Asia', Studies in Conflict & Terrorism (2019).

This chapter proceeds by explaining the present study's methodology before examining the AU's legal instruments applicable to terrorism. Thereafter, the chapter examines nine types of organized crime which provide clear empirical links with terrorism. Understanding the types of links at issue is critical for contextualizing the evaluation of the applicability and effectiveness of the AU's legal instruments.

2 Methodology: Researching the Links between Terrorism an Organized Crime in Africa

This is an in-depth qualitative study of (1) the links between terrorism and organized crime in East and West Africa and the Sahel and (2) the applicability and effectiveness of the AU's legal instruments in combatting the phenomenon. These research aims require empirical study. In order to address them, the author gathered empirical data using a mixed methods approach. This part explains the research process and aims to shed new light on some of the methodological challenges in researching the links between terrorism an organized crime in Africa, including the interview method with 'elites' as a data collection technique, when the norm in scholarship and research commissioned by policymakers appears to be to exclude such details.[61] As will be shown, one of the more fundamental empirical findings is that both the AU and many of its member states are unwilling and/or lack the capacity to participate in the research process and collect or share relevant and reliable data (with each other and the present author) both on the links between terrorism and organized crime and the applicability and effectiveness of the AU's legal instruments in combatting the phenomenon. The result is the lack of a clear and common understanding of the links and African responses are likely to remain fragmented and inadequately informed by evidence-led research.

2.1 *Interviews as a Data Collection Technique*

This study utilized semi-structured interviews with key informants, who are subject-matter experts in understanding and combatting both terrorism and its links with organized crime in Africa, as the most appropriate qualitative method of gathering primary source data due to their flexible nature, ensuring that major topics were covered while not limiting participants to

61 D.J. Harris, P. Simi and G. Ligon, 'Reporting Practices of Journal Articles that Include Interviews with Extremists', 39 Studies in Conflict & Terrorism 602 (2016).

predetermined ideas or theories.[62] Additionally, this method allows participants to elicit narratives about their experiences. Due to travel restrictions resulting from Covid-19, interviews were conducted by Zoom with a total of 44 participants. This group of participants included senior officials of various government agencies in the areas of policy, law enforcement, counterterrorism, prosecution and the judiciary from Kenya, Mali, Nigeria, South Africa, Tanzania and the UK.[63] Interviews were also conducted with a range of other participants who have (1) knowledge of the links between terrorism and organized crime and (2) the operation of the law on the ground, including representatives of the EU (Counter-Terrorism Coordinator and External Action Service), Global Counterterrorism Forum Working Groups in East and West Africa, Interpol, UN Interregional Crime and Justice Research Institute (UNICRI) and UNODC regional offices in East, West and Central Africa.

Interviewing elite participants presents distinctive methodological challenges, which is exacerbated when individuals occupy relatively powerful government or institutional positions and the research involves highly sensitive issues concerning national security and the personal safety and confidentiality of the state's intelligence and law enforcement personnel, on the one hand, and widespread allegations of the serious and systematic misuse of counterterrorism powers and corrupt activities of public officials, on the other.[64] Therefore, interview participants also included representatives from civil society who conduct research on the ground in Africa (Global Initiative against Transnational Organized Crime, Global Witness, Human Rights Watch, Institute for Security Studies and International Crisis Group). The interviews were completed between September 2020 and May 2021.

After a preliminary review of the literature and based on information gleaned from the author's participation in a series of high-level meetings organized by the Global Counterterrorism Forum, Royal United Services Institute and UNODC between 2017 and 2019—attended by the representatives of government agencies from numerous countries (including some AU member states), civil society and academia—a total of 98 prospective interview participants were identified for inclusion in the current study. This sample included

62 E. Drever, *Using Semi-Structured Interviews in Small-Scale Research: A Teacher's Guide* (1995).

63 The UK was included because the government has provided funding to support various projects to counter terrorism and transnational organized crime in the Lake Chad Basin and other sub-regions.

64 See, e.g., R. Milkecz, 'Interviewing Elites: Addressing Methodological Issues', 18 Qualitative Inquiry 482 (2012).

54 representatives of the AU and the government agencies of 18 AU member states who are affected by terrorism and/or organized crime in East or West Africa or the Sahel, providing a sample of participants who are potentially information rich and could best help to understand the aims of this study.[65] However, for reasons explained below, it is rather disappointing that 38 of these participants, comprising all representatives of the AU and twelve AU member states, declined to participate or chose not to respond to multiple interview requests, resulting in a final sample of 44 participants.

A variety of non-probability sampling techniques were used to construct the pool of participants, including expert sampling, purposive sampling and snowball sampling. Participants were identified and selected based on their professional activities and expertise, or publication record, or recommendation by other prospective interviewees, in this case their knowledge and experience of the links between terrorism and organized crime and/or the applicability and effectiveness of AU instruments in combatting this phenomenon.[66] In addition to national perspectives, the representatives of some government agencies (as well as the EU and UNODC) have knowledge in one of two sub-regional cross-border joint counterterrorism operations in West Africa and the Sahel. The first of these operations is the Multinational Joint Task Force (MJTF) which was launched in 2015 by Benin, Cameroon, Chad, Niger and Nigeria with the aim of combating Boko Haram in the Lake Chad Basin. The second operation is the Group of Five Sahel Joint Force (G5 Sahel Joint Force) which was launched in 2017 by Burkina Faso, Chad, Mali, Mauritania and Niger to counter the growing threat of transnational terrorism, organized crime and human trafficking, and the increasing links between these phenomena, in the Sahel.[67]

Additionally, the EU was identified because it has provided substantial funding and external action to the AU and in strategic partnership with AU member states to counter terrorism, organized crime and the links between these phenomena in Africa.[68] In paritucIar, the EU has funded a project enhancing African capacity to counter transnational organized crime (ENACT), delivered by Interpol in affiliation with the Global Initiative against Transnational

65 The AU member states are as follows: Algeria, Benin, Burkina Faso, Cameroon, Chad, DRC, Egypt, Kenya, Libya, Mali, Mozambique, Niger, Nigeria, Somalia, South Africa, Sudan, Tanzania and Uganda.

66 For instance, the representatives of the EU and government agencies in South Africa and the UK were recommended by other prospective interviewees.

67 SC/RES/2359 (2017).

68 Council of the EU, EU-Africa Relations, https://www.consilium.europa.eu/en/policies/eu-africa/.

Organized Crime and Institute for Security Studies.[69] ENACT recognizes that the links between terrorism and organized crime pose serious challenges to Africa's peace and security and has aimed to build up the evidence base on the enabling factors which increase the likelihood of such links occurring within specific African contexts. The final interview sample included a combined total of 11 participants from all of the organizations responsible for delivering ENACT.

The interviews with key informants had two objectives: first, to obtain up-to-date and reliable information on issues that were not sufficiently addressed in the existing literature. Second (and if applicable), discuss potential future improvements to the AU's legal instruments relevant to combatting the links between terrorism and organized crime in the area of the participant's expertise. Interviews with participants who have first-hand knowledge are essential given the mounting recognition for the need to gather new evidence. Additionally, obtaining relevant information using data collection methods other than interviews in the geographical locations under study pose significant practical challenges.[70] As one participant suggested, the links are 'rarely clear' and 'often unseen' due to the clandestine nature of both the actors and the activities involved.[71] Another participant explained that there are no 'smoking gun' examples of the links in Africa and evidence has to be pieced together using multiple sources of data from intelligence, law enforcement, counterterrorism and customs and border agencies and even former members of a terrorist group.[72] As terrorist groups and criminal activities exploit long porous borders and territory with little or no state presence, a state may even be unaware that links are occurring in its territory.[73] Further, the occurrence

69 ENACT, 'The Nexus between Organized Crime and Terrorism', https://enactafrica.org/research/explainers/the-nexus-between-organised-crime-and-terrorism.

70 See also Hague Good Practices, *supra* note 55, at 1.

71 Interview (Nigeria National Counter Terrorism Centre representative). The same view was expressed in other interviews, e.g., Interview (Global Counterterrorism Forum Capacity-Building in the East Africa Region Working Group representative); Interview (Global Counterterrorism Forum Capacity-building in the West Africa Region Working Group representative); Interview (Interpol representative); Interview (UNICRI representative). See also GIABA Report, 'The Nexus Between Small Arms and Light Weapons and Money Laundering and Terrorist Financing in West Africa' (2013), para. 66 (the operations of terrorist and armed groups are 'shrouded in mystery').

72 Interview (EU Counter-Terrorism Coordinator representative).

73 Interview (Kenya National Counter-Terrorism Centre representative); Interview (Mali Specialized Judicial Unit to Combat Terrorism and Transnational Organized Crime representative); Interview (Nigeria National Counter Terrorism Centre representative); Interview (UNICRI representative).

of links in territory partially controlled by terrorist or armed groups makes evidence and intelligence collection challenging.[74] Some AU member states lack the capacity to gather information in order to establish the existence and nature of links within their jurisdiction.[75] Corruption among law enforcement, military, customs and border officials may result in potential links going unreported.[76]

Criminal investigations and court records provide little relevant or reliable information on the links between terrorism and organized crime.[77] For instance, several participants explained that there are a lack of recorded criminal trials involving terrorism and the links between terrorism and organized crime because such cases are hard to prove evidentially and due to the underdeveloped criminal justice system in many countries, compounded by insufficient expertise and training in investigating, prosecuting and adjudicating terrorism-related trials.[78] Suspects are usually charged with a variety of broadly and vaguely defined precursor and inchoate crimes in domestic law that require little or no connection to future terrorist acts and, therefore, remove the burden of proving a special terrorist intent.[79] More concerning, some AU member states evade the law enforcement provisions required by

74 Interviews, *ibid.*; Interview (Interpol representative).

75 Interview (Global Counterterrorism Forum Capacity-Building in the East Africa Region Working Group representative); Interview (Global Counterterrorism Forum Capacity-building in the West Africa Region Working Group representative); Interview (UNICRI representative). See also UN Secretary-General Report, Action taken by Member States and United Nations entities to address the issue of linkages between terrorism and organized crime, *supra* note 17, para. 6.

76 Interviews, *ibid.*; Interview (European External Action Service representative); Interview (Institute for Security Studies representative); Interview (UNODC Regional Office for West and Central Africa representative). See also Hague Good Practices, *supra* note 55, at 2–3.

77 See also FATF Report, 'Financial Flows From Human Trafficking' (2018), at 38.

78 Interview (Global Counterterrorism Forum Capacity-Building in the East Africa Region Working Group representative); Interview (Global Counterterrorism Forum Capacity-building in the West Africa Region Working Group representative); Interview (Institute for Security Studies representative); Interview (Mali Specialized Judicial Unit to Combat Terrorism and Transnational Organized Crime representative); Interview (Nigeria Complex Case Working Group within the Office of the Attorney-General of the Federation representative); Interview (Nigeria Federal High Court representative); Interview (Nigeria National Counter Terrorism Centre representative); Interview (UNICRI representative); Interview (UNODC Regional Office for West and Central Africa representative). See also *Communiqué (2021), supra note 21*, para. 15(a); Maza et al., *supra* note 16, at 10–11.

79 Interviews (2 Global Initiative against Transnational Organized Crime representatives); Interview (Human Rights Watch representative); Interviews (2 Institute for Security Studies representatives); Interview (International Crisis Group representative).

AU legal instruments and, instead, employ various practices which violate the protection norms of human rights law in combating the growing links between terrorism and organized crime. Such practices include extrajudicial killing and the mass arbitrary arrest and detention without trial of individuals who are suspected of supporting terrorist groups. The relatively small number of individuals who are eventually tried tends to be based on weak or confessional evidence, including evidence obtained through torture, and absent procedural safeguards.[80]

Interviews were preferred to alternative data collection techniques such as questionnaires. The method of questionnaires has previously been utilized in studies commissioned by the UN Counter Terrorism Executive Directorate (CTED), Global Counterterrorism Forum and UNODC to collect data on the links between terrorism and organized crime.[81] However, the number of completed questionnaires returned tends to be relatively low and the responses often lack specific and relevant information.[82] Additionally, interviews provide an opportunity to establish the trust and rapport of a participant and, in turn, enhance the potential of gathering richer and more detailed information. A participant can be asked to elaborate on a parituclar issue and enable the interviewer to ask follow-up questions. Undertaking field research to interview or otherwise interact with known terrorists in hostile and remote territory poses a personal danger to researchers. Indeed, Western nationals are especially targeted with KFR. Furthermore, there are considerable practical difficulties involved with finding members of an active (or former) terrorist group and convincing them to allow a researcher to study them for a prolonged period of time.

The data gathered using semi-structured interviews was combined with the analysis of data gathered using unstructured interviews with a total of 53 participants as part of the completion of two major studies as an independent expert at the UN examining the links between terrorism and organized crime from a global perspective with a particular focus on Africa. Both studies were precipitated by UN Security Council resolution 2195.[83]

---

80 Interviews, *ibid.* See also Nozawa and Lefas, *supra* note 31.

81 Hague Good Practices, *supra* note 55; Counter-Terrorism Executive Directorate, 'Identifying and Exploring the Nexus Between Human Trafficking, Terrorism and, Terrorism Financing', *supra* note 17; Y. Dandurand and V. Chin, 'Links between Terrorism and Other forms of Crime: A Report to Foreign Affairs Canada and UNODC', International Centre for Criminal Law Reform and Criminal Justice Policy (2004).

82 Counter-Terrorism Executive Directorate, 'Identifying and Exploring the Nexus Between Human Trafficking, Terrorism and, Terrorism Financing', *ibid.*, at 9.

83 SC/RES/2195 (2014), para. 20.

The first of these studies was commissioned by the UNODC and resulted, in 2019, in the publication of an extensive report. Although this report was not published as an open source, the report has been referenced in subsequent UN publications.[84] In preparation and during the completion of the UNODC study, the author completed unstructured interviews with a total of 41 participants, comprising representatives of UN entities, the civil society and academia, with expertise in terrorism or organized crime. The bulk of these interviews were conducted at the UN Office in Vienna during the author's participation in high-level meetings, while 14 of the interviews were conducted by Skype. The interviews were conducted between February 2017 and September 2019.[85]

The second study, led by the Netherlands and developed in collaboration with UNICRI and the Global Counterterrorism Forum, resulted in the publication of the Hague Good Practices and a policy toolkit to facilitate the development of national strategies to counter links between terrorism and organized crime.[86] This study was based on primary source data gathered through completed questionnaires with subject-matter experts followed by discussions at four regional meetings, two of which were held in Africa (Algiers and Nairobi focusing respectively on West Africa and the Sahel and the Horn of Africa and East Africa). The discussions of these meetings are not published as an open source. The author conducted 12 unstructured interviews with some of the discussants who contributed to the two African meetings, comprising the representatives from civil society and academia, as well as with representatives from UNICRI and the Global Counterterrorism Forum's capacity-building working groups in the East and West Africa regions. All of these interviews were conducted by Skype. The interviews were conducted between July 2018 and October 2019.

All of the interviews were recorded by the author with extensive handwritten notes, rather than audio-recorded, always with the participant's informed consent. The interview notes were later entered into electronic format. The interview transcripts were analyzed using the method of thematic analysis to identify key themes relating to the links between terrorism and organized crime in Africa and the applicability and effectiveness of AU instruments in combatting this phenomenon. These themes were extracted

84 E.g., UN Secretary-General Report, Action taken by Member States and United Nations entities to address the issue of linkages between terrorism and organized crime, *supra* note 17, para. 72.

85 It must be said that the interview data was not included in the UNODC study, as that study was ultimately limited to data gathered using the literature review method.

86 Hague Good Practices, *supra* note 55.

using *NVivo*, a software program for coding and analyzing text. After importing the interview transcripts into *NVivo*, the author read through each document line-by-line, to identify themes and hierarchically organizing these themes into different analytical units for subsequent interpretation. This coding process produced numerous themes corresponding to various aspects of the links between terrorism and organized crime, including criminal activities, the causes and facilitating mechanisms of the links, the actors and groups involved, legislative and law enforcement responses to the links, and events of interest. Many of these themes and sub-themes are not included in the present study as they do not directly relate to its aims. After coding, the thematically organized data extracts were reflected on further in an iterative process common in qualitative analysis.

The thematically organized data were triangulated with a comprehensive review of primary and secondary source data published in open sources utilizing the literature review method. Secondary source data includes scholarly research, publications by civil society organizations and media reports. Primary source data includes official publications by the AU, CoE, EU, Financial Action Task Force, Interpol, and various UN entities including Panels of Experts of the Security Council, all of which provide a mounting body of evidence documenting different aspects of the links.[87] Triangulation of multiple sources of data is necessary for two main reasons. The first relates to the anonymity of interview participants. The ability of the wider academic community to independently assess the validity and accuracy of findings and replicate the research design is based upon access to the same primary data sources. There is no completely satisfactory way to address this issue. Where possible, an effort was made to reference open sources which contain similar information. Second, the triangulation of multiple data sources is important to mitigate potential bias, resulting in overstating the extent of any links between terrorism and organized crime.[88] For instance, elite individuals in government agencies may be reliable but are not necessarily a neutral source of information. In an effort

87 E.g., Reitano *et al.*, *supra* note 17; A. Salinas de Frias, 'Report on Links Between Terrorism and Transnational Organized Crime,' Council of Europe Second International Conference on Terrorism and Organised Crime (2017); A. Salinas de Frias, 'Legal Instruments Combating TOC and Terrorism: Overlapping, Lacunae or Opportunities?', Council of Europe, Background Information Report on the Linkages between Terrorism and Transnational Organised Crime (2016); T. Makarenko, 'Europe's Crime-Terror Nexus: Links between terrorist and organized crime groups in the European Union', European Parliament (2012).

88 E.g., Williams, supra note 14, suggests that the links have been exaggerated based on 'confirmation bias' by which those attempting to look for a relationship will invariably find one. See also UN Special Rapporteur, *supra* note 11, at 8–9.

to control bias, interview participants were not made aware of each other's identity and the information given by one participant was not shared with the other participants. The method of triangulation can provide some means of cross-validation and the verification of facts from multiple sources, thus further strengthening the objectivity and reliability of findings in the research process.[89]

2.2 *Challenges to the Use of the Interview Method*

Researching the links between terrorism an organized crime in Africa using the interview method as a data collection technique poses unique methodological challenges, which are exacerbated when participants are elites in relatively powerful positions who guard their external image very carefully and who may not want to share potentially highly sensitive information with outsiders. As Mikecz explains, '[g]aining access to elites is hard enough; gaining their trust and building rapport with them is even more difficult'.[90] AU member states have long experienced a 'severe trust deficit' both with each other and the AU, which is hampering the implementation of AU legal instruments countering terrorism at the operational level as states are reluctant to cooperate and exchange information including in the investigation and prosecution of suspects.[91] AU member states are even less willing to trust and share information with outsider researchers.

Approaching and gaining access to elites, including convincing them that participation would come at negligible risk to themselves or the reputation of their respective government or institution, proved to be one of the most challenging and time-consuming aspects of the research process. The representatives of several government agencies and AU organs and departments declined to participate in interviews for a variety of reasons. For some of these elites, understanding and countering terrorism and its links with organized crime is not a high political priority; others lack awareness of the links due to investigative capacity and resource constraints and therefore felt unable to make a meaningful contribution.[92] A further indication of such unwillingness and/or

89 See also Maza et al., *supra* note 16, at 2.

90 Milkecz, *supra* note 62, at 482.

91 UN Counter-Terrorism Implementation Task Force, 'Summary and Conclusions Workshop on the Regional Implementation of the United Nations Global Counter-Terrorism Strategy in Southern Africa' (2011). See also Maza et al., *supra* note 16, at 8–11; Solomon, *supra* note 8, Ch. 6.

92 See also UN Secretary-General Report, Action taken by Member States and United Nations entities to address the issue of linkages between terrorism and organized crime, *supra* note 17, paras. 6, 108; UN Special Rapporteur, *supra* note 11; Counter-Terrorism Executive

inability is illustrated by the relatively low level of AU and AU member state participation in UN Security Council meetings addressing the links between terrorism and organized crime.[93]

More disconcerting, for some states the subject may be politically sensitive either because they have provided support to a group which is designated as a 'terrorist group' or be involved in or benefit from organized crime including crime committed by a terrorist group.[94] Therefore, states may not wish to see government officials' involvement in these phenomena become the subject of external scrutiny. In the current study, several participants explained that state officials of various rank have been involved criminal activities relating to drug and weapons trafficking, migrant smuggling and the exploitation of natural resources.[95] States have long resisted the creation of a treaty monitoring body or any form of formal follow-up in the text of treaties relating to terrorism and organized crime to monitor the efforts taken domestically to implement them. Indeed, it took a binding UN Security Council resolution, adopted under Chapter VII of the UN Charter, to create a Counter-Terrorism Committee of the Council mandated to monitor the national implementation of terrorism related treaties by all states.[96] Even then, the review process lacks transparency and national reports are not publicly available to avoid wider scrutiny independent of the Security Council. Following the establishment of the Counter-Terrorism Committee, the AU adopted a 'Protocol Relating to the Establishment of the Peace and Security Council of the African Union' which has a monitoring role in the implementation and harmonization of continental and international legal instruments relating to terrorism.[97] Yet, many AU

Directorate, 'Identifying and Exploring the Nexus Between Human Trafficking, Terrorism and, Terrorism Financing', *supra* note 17, at 7–9.

93 E.g., UNSC, 74th Year, 8569th Meeting, UN Doc. S/PV.8569 (9 July 2019); UNSC, 69th Year, 7351st Meeting, UN Doc. S/PV.7351 (19 December 2014).

94 Interview (Global Witness representative); Interviews (2 Global Initiative against Transnational Organized Crime representatives); Interviews (3 Institute for Security Studies representatives); Interview (UNICRI representative). See also Maza et al., *supra* note 16, at 10; C. Rose, 'The Creation of a Review Mechanism for the UN Convention Against Transnational Organized Crime and Its Protocols', 114 AJIL 51 (2020), at 64–65.

95 Interviews, *ibid.*; Interview (UNODC Regional Office for East Africa); Interview (UNODC Regional Office for West and Central Africa representative). See also UNODC, 'Transnational Organized Crime in West Africa: A Threat Assessment' (2013), at 9–10.

96 S/RES/1373 (2001), para. 6; SC/RES/1535 (2004). See also I. Roele, 'Disciplinary Power and the UN Security Council Counter Terrorism Committee', 19 J. CONFLICT & SEC. L. 49 (2013).

97 AU Protocol, Art. 2.

member states are unwilling and/or unable to submit annual reports to the Peace and Security Council.[98]

Conversely, states expressed strong resistance to the creation of a treaty monitoring body responsible for reviewing the implementation of the UNTOC. The monitoring body that was eventually created, some two decades after the adoption of the UNTOC, lacks transparency and is unable to substantially pressure or coerce states into improving compliance.[99] The resistance to UN Security Council encroachment in respect of national measures taken to counter organized crime is reflected during negotiations of the draft text of resolution 2482 as part of the Council's efforts to address the links between terrorism and organized crime.[100] In the original draft resolution circulated by Peru, a preambular paragraph stated that terrorism and organized crime have different motivations and applicable legal regimes but stressed that they should not be treated in isolation from each other. This paragraph was ultimately deleted as some Council members view organized crime as a law enforcement issue, the regulation of which is part of the internal affairs of states, and are wary of perceived Council encroachment if organized crime and the domestic implementation of the UNTOC were included as part of its counter-terrorism agenda. As a result, resolution 2482 omits any reference to the relationship between the legal regimes regulating terrorism and organized crime or the applicability of these regimes to the links between terrorism and organized crime.

The reluctance of states to share information regarding the links between terrorism and organized crime with researchers (or with each other and organizations such as the UN) is a common problem. For instance, in preparation for the development of the Hague Good Practices at the East Africa and Horn of Africa regional meeting, held in Nairobi, the representatives of only four AU member states participated in the meeting and only one of them provided some general observations about the links between terrorism and organized crime involving Al-Shabaab. In the West Africa and Sahel regional meeting, held in Algiers, the representative of only one AU member state participated in the meeting.

The elites who eventually agreed to an initial interview in the current study did so only after months of email exchanges. Gaining the trust of participants

---

98 Interviews (2 Institute for Security Studies representatives).

99 For a useful explanation of why the creation of a treaty monitoring body for UNTOC proved to be so controversial and some insights into the compromise ultimately struck by states party, see Rose, *supra* note 94.

100 S/RES/2482 (2019).

was essential for gaining access. The present author's positionality as an independent expert at the UN and the establishment of informal networks during the participation of various high-level meetings undoubtedly facilitated this process. In an effort to create a trusting relationship with participants, as well as alleviate concerns regarding personal security and privacy and encourage a detailed and candid account in discussion during interviews, participants were given reassurances both in email communications and in interview consent forms that anonymity would be a prerequisite for participation. Additionally, participants were sent a certificate of ethical approval, information about the research aims and an indicative agenda for the interviews. Participants were informed that interviews would be conducted under the Chatham House Rule and an audio-recording device would not be used. As a result, the information given by participants is not attributed by name. Moreover, participants were assured that confidential information would not be included in the current study.

Despite the measures taken to ensure participant safety, anonymity and confidentiality, some participants were more accessible than others. Conspicuously absent from the sample of participants is a representative of the AU. Interviews were originally planned with a view to speaking to AU representatives. Interview requests were repeatedly transmitted to 16 potential participants from several AU organs and departments, as well as the ACSRT and African Police Cooperation Mechanism.[101] In total, 14 of these participants chose not to respond to such requests, despite them being identified by other AU officials as relevant sources of information. At the start of the interview process, one official from the Policy Development Unit agreed to participate in an initial interview, but subsequently failed to attend the scheduled interview and all lines of communication ended without any explanation. Another official from the Peace and Security Council declined to participate in an interview and instead requested that a questionnaire be transmitted. However, the completed questionnaire was never returned, and all lines of communication abruptly ended.

The lack of AU participation in the current study is despite the AU Chairperson of the Commission on Terrorism and Violent Extremism in Africa highlighting, in 2014, that terrorism in Africa is influenced by the growing links

---

101 The relevant AU organs and departments include: Commission; Peace and Security Council; Department for Policy; Department for Political Affairs, Peace and Security; Department for Trade, Industry and Mining; Permanent Observer Mission of the AU to the UN; and Committee of Intelligence and Security Services of Africa.

with organized crime.[102] Since that time, the AU Peace and Security Council has adopted several *Communiqués* expressing 'deep concerns over the growing linkages between terrorism and transnational organized crime' and noting with 'serious concern the growing capacity of terrorist organizations in Africa to finance their activities by, among others, running criminal/illicit economies in areas under their control, engaging in illegal exploitation of, and trade in, natural resources, kidnaping for ransom, arms, drugs and human trafficking'.[103] However, the AU Commission has not taken any action in this regard. Several participants explained that the ACSRT, which serves as the technical arm of the AU with the purpose of conducting research and reviewing the continental counterterrorism legal framework, severely lacks resources to perform its designated role as international donors have withdrawn funding due to the ACSRT's inability to perform adequately.[104] It is likely that the AU does not wish to draw attention to its inaction or to become the subject of external scrutiny and criticism. Other participants explained that elites in the AU typically reflect the political attitude of its member states; and, for the same reasons explained above, such individuals are unwilling to discuss terrorism and organized crime because it would not be in the interest of many member states.[105]

2.3 *Limitations*

The primary limitations of the current study are (1) the relatively small sample size regarding participants from African states and the absence of AU representatives; (2) the quality of the data that could be included in the present study because it was deemed highly sensitive or confidential; and (3) the accuracy of the data provided by participants and their motivation for providing it is often difficult to ascertain. For these reasons, the data should be treated with caution. The selection of interview participants from a limited number of countries means that there will be perspectives that have been missed and raises issues about the generalizability of the data. The author sought to mitigate this limitation by including a diverse range of participants including

102 Report of the Chairperson of the Commission on Terrorism and Violent Extremism in Africa, *supra* note 21, para. (I)5.

103 *Communiqué* (2021), *supra* note 21, para. 2; Peace and Security Council, *Communiqué*, PSC/PR/COMM. (CMLXXV), 975TH Meeting, Ethiopia (27 January 2021), paras. 2, 4; *Communiqué* (2019), *supra note 21, para. 2.*

104 Interview (European External Action Service representative); Interviews (2 Global Initiative against Transnational Organized Crime representatives); Interview (2 Institute for Security Studies representative). See also Solomon, *supra* note 8, at 115.

105 Interviews (Global Initiative against Transnational Organized Crime representatives); Interview (Institute for Security Studies representative).

nonelite participants and those who challenged the status quo. The sample is representative of some of the sub-regions of Africa which are most affected by links between terrorism and organized crime and is sufficient to inform the evaluation of the applicability and effectiveness of AU legal instruments in countering aspects of this phenomenon. Unlike the Hague Good Practices, which are based on a smaller sample size than the present study, the data garnered from the sample is not intended to be generalized globally. The data are insufficient to measure in quantitative terms the density and scale of the links between terrorism and organized crime.

3 The AU Counterterrorism Framework

This part considers the principal legal instruments forming part of the AU's counterterrorism framework before providing a contextualized evaluation of the applicability and effectiveness of these instruments to the links between terrorism and organized crime in Africa. Since much has been written on these instruments, it suffices here to consider the definition of 'terrorist act' and the requirement of a special intent.[106]

3.1 *OAU Convention on the Prevention and Combating of Terrorism 1999*

Prior to the 1990s, the predecessor to the AU—the Organization of African Unity—had been silent on matters relating to terrorism.[107] Terrorist acts against African states escalated in number, frequency and sophistication in the 1990s, resulting in some high profile and mass casualty attacks such as the attempted assassination of President Mubarak of Egypt in 1995 and the Al Qaeda bombings of the United States embassies in Kenya and Tanzania in 1998, both of which involved alleged Sudanese complicity during Osama bin Laden's residence in Sudan from 1992 to 1995. The OAU responded by adopting the OAU

106 See, e.g., B. Saul, 'The Crime of Terrorism within the Jurisdiction of the African Court of Justice and Human and Peoples' Rights', in C.C. Jalloh et al. (eds.), *The African Court of Justice and Human and Peoples' Rights in Context* (2019), Ch. 15; M. Ewi and A. du Plessis, 'Criminal Justice Responses to Terrorism in Africa: The Role of the African Union and Sub-Regional Organizations', in A.M. Salinas, K.L.H. Samuel and N.D. White (eds.), *Counter-Terrorism: International Law and Practice* (2012), Ch. 36.

107 M. Ewi and A. du Plessis, 'Counter-terrorism and Pan-Africanism: From Non-Action to Non-Indifference', in B. Saul (ed.), *Research Handbook on International Law and Terrorism* (2014).

Convention, which remains the principal continental legislative instrument on preventing and combating terrorism in Africa.[108]

The OAU Convention was drafted by a sub-committee of the OAU Central Organ of the Mechanism for Conflict Prevention, Management and Resolution, comprising five states (Algeria as chair, Burundi, Namibia, Senegal and Tanzania), in collaboration with the OAU legal division.[109] At the time, Algeria was one of the few African states that had already enacted legislation criminalizing subversive and terrorist acts.[110] The drafting of the OAU Convention was, in turn, heavily influenced by Algeria's leadership.[111]

Article 1(3)(a) defines a 'terrorist act' as follows:

> [a]ny act which is a violation of the criminal laws of a State Party and which may endanger the life, physical integrity or freedom of, or cause serious injury or death to, any person, any number or group of persons or causes or may cause damage to public or private property, natural resources, environmental or cultural heritage.[112]

To constitute a terrorist act, the prohibited conduct must be 'calculated or intended to':

> (i) intimidate, put in fear, force, coerce or induce any government, body, institution, the general public or any segment thereof, to do or abstain from doing any act, or to adopt or abandon a particular standpoint, or to act according to certain principles; or
> (ii) disrupt any public service, the delivery of any essential service to the public or to create a public emergency; or
> (iii) create general insurrection in a State.[113]

---

108 OAU Convention, *supra* note 9.

109 H. Boukrif, 'Quelques commentaires et observations sur la Convention de l'Organisation de l'Unite africaine sur la Prevention et la Lutte Contre le Terrorism', 11 *African Journal of International and Comparative Law* 753 (1999).

110 Saul, *supra* note 106, at 413.

111 *Ibid.*

112 *Ibid.* The OAU Convention follows the Arab and OIC Conventions in referring to instilling fear in the public; endangering life, physical security or freedom; harming public or private property, or the environment; and endangering natural resources. The definition of terrorist act in the OAU Convention is replicated in the Protocol on Amendments to the Protocol on the Statute of the African Court of Justice and Human Rights, 27 June 2014, Art. 28G.

113 *Ibid.*, Art. 1(3)(a)(i)–(iii).

Terrorist acts are further defined to include various extended modes of criminal liability, including 'any promotion, sponsoring, contribution to, command, aid, incitement, encouragement, attempt, threat, conspiracy, organizing, or procurement of any person, with the intent to commit any act referred to' above.[114]

As discussed in the introduction, there is still no agreement on a definition of 'terrorism' in international law.[115] This is so despite episodic efforts by the UN since the 1960s through to the ongoing negotiations, since 2000, on a Draft Comprehensive Terrorism Convention.[116] The two fundamental problems afflicting attempts to establish a definition of terrorism in international law to this day are whether states can commit terrorism, and whether acts of violence committed by freedom fighters struggling against foreign aggression or an oppressive regime qualify as terrorism.[117] The 120 states who are members of the Non-Aligned Movement (whose membership includes African states and the AU as an observer organization), refuse to include in the legal concept of terrorism acts of violence committed by liberation and freedom fighters.[118] The exclusion of freedom fighters is based on unique historical experience regarding centuries of foreign control and colonialism and national anti-colonial and liberation struggles for independence.

The OAU Convention was able to circumvent the definitional problem in Africa by defining what conduct constitutes a 'terrorist act' rather than 'terrorism', while giving each state party discretion to determine, in accordance with its national law, precisely what crimes are included in the meaning of 'terrorist act'.[119] Underlying this approach is the rather simplistic idea that member states would align national legislation and practice with the Convention and each other in order to create harmonization. However, the empirical record suggests that this is not the case.[120] Additionally, Article 3(1) excludes from the definition of terrorist acts 'the struggle waged by peoples in accordance with the principles of international law for their liberation or self-determination,

114 *Ibid.*, Art. 1(b).

115 *R v. Gul*, [2013] UKSC 64, 18.

116 See, e.g., Sixth Committee Report, Measures to eliminate international terrorism, UN Doc. A/71/518 (11 November 2016).

117 A. Greene, 'Defining Terrorism: One Size Fits All?, 66 INT'L & COMP. L. Q. 411 (2017), at 413.

118 See also K.L.H. Samuel, *The OIC, the UN and Counter-Terrorism Law-Making: Conflicting or Cooperative Legal Orders?* (2013), at 233.

119 Conversely, other regional instruments relevant to African states contain wide and generic definitions of 'terrorism': OIC Convention, *supra* note 9; Arab Convention, *supra* note 46.

120 Interviews (3 Institute for Security Studies representatives).

including armed struggle against colonialism, occupation, aggression and domination by foreign forces'.[121] This exclusion exists despite Article 3(2) stating that '[p]olitical, philosophical, ideological, racial, ethnic, religious or other motives shall not be a justifiable defence against a terrorist act'. The exemption in Article 3(1) means that the OAU Convention could exclude the acts of some of the most violent terrorist groups in Africa, including well-organized and heavily armed groups who benefit, directly or indirectly, from organized crime, on the pretext that they are fighting for liberation or self-determination.[122]

Informed by Algeria's experience in the early 1990s, the OAU Convention includes in the definition of 'terrorist act' any act calculated or intended to intimidate or coerce a government to do or abstain from doing any act or 'create general insurrection in a State'. The latter offence is focused on protecting the government of a state party from rebellion, revolution or any other offences concerning challenges to a state's political authority or constitutional order. And no distinction is drawn between insurrection against democratic governments and those against authoritarian or repressive ones. Therefore, the OAU Convention gives a state party the discretion to exempt violence committed by freedom fighters when that party is facing 'occupation', 'aggression' or 'domination' by foreign forces (irrespective of whether such forces are state or non-state actors), on the one hand, and qualify the exact same violence as a 'terrorist act' if it is directed against the government in power, on the other. This interpretation of the OAU Convention is supported by the approach of a number of repressive African (and Middle East) states in the aftermath of the 'Arab Spring' and attempts—both successful and unsuccessful—to usher in internal regime change by various armed opposition groups. Additionally, there is no exclusion in the OAU Convention of conduct in armed conflict covered by international humanitarian law (IHL). The omission is significant because counterterrorism operations are frequently undertaken in the context of non-international armed conflicts in which IHL applies and non-state actors are designated by some governments or the UN as 'terrorist', leading to a potentially troubling conflation between the two legal regimes. One of the effects is that the activities of armed groups who are fighting against the government of a state party could be denied any of the protective norms of both IHL and international human rights law and, instead, criminalized as 'terrorist

121 The same exclusion clause is included in the OIC and Arab Conventions, *ibid.*, Arts. 2(a) and 2(a) respectively.

122 Saul, *supra* note 106, at 415.

acts'.[123] The application of terrorist acts in the OAU Convention to the conduct of a non-state actor in armed conflict could create a further undesirable disincentive to abide by IHL and impede post-conflict reconciliation.[124]

The discretion to designate groups as 'terrorist' and pick and choose which acts of violence are qualified as a 'terrorist act' may not result in neutral outcomes; rather, it has the potential to form an essential aspect of the misuse of counterterrorism law and undermine the range of ways that states must cooperate in preventing and countering acts of terrorism. These obligations require states, for instance, to refrain from the provision of funding and logistical support, including weapons and safe havens, to terrorists; the establishment of databases for the collection and exchange of information; and law enforcement cooperation in the investigation and extradition or prosecution of an alleged offender who is present on a state's territory.[125] The ability to exempt a group from the definition of terrorist acts also has important implications for operational responses to the links between terrorism and organized crime. Indeed, a state may even be willing to facilitate or at least tolerate the activities of a group who engage in or benefit from organized crime because of their designation as freedom fighters.

The operative provisions of the OAU Convention make no reference to the links between terrorism and organized crime. This is despite the preamble to the Convention expressing a determination to eliminate 'terrorism is all its forms and manifestations' and noting the 'growing links' between terrorism and organized crime, including arms and drug trafficking and money laundering.[126] The Convention's narrow emphasis on eliminating state funding and support of terrorist acts is important and understandable given the number of African states which had been accused, at the time, of providing various support and safe haven to terrorists. Nonetheless, the Convention glosses over the fact that some terrorist groups place reliance on organized crime in addition or as an alternative to states as a source of funding and logistical support. In this regard, a further important regulatory gap in the OAU Convention is

123 E.g., see Report of the Special Rapporteur on the Promotion and Protection of Human Rights and Fundamental Freedoms while Countering Terrorism, UN Doc. A/75/337 (3 September 2020).

124 B. Saul, 'Order from Chaos: The Optimal Relationship between International Counter-Terrorism Law and International Humanitarian Law', (forthcoming) International Review of the Red Cross (2021).

125 OAU Convention, *supra* note 9, Art. 4.

126 *Ibid.*, preambular para. 11.

terrorist financing including organized crime as a source of funding.[127] The OAU Convention was adopted in the same year as the UN Convention for the Suppression of the Financing of Terrorism (CTF Convention). It is unclear why the OAU Convention does not include acts criminalized in the CTF Convention. Given the widely held belief by national governments and international organizations that financing is a key requisite of terrorist activity, this omission represents a striking gap.

As part of the response to resolution 1373, adopted by the UN Security Council under Chapter VII of the UN Charter in reaction to the terrorist attacks on 11 September 2001, as well as the dire ratification and implementation of the OAU Convention, the AU adopted the Plan of Action in 2002.[128] The Plan of Action, among other things, acknowledged that terrorism exploits 'informal and illegal trade and financing networks' and requires states to 'take into consideration the intimate relationship between terrorism and related scourges such as drug trafficking, illicit proliferation and trafficking of small arms and light weapons, corruption and money laundering—all of which are variants of transnational organized crime'.[129] However, the Plan of Action does not provide for any actionable recommendations for the prevention and combating of the links between terrorism and organized crime.[130]

The AU Protocol 2004 to the OAU Convention was spurred in part by concerns about the slow domestic implementation of the Convention.[131] The Protocol creates no new offences, but aims to enhance the implementation of the OAU Convention and to coordinate and harmonize African efforts to prevent and combat terrorism.[132] States undertake to implement a range of measures on terrorist training and financing, mercenarism, weapons of mass destruction, preventing the entry of terrorists, and exchange of information and cooperation. Like the OAU Convention, the Protocol excludes any references in the operative provisions to the links between terrorism and organized crime. This is despite a preambular reference recognizing the growing threat of

127 Interviews (3 Institute for Security Studies representatives). See also UN Counter-Terrorism Implementation Task Force, *supra* note 91.

128 Plan of Action, *supra* note 10.

129 *Ibid.*, para. 10(d).

130 In order to implement the obligations in UN Security Council resolution 1373 (2001), the Plan of Action provides that states undertake to implement the CTF and introduce national legislation criminalizing the financing of terrorism.

131 Protocol to the OAU Convention on the Prevention and Combating of Terrorism 2004.

132 *Ibid.*, Art. 2. The Protocol tries to address a major weakness of the OAU Convention: its failure to include an implementation mechanism. The Protocol mandates the AU's Peace and Security Council to monitor and facilitate implementation.

terrorism in the continent and 'the growing risks of linkages between terrorism and mercenarism, weapons of mass destruction, drug trafficking, corruption, transnational organized crimes, money laundering, and the illicit proliferation of small arms'.[133] States have a general undertaking to detect, freeze and confiscate any funds or assets 'allocated for the purpose of the committing a terrorist act'; however, the Protocol does not mention, either directly or indirectly, the prevention and criminalization of the financing of individual terrorists or of terrorist groups in the absence of a link to terrorist acts.

The effectiveness of the Protocol in facilitating the harmonization of national legislation implementing the OAU Convention is open to question, given that the Protocol only entered into force in 2014 and at the time 41 AU member states had already ratified the Convention, while a number of important states which are actively fighting terrorism have not ratified the Protocol.[134] In an effort to stimulate the ratification of the OAU Convention and remedy the lack of harmonization in national legislation in the implementation of continental and international treaty obligations, at a 'soft' law level the AU adopted a 'Model Anti-Terrorism Model Law' (Model Law) in 2011.[135] The Model Law includes provisions relevant for combatting some of the links between terrorism and organized crime, including terrorist financing, the payment of ransom to terrorists and a broad offence when a person 'does anything which will, or is likely to enhance the ability of any entity to engage in a terrorist act, including to provide or offering to provide a skill or an expertise'.[136] However, the Model Law requires offences to be connected to the commission of a 'terrorist act' as defined in the OAU Convention. Moreover, the Model Law is significantly narrower in scope than the OAU Convention through the inclusion of an additional special terrorist intent requirement: namely, an act must be committed 'to advance a political, religious or ideological cause'.[137] Consequently, the Model Law may be inapplicable to many of the organized crime activities benefitting terrorist groups. And the Model Law's inclusion of an additional special intent requirement could inadvertently exacerbate the lack of national harmonization, not only in legislative practice but also in respect of the investigation

133 *Ibid.*, preambular para. 1.

134 E.g., CAR, Chad, DRC, Egypt, Kenya, Nigeria, Sierra Leone, Sudan, Uganda and Somalia. Interviews (2 Institute for Security Studies representatives).

135 See Decision on the Report of the Peace and Security Council on its Activities and the State of Peace and Security in Africa, Assembly of the African Union Decision 369 (XVII) (30 June–1 July 2011).

136 *Ibid.*, section 9.

137 *Ibid.*, section 4(xxxix). This motive element is drawn from the law in South Africa which, in turn, was replicated from the law in the UK.

and extradition or prosecution of suspects, depending upon whether member states decide to implement the special intent requirement contained either in the OAU Convention or the Model Law, or both, or neither of them.[138]

The breadth of the definition of 'terrorist act' in the OAU Convention and its extended modes of liability mean that the Convention is applicable to terrorist acts committed by both terrorist and organized crime or armed groups. Additionally, the Convention may be applicable to some organized crime activities, such as KFR or illegal taxation, providing that they also fulfil the constituent elements of a 'terrorist act' including the special intent requirement. However, one of the major themes emerging out of the interview data is that the Convention is both inapplicable and ineffective for combatting these links.[139] In particular, the Convention and its Protocol, as well as the Model Law, embrace the conventional assumption that terrorism and organized crime are conceptually and legally distinct phenomena, with differing motivations, and are subject to different legal regimes: terrorism is committed with the intent of causing fear among the population or to compel the government or an international organization to do or refrain from doing something, the aim of which is to further an underlying political or ideological goal. Conversely, organized crime focuses on financial and material gain. A terrorist group engages in organized crime, if at all, to raise the necessary funds required as a means to achieve its political or ideological goals, rather than the goal itself. According to this conventional view, the requirement of a special intent is needed to distinguish terrorism from ordinary crime and to prevent the unnecessary expansion and further widespread misuse and misapplication of exceptional counterterrorism law and practice.[140]

Yet, as discussed in the introduction, the distinction between terrorism and organized crime in Africa is blurred. The most powerful and resilient terrorist

---

138 Interview (Global Counterterrorism Forum Capacity-Building in the East Africa Region Working Group representative); Interview (Global Counterterrorism Forum Capacity-building in the West Africa Region Working Group representative); Interview (Institute for Security Studies representative); Interview (UNODC Regional Office for East Africa representative); Interview (UNODC Regional Office for West and Central Africa representative).

139 Interviews (3 Institute for Security Studies representatives); Interview (Kenya Anti-Terrorism Police Unit representative); Interviews (2 Kenya National Counter-Terrorism Centre representatives); Interview (Nigeria Complex Case Working Group within the Office of the Attorney-General of the Federation representative); Interviews (2 Nigeria National Counter Terrorism Centre representatives).

140 The UN Special Rapporteur on the Protection of Human Rights and Fundamental Freedoms while Countering Terrorism, UN Doc. A/61/267, para. 44 (16 August 2006); UN Special Rapporteur, *supra* note 11.

groups are financially and materially motivated; in addition to terrorist groups benefitting from organized crime financially, logistically or operationally in the commission of terrorist acts, they exploit and benefit from organized crime, both directly and indirectly, for a variety of other purposes ranging from subsistence and personal enrichment for individual members and their families, to the purchase of property, vehicles and travel, to the funding of licit business, to the provision of services such as health and education in territory under their influence or control, to the payment of corrupt state agents.[141] Additionally, terrorist groups are, with increasing frequency, successfully using funds generated from organized crime in order to recruit 'guns for hire' (foreign terrorist fighters and mercenaries) who are seeking financial and material gain rather than furthering a political or ideological goal.[142] As such, some of what is distinctive about terrorism—the requirement of a special intent—renders the AU counterterrorism framework potentially inapplicable to many of the links between terrorism and organized crime. Indeed, the criminal activities that benefit terrorist groups may be far removed from the commission of a terrorist act. The requirement of a special intent is, moreover, inconsistent with international approaches to countering terrorism.[143] It is perhaps for this reason that the UN Security Council has urged states to ratify and implement international instruments as a priority in order to address the links.[144]

From a law enforcement and prosecution perspective, there are practical problems in proving that the immediate aim of a terrorist group's criminal activity is to coerce or intimidate a government or part of the population, or that an act was committed to advance a political, religious or ideological cause. As one participant from law enforcement explained, 'in most instances, and absent confessional evidence, it would be difficult, if not impossible, to prove that a criminal activity, such as the trafficking of weapons or drugs or

141 Interviews (2 Global Initiative against Transnational Organized Crime representatives); Interviews (3 Institute for Security Studies representatives); Interview (International Crisis Group representative); Interviews (2 Kenya National Counter-Terrorism Centre representatives); Interview (Mali Specialized Judicial Unit to Combat Terrorism and Transnational Organized Crime representative); Interviews (2 Nigeria National Counter Terrorism Centre representatives); Interview (UNODC Regional Office for East Africa representative); Interview (UNODC Regional Office for West and Central Africa representative).

142 Interviews, *ibid.*

143 The vast majority of international treaties and binding UN Security Council resolutions relating to terrorism do not contain a special terrorist intent requirement (i.e., these offences do not require the prosecution to prove that the perpetrator committed the act with a terrorist purpose).

144 S/RES/2195 (2014), para. 3.

the taxation of criminal networks for safe passage, is connected to the commission of terrorism'.[145] The difficulty of establishing a special terrorist intent is compounded by difficulties in the collection of evidence located in remote areas or in the territory of neighbouring countries, combined with the lack of specialized training and expertise on the part of relevant state agencies.[146] A similar view was echoed by other participants.[147] It is precisely for this reason that alleged terrorists and affiliates who are involved in organized crime tend to be prosecuted (if at all) with offences unrelated to the OAU Convention that require little or no connection to future terrorist acts, thereby removing the burden of proving a special terrorist intent.[148]

Nonetheless, for some two decades the AU has stressed the relevance of the OAU Convention and its Protocol for the prevention and combating of terrorism in Africa, including the growing links between terrorism and organized crime, and reiterated its call for states to sign and ratify, without delay, these instruments.[149] In 2018 the AU Peace and Security Council adopted a *Communiqué* acknowledging for the first time, it would appear, *the* potential ineffectiveness of AU legal instruments in combatting the links between terrorism and organized crime.[150] Thus, the Peace and Security Council requested the AU Commission, through the ACSRT, to review the efficacy of

145 Interview (South Africa Directorate for Priority Crime Investigation participant).

146 *Ibid.* Interview (Global Counterterrorism Forum Capacity-Building in the East Africa Region Working Group representative); Interview (Global Counterterrorism Forum Capacity-building in the West Africa Region Working Group representative); Interview (UNODC Regional Office for East Africa representative); Interview (UNODC Regional Office for West and Central Africa representative).

147 Interview (Global Initiative against Transnational Organized Crime representative); Interview (Institute for Security Studies representative); Interview (Kenya Customs and Border Control representative); Interview (2 Kenya National Counter-Terrorism Centre representatives); Interview (Mali Bamako Court of Appeal representative); Interview (Mali Specialized Judicial Unit to Combat Terrorism and Transnational Organized Crime representative); Interview (Nigeria Complex Case Working Group within the Office of the Attorney-General of the Federation representative); Interview (Nigeria Federal High Court representative); Interview (Nigeria National Counter Terrorism Centre representative).

148 Interview (Institute for Security Studies representative); Interview (Kenya Anti-Terrorism Police Unit); Interview (Mali Specialized Judicial Unit to Combat Terrorism and Transnational Organized Crime representative); Interview (Nigeria Complex Case Working Group within the Office of the Attorney-General of the Federation representative); Interview (Nigeria Federal High Court representative); Interview (South Africa Directorate for Priority Crime Investigation participant); Interview (South African Police Service representative).

149 *Supra* note 21 and the sources cited therein.

150 *Communiqué (2018), supra note 21*, para. 15.

all continental legal instruments relating to the prevention and combating of terrorism, 'so as to make them also relevant in fighting the new methods and techniques of terrorist financing'; and that the Commission 'urgently' update the AU Plan of Action.[151] Since that time, however, the AU Commission has not undertaken any action in this regard.[152] The following year, the Peace and Security Council adopted a Communiqué expressing 'deep concern' over the growing threat posed by transnational organized crime to peace and security in Africa, 'particularly its increasingly direct linkages and collusion with terrorism' and 'the ability of terrorist organizations and other armed groups to finance their activities through criminal activities'; and urged states to ensure that necessary steps are taken to domesticate the UNTOC in the fight against transnational organized crime including the commission of such crime by terrorist groups.[153]

Therefore, the Peace and Security Council's Communiqués are underpinned by the twin (mistaken) assumptions that the links between terrorism and organized crime are purely financial and that the UNTOC is capable of targeting terrorist groups who benefit from transnational organized crime as a source of financing, thereby filling any regulatory gaps left by the OAU Convention. The extent to which terrorism can be effectively addressed through the UNTOC and its three protocols on human and trafficking and migrant smuggling has been little explored in scholarship. It is certainly true that the UNTOC could target transnational organized crime by terrorist groups in some contexts, when the immediate aim of the terrorist group's criminal activity is to obtain a financial or material benefit.[154] Both the preamble to the UNTOC and the General Assembly resolution adopting the UNTOC recognize the growing links between terrorism and transnational organized crime, indicating that some states were in favour of the instrument covering criminal activities committed by terrorist groups. Additionally, some scholars and the UN Special Rapporteur on the protection of human rights while countering terrorism have suggested

151 *Ibid.*, para. 15.

152 The Peace and Security Council repeated the same request in *Communiqué* (*2021*), *supra note 21*.

153 *Communiqué* (*2019*), *supra note 21*, para. 2. See also *Communiqué* (*2014*), *supra note 21, para. 16*.

154 Similarly, the CoE, *supra* note 17, suggests that 'terrorism is often a form of organised crime'; therefore, states should target terrorism by using the operational methods and legal instruments that already have proved to be effective in the fight against transnational organised crime.

that many of the criminal activities committed by terrorist groups can be substantially targeted and repressed under the UNTOC and its protocols.[155]

On the other hand, placing weighty reliance on the UNTOC to fill potential lacunae in the OAU Convention is problematic. The UN Security Council has made repeated references to the UNTOC, but it is apparent on close reading that its relevant resolutions do not adopt the terminology used in the UNTOC or express that the UNTOC is applicable for combatting the links between terrorism and organized crime.[156] The UNTOC regime does not capture some types of organized crime benefitting terrorist groups identified by the present study, such as the sourcing, manufacture and illicit traffic of light weapons, military grade materiel and IED components; KFR; the taxation of criminal networks for safe passage or of local communities and business; the traffic and supply of drugs; and the exploitation of natural resources. These and other criminal activities may also be purely domestic organized crime and, thus, fail to qualify as 'transnational in nature'. Likewise, some organized crime benefitting terrorist groups in Africa may not fulfil the specific intent requirement of a 'financial or other material benefit' that is central to the definition under the UNTOC. A terrorist group may benefit from organized crime for logistical or operational purposes. For instance, it is open to question whether a 'material benefit' would result from a terrorist group who engages in KFR with the aim of securing the release of imprisoned members, which has occurred on numerous instances in various AU member states in East and West Africa and the Sahel.[157] Similarly, a terrorist group who purchases military grade materiel or IED components intending that they are to be used against a rival group or to repel state security and defence forces may not satisfy UNTOC's material benefit requirement. The UNTOC regime certainly does not target organized crime organized crime by the 'shadow state' or public and private corruption which facilitate the links between terrorism and organized crime.[158]

---

155 UN Special Rapporteur, *supra* note 11, at 9–10; Schmid, *supra* note 6, at 13; Saul, *supra* note 11, at 3.

156 See also UN Special Rapporteur, *supra* note 11, at 6.

157 Interview (Institute for Security Studies representative); Interview (Nigeria National Counter Terrorism Centre representative). See also H. van der Wilt and C. Paulussen, 'The role of international criminal law in responding to the crime–terror nexus', 16 European Journal of Criminology 315 (2019), at 319.

158 Interview (1 Global Counterterrorism Forum Capacity-Building in the East Africa Region Working Group representative); Interviews (2 Global Counterterrorism Forum Capacity-building in the West Africa Region Working Group representatives); Interviews (2 Global Initiative against Transnational Organized Crime representatives); Interviews (3 Institute for Security Studies representatives). See also Izenman and Keatinge, *supra* note 26, at 13–18; Rose, *supra* note 87.

Ultimately, the UNTOC regime is only as effective in enhancing cooperation among states in combatting the links between terrorism and organized crime as its national implementation, the external and transparent monitoring and scrutiny of which has been resisted by states.[159] The UNTOC has been ratified by the majority of AU member states. There are indications, however, that the absence of a definition of 'organized crime' in the UNTOC has resulted in much disparity in national legislation and practice.[160] Additionally, the legislation of most AU member states does not criminalize 'organized crime'.[161] Often, domestic legislation regulating certain criminal activities is detached from terrorism. Hence, the UNODC suggests that, in order to strengthen the response to the links, as a priority the UNTOC and its three protocols should be 'better used' to promote more coherence between domestic anti-crime and counter-terrorism legislation.[162]

4 The Applicability and Effectiveness of the AU Counterterrorism Framework in Combatting Terrorism-Organized Crime Links in Africa

The final section of this chapter evaluates the applicability and effectiveness of the OAU Convention in preventing and combatting the links between terrorism and organized crime. As discussed in the introduction, effectiveness is measured based on the extent to which the OAU Convention provides a legal basis to facilitate coordinated practice according to two criteria: (1) harmonization in the criminalization of activity relating to the links between terrorism and organized crime and (2) the operation of the law 'on the ground' in terms of law enforcement cooperation in the investigation, prosecution and extradition of suspects. The evaluation is contextualized by reference to empirical

159 Part 2(B).

160 Interview (Global Initiative against Transnational Organized Crime representative); Interviews (2 Institute for Security Studies representatives); Interview (UNODC Regional Office for East Africa representative); Interview (UNODC Regional Office for West and Central Africa representative). See also L. Adal, 'Organized Crime in Africa: Weak Laws Make Tackling Organized Crime Harder', Institute for Security Studies (2018); A. Salinas de Frias, 'Report on links between Terrorism and Transnational Organized Crime', 2nd INTERNATIONAL CONFERENCE ON TERRORISM AND ORGANISED CRIME, Spain, at 3 (21–22 September 2017).

161 Interviews, *ibid.* However, some AU member states criminalize 'organized criminal activities'; e.g., Prevention of Organised Crimes, Act No. 6 of 2010 (Kenya).

162 UNSC, 74th Year, 8569th Meeting, UN Doc. S/PV.8569, at 3 (9 July 2019).

evidence of the following categories of organized crime which in practice benefit terrorists in Africa financially, logistically or operationally: weapons and ammunition (including small and light weapons and military grade materiel and IED components); KFR; illegal taxation; illicit traffic of humans and drugs; migrant smuggling; and exploitation of natural resources. In consideration of some of these categories, reference will also be made to two further types of organized crime, both of which enable and facilitate terrorist groups to benefit from organized crime: namely, public and private corruption and money laundering.

4.1 *Weapons*

One of the major themes emerging from the interview data is small and light weapons and ammunition and, with increasing frequency, military grade materiel, explosives and IED components, referred to collectively in the present context as 'weapons'. The manufacture, possession, illicit traffic, provision or receiving of training or technical expertise and use of weapons represents one of the most important links between terrorism and organized crime.[163] Terrorist groups in Africa are not generally involved in the illicit traffic of weapons as a source of funding.[164] Rather, the link between terrorism, organized crime and weapons has wider dimensions.

For instance, terrorist groups use weapons to gain and maintain control of territory and spheres of influence, including in the struggle for power against other terrorist and armed groups.[165] Similarly, terrorist groups use weapons in

---

163 In the present study, 'illicit traffic' has the same meaning as Article 3 of the UNTOC firearms protocol, *supra* note 44. Interview (European External Action Service representative); Interviews (3 Global Initiative against Transnational Organized Crime representatives); Interviews (3 Institute for Security Studies representatives); Interview (International Crisis Group representative); Interview (2 Kenya National Counter-Terrorism Centre representatives); Interview (Mali Bamako Court of Appeal representative); Interview (Mali Specialized Judicial Unit to Combat Terrorism and Transnational Organized Crime representative); Interview (Nigeria Complex Case Working Group within the Office of the Attorney-General of the Federation representative); Interviews (2 Nigeria National Counter Terrorism Centre representatives); Interview (South Africa Directorate for Priority Crime Investigation representative); Interview (UNODC Regional Office for East Africa representative); Interview (UNODC Regional Office for West and Central Africa representative).

164 Interviews, *ibid.* However, the members of some terrorist groups, such as AQIM, Boko Haram and Islamic State, engage in the illicit traffic of weapons for their own use and to supply allied or affiliated groups in exchange for training and technical expertise, *ibid.*

165 Interviews (3 Global Initiative against Transnational Organized Crime representatives); Interviews (3 Institute for Security Studies representatives); Interview (International Crisis Group representative); Interview (2 Kenya National Counter-Terrorism Centre

the fight with criminal networks over lucrative smuggling routes, contraband and the protection of convoys. These routes, which traverse porous and vast ungoverned spaces along borders, are used to smuggle across borders and sub-regions various commodities ranging from drugs and cigarettes, to vehicles and fuel, to weapons, food and migrants.[166] Terrorist groups are able to exploit the commodities that transit through these routes and generate revenue by taxing criminal networks for 'safe passage'.[167] For instance, several participants explained that it is 'impossible' for cocaine to transit through West and North Africa, sourced from Latin America and destined for Europe, without taxes being paid to terrorist groups.[168] As one of these participants explained, 'the ability to impose taxes on criminal groups smuggling illicit goods, particularly drugs, is how most terrorist groups in West Africa and the Sahel really make their money'.[169] In this regard, the AU Peace and Security Council has acknowledged that the control of cross-border smuggling routes means that terrorist groups in the Sahel are 'thriving' and gives them 'the capacity of regeneration'.[170] One of the most prominent terrorist groups in the Sahel is AQIM. Heavily armed AQIM operatives have the ability to continually tax smuggling routes in the Sahel, in paritucular the tri-border area between Algeria, Libya and

---

representatives); Interview (Mali Specialized Judicial Unit to Combat Terrorism and Transnational Organized Crime representative); Interviews (2 Nigeria National Counter Terrorism Centre representatives).

166 Interviews, *ibid.* Interview (UNODC Regional Office for East Africa representative); Interview (UNODC Regional Office for West and Central Africa representative). See also FATF-GIABA-GABAC, Terrorist Financing in West and Central Africa, *supra* note 11, at 19; Letter dated 15 February 2014 from the Panel of Experts on Libya established pursuant to resolution 1973 (2011) addressed to the President of the Security Council, UN Doc. S/2014/106, paras. 102, 113, 132, 136, 146 (19 February 2014); Letter dated 23 March 2012 from the Chairman of the Security Council Committee established pursuant to resolution 1970 (2011) concerning Libya addressed to the President of the Security Council, UN Doc. S/2012/178, paras. 29–32, 45 (26 March 2012).

167 Interviews, *ibid.*; Interview (European External Action Service representative). See also Twenty-fifth report of the Analytical Support and Sanctions Monitoring Team submitted pursuant to resolution 2368 (2017) concerning ISIL (Da'esh), Al-Qaida and associated individuals and entities, UN Doc. S/2020/53, paras. 29–30 (29 January 2020); W. Assanvo et al., 'Violent extremism, organized crime and local conflicts in Liptako-Gourma', Institute for Security Studies (2019), at 9; FATF-GIABA-GABAC, *ibid.*, at 21.

168 Interviews, *ibid.* See also P. Tinti, 'Drug Trafficking in Northern Mali: A Tenuous Criminal Equilibrium', ENACT Research Paper No. 14 (2020).

169 Interview (Global Initiative against Transnational Organized Crime representative). See also FATF, 'Emerging Terrorist Financing Risks' (2015), at 16.

170 Peace and Security Council Report on Mali and the Sahel and the Activities of the African Union Mission for Mali and the Sahel, *supra* note 24, para. 9.

Niger, as part of AQIM's operations.[171] In recent years, some terrorist groups in the Sahel have begun to 'invest heavily' in the supply of armed convoys, in return for payment, to ensure that goods are not attacked by rival groups.[172] In East Africa, heavily armed Al-Shabaab operatives employ a lucrative system of checkpoint taxation across both smuggling and transport routes in Somalia and at the territorial border with neighbouring countries. The group applies a rate of taxation based on the type of transiting vehicle and the goods carried (both licit and illicit).[173] Al-Shabab is able to maintain checkpoint taxation despite numerous air strikes by the United States.[174]

Weapons are also used by terrorist groups as an enabler of other criminal activities such as the imposition of illegal taxes on local communities and businesses, KFR, armed robbery and the illicit exploitation of natural resources.[175] The ability of terrorist groups to purchase or acquire weapons through organized crime is fuelling these and other criminal activities to the extent that illegal taxation and KFR are 'rampant' in Burkina Faso, Mali, Niger, Nigeria and Somalia.[176] The funding generated from these criminal activities, in turn, enables terrorist groups to purchase higher quantities of weapons and military

---

171 Twenty-fifth report of the Analytical Support and Sanctions Monitoring Team submitted pursuant to resolution 2368 (2017) concerning ISIL (Da'esh), Al-Qaida and associated individuals and entities, *supra* note 167.

172 Interview (Global Initiative against Transnational Organized Crime representative); Interview (Institute for Security Studies representative); Interview (International Crisis Group representative); Interview (Mali Specialized Judicial Unit to Combat Terrorism and Transnational Organized Crime representative); Interviews (2 Nigeria National Counter Terrorism Centre representatives).

173 Interview (Kenya Customs and Border Control representative); Interviews (2 Kenya National Counter-Terrorism Centre representatives).

174 Interviews (2 Kenya National Counter-Terrorism Centre representatives).

175 Interviews (2 Global Initiative against Transnational Organized Crime representatives); Interviews (3 Institute for Security Studies representatives); Interview (International Crisis Group representative); Interview (Kenya Customs and Border Control representative); Interviews (2 Kenya National Counter-Terrorism Centre representatives); Interview (Mali Specialized Judicial Unit to Combat Terrorism and Transnational Organized Crime representative); Interview (Mali Bamako Court of Appeal representative); Interview (Nigeria Federal High Court representative); Interviews (2 Nigeria National Counter Terrorism Centre representatives).

176 Interviews (2 Kenya National Counter-Terrorism Centre representatives); Interview (Mali Specialized Judicial Unit to Combat Terrorism and Transnational Organized Crime representative); Interviews (2 Nigeria National Counter Terrorism Centre representatives); Interview (UNODC Regional Office for East Africa representative); Interview (UNODC Regional Office for West and Central Africa representative). See also UN Secretary-General Report, Situation in Mali, UN Doc. S/2021/519, para. 43 (1 June 2021).

grade materiel and vehicles.[177] The circular flow of weapons, organized crime and funding is illustrated by Al-Shabaab. The group's annual operational expenditure in 2019 was approximately $21 million. Of that total, $16.5 million was allocated to Al-Shabaab's military and logistical support units, with 40 per cent of the funds allocated to the purchase of weapons and ammunition. These funds were generated primarily through illegal taxation and KFR.[178] In turn, Al-Shabaab has used these weapons to maintain and expand its areas of influence including a sophisticated and diversified system of illegal taxation.[179]

Remarkably, the OAU Convention does not address specifically the manufacture, possession, illicit traffic, provision or receiving of training or technical expertise and use of weapons, including when they are intended for the commission of a domestic or transnational terrorist act or organized crime activity. Additionally, the Convention does not address the various sources on which terrorist groups place reliance in order to obtain weapons, including the 'widespread' problem of illegal cross-border trade and transportation. For the past two decades, questions about how terrorist groups in Africa obtain weapons have generated speculation. The empirical evidence gathered by this study suggests that terrorist groups typically purchase or acquire weapons from criminal networks who specialize in the trade and supply of weapons from four main sources: (1) weapons recirculated from past and current armed conflicts; (2) weapons 'diverted' by governments both within and outside the continent; (3) weapons manufactured locally; and (4) weapons sold or rented by corrupt public officials in law enforcement and military services as well as the employees of private security companies.[180] In order to supply terrorist

177 Interviews, *ibid.*

178 Letter dated 28 September 2020 from the Panel of Experts on Somalia addressed to the Chair of the Security Council Committee pursuant to resolution 751 (1992) concerning Somalia, UN Doc. S/2020/949, para. 31 (28 September 2020).

179 Interviews (2 Kenya National Counter-Terrorism Centre representatives); Interview (UNODC Regional Office for East Africa representative).

180 Interviews (2 Global Counterterrorism Forum Capacity-Building in the East Africa Region Working Group representatives); Interviews (3 Global Counterterrorism Forum Capacity-building in the West Africa Region Working Group representatives); Interviews (2 Global Initiative against Transnational Organized Crime representatives); Interviews (3 Institute for Security Studies representatives); Interview (International Crisis Group representative); Interview (Interpol representative); Interviews (2 Kenya National Counter-Terrorism Centre representatives); Interview (Mali Specialized Judicial Unit to Combat Terrorism and Transnational Organized Crime representative); Interview (Mali Bamako Court of Appeal representative); Interview (Nigeria Federal High Court representative); Interviews (2 Nigeria National Counter Terrorism Centre representatives); Interview (UNODC Regional Office for East Africa representative); Interview (UNODC Regional Office for West and Central Africa representative). Although there are instances, for

groups with weapons, highly diversified and dynamic methods are used for moving weapons across national borders and a complex chain of intermediaries, ranging from the small 'ant trade', to large-smuggling, to professional transporters, who act for profit rather than the commission of a terrorist act.[181] In practice, therefore, it has proven difficult to distinguish people acting for profit and those associated with terrorism. Equally problematic is establishing that people have a special terrorist intent or even a link to a terrorist group, rendering the OAU Convention inapplicable.[182]

As a result, the Convention has not provided a legal basis to facilitate coordination in the criminalization of activity relating to the links between terrorism and organized crime in the context of weapons. Several participants explained that the existence and extent of the regulatory approaches of member states in criminalizing, inter alia, the manufacture, illicit traffic, obliteration of serial numbers and possession of different categories of weapons are rather divergent and sometimes outdated.[183] Some member states, such as Cameroon, criminalize the possession or use of 'weapons of war' but only if the accused has a special terrorist intent.[184] Additionally, most member states lack comprehensive legislation criminalizing light weapons, military grade materiel and IEDs, as well as public and private corruption as a facilitator in the sourcing

---

example, when individual police and military personnel in Nigeria and Somalia have sold weapons to terrorist groups, *ibid.* With increasing frequency, however, terrorist groups are mounting coordinated and violent attacks in order to steal weapons from state stocks (military bases, garrisons, barracks and outposts and police stations). See also Assanvo et al., *supra* note 167, at 9–11; GIABA Report, *supra* note 71, paras. 16–27; H. Kone, 'Where do Sahel terrorists get their heavy weapons?', Institute for Security Studies (2020).

181 Interviews, *ibid.* See also Final report of the Panel of Experts on Libya established pursuant to resolution 1973 (2011), UN Doc. S/2017/466, para. 180 (1 June 2017).

182 Interviews, *ibid.*; Interview (Kenya Anti-Terrorism Police Unit); Interview (Kenya Customs and Border Control representative); Interview (Nigeria Complex Case Working Group within the Office of the Attorney-General of the Federation representative); Interview (South Africa Directorate for Priority Crime Investigation representative).

183 Interview (Global Counterterrorism Forum Capacity-Building in the East Africa Region Working Group representative); Interview (Global Counterterrorism Forum Capacity-building in the West Africa Region Working Group representative); Interviews (2 Global Initiative against Transnational Organized Crime representatives); Interviews (2 Institute for Security Studies representatives); Interview (UNODC Regional Office for East Africa representative); Interview (UNODC Regional Office for West and Central Africa representative). See also UN Security Council Counter-Terrorism Committee, 'Global survey of the implementation of Security Council resolution 1373 (2001) and other relevant resolutions by Member States' (2021); GIABA Report, *supra* note 71, Ch. 5.

184 Law No. 2014/028 of 23 December 2014 on the Suppression of Acts of Terrorism in Cameroon (Cameroon).

and cross-border illicit traffic of weapons.[185] Likewise, the Convention is also ineffective in coordinating law enforcement cooperation among source, transit and destination countries from within and across different subregions in the investigation and extradition or prosecution of the actors involved.[186] In an effort to develop a comprehensive and harmonized approach across domestic legal systems with the aim of ensuring a more effective approach in countering terrorism, the UN Security Council's Counter-Terrorism Committee has included the assessment of legislative frameworks and their enforcement relating to weapons as part of its mandate in monitoring the domestic implementation of resolution 1373.[187]

Particularly problematic is the Convention's inapplicability to the illicit traffic of IED components (fertilizers, chemicals and explosives that are normally intended for farming, mining and commercial use) and the manufacture of IEDs including in 'logistical depots' used by terrorist groups.[188] The Convention's silence on such activity is striking given the prominence of IEDs as the 'weapon of choice' for terrorist groups in East and West Africa and the growing technical capability of these groups to manufacture them.[189] It is probably for this reason that the AU Peace and Security Council has recently adopted a *Communiqué* requesting member states to enact legislation and traceability control measures that include importation, movement, storage, distribution and use of materials and components used for making IEDs.[190] In the absence of a continental-wide instrument with adequate monitoring, however, national measures are likely to be deficient and haphazard.

185 Interview (Global Counterterrorism Forum Capacity-Building in the East Africa Region Working Group representative); Interview (Global Counterterrorism Forum Capacity-building in the West Africa Region Working Group representative); Interviews (2 Global Initiative against Transnational Organized Crime representatives); Interviews (2 Institute for Security Studies representatives); Interview (UNODC Regional Office for East Africa representative); Interview (UNODC Regional Office for West and Central Africa representative).

186 Interviews, *ibid.*

187 UN Security Council Counter-Terrorism Committee, Global survey of the implementation of Security Council resolution 1373 (2001) and other relevant resolutions by Member States, *supra* note 183.

188 Interview (Global Counterterrorism Forum Capacity-Building in the East Africa Region Working Group representative); Interview (Global Counterterrorism Forum Capacity-building in the West Africa Region Working Group representative).

189 Letter dated 28 September 2020 from the Panel of Experts on Somalia addressed to the Chair of the Security Council Committee pursuant to resolution 751 (1992) concerning Somalia, *supra* note 178, para. 44.

190 *Communiqué (2021), supra note 21.*

4.2 *Kidnapping for Ransom* (*KFR*)

Terrorist and criminal groups across Africa are, with increasing frequency, engaging in KFR.[191] According to participants, KFR is a thriving 'business model' in countries such as Cameroon, Burkina Faso, Mali, Mauritania, Niger, Nigeria and Somalia and one of the most important, if not the single main source, of terrorist funding.[192] Little information is known about the ransom payments, including the number of successful ransoms, the amounts paid, the conditions of the ransoms and the manner in which the money is transferred to kidnappers and through whom.[193] Generally, states are unwilling to disclose such information or even acknowledge that ransom payments are made at all.[194] Partly with the aim of 'profile-raising', the AU adopted a Decision to combat the payment of ransom to terrorist groups and contributed to the Algiers Memorandum on Good Practices on Preventing and Denying the Benefits of Kidnapping for Ransom by Terrorists, issued by the Global Counterterrorism Forum.[195] Similar to some of the Global Counterterrorism Forum's other 'soft law' initiatives, which are developed with little transparency,[196] the UN Security Council subsequently began the process of transposing the Algiers Memorandum into more formal and binding law. Thus, in resolution 2133 the Council expressed concern that 'ransom payments to terrorist groups are one of the sources of income which supports their recruitment efforts, strengthens

191 Interview (Global Counterterrorism Forum Capacity-Building in the East Africa Region Working Group representatives); Interview (Global Counterterrorism Forum Capacity-building in the West Africa Region Working Group representative); Interviews (2 Institute for Security Studies representatives); Interviews (2 Kenya National Counter-Terrorism Centre representatives); Interview (Mali Bamako Court of Appeal representative); Interview (Mali Specialized Judicial Unit to Combat Terrorism and Transnational Organized Crime representative); Interview (Nigeria Federal High Court representative); Interviews (2 Nigeria National Counter Terrorism Centre representatives); Interview (UNODC Regional Office for East Africa representative); Interview (UNODC Regional Office for West and Central Africa representative). See also FATF Report, 'Terrorist Financing in West Africa' (2013); FATF-GIABA-GABAC, Terrorist Financing in West and Central Africa (2016).

192 Interviews, *ibid.* See also UNSC, 69th Year, 7351st Meeting, UN Doc. S/PV.7351 (19 December 2014).

193 FATF-GIABA-GABAC, Terrorist Financing in West and Central Africa, *supra* note 191.

194 Interviews (3 Institute for Security Studies representatives). See also A. Shortland and T. Keatinge, 'Closing the Gap: Assessing Responses to Terrorist-Related Kidnap-for-Ransom', RUSI Occasional Papers (2017).

195 Global Counterterrorism Forum, 'Algiers Memorandum on Good Practices on Preventing and Denying the Benefits of Kidnapping for Ransom by Terrorists' (2012).

196 Report of the Special Rapporteur on the promotion and protection of human rights and fundamental freedoms while countering terrorism, UN Doc. A/74/335 (29 August 2019).

their operational capability to organize and carry out terrorist attacks, and incentivizes future incidents of kidnapping for ransom'.[197] To that end, it stressed states' obligations under sanctions regimes and in resolution 1373 to prevent terrorist financing and thus called upon states to 'prevent terrorists from benefiting directly or indirectly from ransom payments or from political concessions'.[198] In resolution 2195, the Council went one step further and intimated that the safe release of hostages kidnapped by terrorists without ransom payments or political concessions is in accordance with international law.[199] Nonetheless, KFR is increasing in East and West Africa and the Sahel and terrorist groups continue to raise substantial funds in this way.[200] And the profits generated have transformed some terrorist groups into major military forces.[201]

The OAU Convention does not address KFR. However, the Convention could be indirectly applicable to KFR in circumstances where an act of kidnaping fulfils the constituent elements of a terrorist act. That is to say, it would need to be proven that the kidnapping endangers the life, physical integrity or freedom of any person and is intended to 'intimidate' or 'put in fear' a segment of the public or to induce a government to do or abstain from doing any act. For instance, Al-Shabaab, Boko Haram and the Lord's Resistance Army engage in kidnapping for purposes of forced recruitment, child soldiers, servitude, sexual slavery, as well as for political concessions such as the release of imprisoned members (in parituclar members in leadership roles) and the provision of logistical equipment such as vehicles, fuel and food.[202] As one participant explained,

197 S/RES/2133 (2014), para. 7.

198 *Ibid.*, paras. 1–3.

199 S/RES/2195 (2014), preliminary para. 19.

200 Interview (Global Counterterrorism Forum Capacity-Building in the East Africa Region Working Group representatives); Interviews (2 Global Counterterrorism Forum Capacity-building in the West Africa Region Working Group representatives); Interviews (2 Global Initiative against Transnational Organized Crime representatives); Interviews (3 Institute for Security Studies representatives).

201 Interviews, *ibid.*

202 Interviews, *ibid.*; Interview (Kenya Anti-Terrorism Police Unit); Interview (Kenya Customs and Border Control representative); Interviews (2 Kenya National Counter-Terrorism Centre representatives); Interview (Nigeria Federal High Court representative); Interview (Nigeria Complex Case Working Group within the Office of the Attorney-General of the Federation representative); Interviews (2 Nigeria National Counter Terrorism Centre representatives); Interview (UNODC Regional Office for East Africa representative); Interview (UNODC Regional Office for West and Central Africa representative). See also FATF-GIABA-GABAC, Terrorist Financing in West and Central Africa, *supra* note 191, at 17–18. Al-Shabaab also kidnaps influential Somali clan elders governing parts of Somalia who resist promulgating Al-Shabaab doctrine and assist in recruiting new members,

in 2014 Boko Haram kidnapped 276 female students from a school in town of Chibok in Borno State, Nigeria. Most of the captives were subjected to servitude, forced labour, and sexual slavery (including through forced marriages to Boko Haram members). The gradual release of some of the captives involved the exchange of five imprisoned Boko Haram leaders in addition to the payment of $3.7 million USD in ransom money.[203] As such kidnappings place local populations in 'constant fear' or are intended to induce a government to act in a parituclar way, the OAU Convention would, prima facie, be applicable to such activity. Nonetheless, the instrument has failed to coordinate the practice of AU member states in the criminalization and the investigation and extradition or prosecution of suspects involved this type of criminal activity.[204]

The OAU Convention is inapplicable, it would appear, to circumstances where a terrorist group engages in kidnapping (in parituclar foreign and Western nationals) for the purpose of fundraising. It is open to question whether such activity would establish the OAU Convention's requisite special terrorist intent. For instance, Al-Shabaab has an expansive and well-resourced network of cells across East Africa aimed at complex kidnapping operations against foreign and Western nationals. Al-Shabaab cells operating in countries such as Djibouti, Ethiopia, Kenya, Tanzania and Uganda are responsible for gathering local intelligence and planning and coordinating operations; they are given wide discretion and autonomy, including the selection of the target.[205] However, such activities are driven by economic motives.[206]

Equally problematic is the extent to which the OAU Convention would be applicable to situations where a criminal network or a contractor or subcontractor conducts the kidnapping operation and a terrorist group has limited or no involvement and benefits indirectly, such as receipt of a share of the profit

Twenty-fifth report of the Analytical Support and Sanctions Monitoring Team submitted pursuant to resolution 2368 (2017) concerning ISIL (Da'esh), Al-Qaida and associated individuals and entities, *supra* note 167.

203 Interview (Nigeria National Counter Terrorism Centre representative).

204 Interviews (2 Global Counterterrorism Forum Capacity-Building in the East Africa Region Working Group representatives); Interview (Global Counterterrorism Forum Capacity-building in the West Africa Region Working Group representative); Interview (Mali Specialized Judicial Unit to Combat Terrorism and Transnational Organized Crime representative); Interviews (2 Nigeria National Counter Terrorism Centre representatives); Interviews (2 Kenya National Counter-Terrorism Centre representatives).

205 Letter dated 28 September 2020 from the Panel of Experts on Somalia addressed to the Chair of the Security Council Committee pursuant to resolution 751 (1992) concerning Somalia, *supra* note 178, para. 137.

206 Interviews (2 Global Counterterrorism Forum Capacity-Building in the East Africa Region Working Group representatives).

or the payment of taxes.[207] Kidnappings can also be complex: a kidnapping may be conducted by a contractor in one country and the ransom paid to an intermediary in second country, while the terrorist group may have its base of operations in a third country; and it is often difficult to link kidnappings to a parituclar terrorist group or 'follow the money' it may receive from an intermediary.[208] For instance, in Nigeria armed groups (known colloquially as 'bandits', 'kidnap gangs' or 'militias', who are comprised of various criminal networks, Fulani herdsmen and Hausa farmers) have adopted Boko Haram's tactic of KFR because it is so lucrative. In some circumstances, bandits plan and conduct kidnapping operations while Boko Haram's role, in return for a share of the profit, includes claiming responsibility or releasing videos in order to negotiate higher ransoms.[209] As one participant explained, in 2020 a group of bandits kidnapped more than 300 children from a school in Katsina, Northern Nigeria; Boko Haram subsequently released a video claiming responsibility, despite having no direct involvement in the kidnapping.[210] AQIM uses local criminal networks as subcontractors including outsourcing the seizure of hostages to criminal actors to mitigate the risk for their members and extract the highest possible price.[211] Al-Shabaab 'permits' local criminal networks who operate in territory under its control to conduct KFR through the imposition of taxes, as can be seen, for instance, by the surge of maritime piracy between 2008 and 2012 off the coast of Somalia.[212] Al-Shabaab's involvement with piracy is complex and contested in scholarship.[213] For instance, Petrich suggests that there are no credible reports that Al-Shabaab has taken to the seas itself.[214] However,

207 Interviews (2 Institute for Security Studies representatives).

208 Interviews (2 Global Counterterrorism Forum Capacity-Building in the East Africa Region Working Group representatives); Interviews (2 Global Counterterrorism Forum Capacity-building in the West Africa Region Working Group representatives); Interview (Mali Specialized Judicial Unit to Combat Terrorism and Transnational Organized Crime representative); Interviews (2 Nigeria National Counter Terrorism Centre representatives); Interviews (2 Kenya National Counter-Terrorism Centre representatives).

209 Interviews (2 Nigeria National Counter Terrorism Centre representatives).

210 Interview (Nigeria National Counter Terrorism Centre representative).

211 Interview (Global Counterterrorism Forum Capacity-building in the West Africa Region Working Group representative); Interview (Mali Specialized Judicial Unit to Combat Terrorism and Transnational Organized Crime representative). See also Keatinge and Danner, *supra* note 16, at 461; Letter dated 23 March 2012 from the Chairman of the Security Council Committee established pursuant to resolution 1970 (2011) concerning Libya addressed to the President of the Security Council, *supra* note 166, para. 47.

212 Interview (Global Counterterrorism Forum Capacity-Building in the East Africa Region Working Group representative).

213 Levy and Yusuf, *supra* note 8, at 2.

214 Petrich, *supra* note 8, at 14.

several participants confirmed that, rather than executing any significant command and control over the operations, Al-Shabaab approaches pirate clans in the same way as it addresses all other revenue generating activity within its area of influence: by taxing those involved, based on the sums they negotiate from foreign governments and private shipping and insurance companies.[215]

The inapplicability of the OAU Convention to such complex activity, combined with the difficulty of establishing the constituent elements of a terrorist act, has resulted in the Nigerian Senate considering the Terrorism Prevention (Amendment) Bill 2021.[216] The Bill seeks to criminalize anyone who transfers funds, makes payment or colludes with an abductor, kidnapper or terrorist to receive any ransom for the release of any person who has been wrongfully confined, imprisoned or kidnapped. Unlike the OAU Convention, the Bill proposes to criminalize any act of payment of ransoms to secure the release of kidnapped persons, without the need for any connection with terrorism or the need for actual or constructive knowledge on the part of the payer.[217] However, the Bill, if enacted, is likely to be frustrated in its application to the cross-border investigation and prosecution of alleged offences, as other AU member states have not criminalized the same behaviour.

4.3 *Illegal Taxation*

A further major theme emerging from the interview data is illegal taxation.[218] As discussed above, terrorist groups extort criminal networks by taxing smuggling routes. Additionally, they tax local communities and businesses. For instance, in Mali the imposition of taxes on local businesses and communities by groups such as AQIM, Ansar Adine and MUJAO is 'rampant', particularly as the groups occupy swathes of territory in the Douentza, Gao and Ménaka regions.[219] Boko Haram extorts businesses in Nigeria and neighbouring Burkina

215 Interviews (2 Global Counterterrorism Forum Capacity-building in the West Africa Region Working Group representatives); Interviews (2 Kenya National Counter-Terrorism Centre representatives). See also Levy and Yusuf, *supra* note 8, at 2; Petrich, *ibid.*; Report of the Chairperson of the Commission on Terrorism and Violent Extremism in Africa, *supra* note 21, para. 13.

216 Interviews (2 Nigeria National Counter Terrorism Centre representatives).

217 *Ibid.*

218 In this context, illegal taxation and extortion are synonymous given that terrorist groups in control of a territory have no recognised legal authority to levy taxes.

219 Interview (Mali Specialized Judicial Unit to Combat Terrorism and Transnational Organized Crime representative); Interview (UNODC Regional Office for West and Central Africa representative).

Faso, Cameroon, Chad and Niger.[220] The most critical factor contributing to Al-Shabaab's resilience is the continuous expansion of sophisticated extortion and taxation systems, providing the group with a secure revenue base and generating a significant budgetary surplus.[221] The group's taxation methods extend beyond the areas in which it has a geographical presence and range in complexity (sometimes with Somali and Kenyan soldiers acting as facilitators), including checkpoint taxation across main transport routes in the country; the taxation of imports and exports, both licit and illicit; the taxation of property on households, businesses, shops, markets, agriculture and livestock; the taxation of flight tickets; and forced zakat collection.[222] Mimicking Al-Shabaab, the Islamic State faction in Somalia has begun a concerted campaign to impose taxes on individuals and businesses in Puntland, using extortion tactics similar to those employed by Al-Shabaab.[223] For instance, the group successfully extorted a Puntland-based telecommunications company into making a payment totalling several hundred thousand USD.[224]

The OAU Convention does not address the provision or collection of funds through the imposition of illicit taxes in order to fund an individual terrorist or a terrorist group, including as a precursor offence when the funds are not linked to the commission of a terrorist act.[225] Likewise, the Convention does not target individuals from within local communities, tribes and clans on

---

220 Interviews (2 Global Counterterrorism Forum Capacity-building in the West Africa Region Working Group representatives); Interview (Nigeria Complex Case Working Group within the Office of the Attorney-General of the Federation representative); Interviews (2 Nigeria National Counter Terrorism Centre representatives).

221 Letter dated 28 September 2020 from the Panel of Experts on Somalia addressed to the Chair of the Security Council Committee pursuant to resolution 751 (1992) concerning Somalia, *supra* note 178.

222 Interviews (2 Global Counterterrorism Forum Capacity-Building in the East Africa Region Working Group representatives); Interviews (2 Kenya National Counter-Terrorism Centre representatives). See also Twenty-fifth report of the Analytical Support and Sanctions Monitoring Team submitted pursuant to resolution 2368 (2017) concerning ISIL (Da'esh), Al-Qaida and associated individuals and entities, supra note 167, para. 39.

223 Letter dated 27 September 2019 from the Panel of Experts on Somalia addressed to the Chair of the Security Council Committee pursuant to resolution 751 (1992) concerning Somalia, UN Doc. S/2019/858, para. 59 (2019).

224 *Ibid.*

225 In order to combat terrorist financing, UN Security Council resolution 1373 requires all states to criminalize participation in the financing of a terrorist act, a terrorist organization or an individual terrorist, whether funds derive from a legitimate or illegitimate source and without requiring proof of a link to a specific terrorist act. Technical guide to the implementation of Security Council resolution 1373 (2001) and other relevant resolutions, UN Doc. S/2019/998, paras. 37–48 (2019).

whom terrorist groups place reliance as intermediaries to act as informants, gather intelligence and collect payments on their behalf.[226] Additionally, the Convention overlooks the laundering of proceeds generated from illegal taxation. For example, Boko Haram and Al-Shabaab invest funds generated from taxation in various licit enterprises, including in businesses and property.[227] As a result, the Convention could only be applicable to illicit taxation when a terrorist group threatens or uses violence to enforce compliance and the constituent elements of a terrorist act are fulfilled. Participants highlighted that the Convention has not provided AU member states with a legal basis to promote and coordinate the criminalization of illegal taxation and the laundering of proceeds, or the extradition or prosecution of suspects.[228] Rather, member states have criminalized, to varying degrees, any means of providing or collecting funds (which is sufficiently broad to include illegal taxation) pursuant to the implementation of international legal obligations, namely the Terrorist Financing Convention and UN Security Council resolution 1373. However, the legislative practice of member states is divergent in this regard particularly with respect to funds requiring a link to a specific terrorist act.[229]

4.4 *Illicit Traffic and Smuggling: Humans and Drugs*

In scholarship, the link between terrorism and human trafficking and migrant smuggling is contested.[230] The present study found a lack of empirical evidence to draw a general finding that terrorist groups in Africa engage in human trafficking and migrant smuggling. However, several participants confirmed

226 Interviews (2 Global Counterterrorism Forum Capacity-Building in the East Africa Region Working Group representatives); Interviews (2 Global Counterterrorism Forum Capacity-building in the West Africa Region Working Group representatives); Interviews (2 Kenya National Counter-Terrorism Centre representatives).

227 Interviews, *ibid.*; Interview (Nigeria Complex Case Working Group within the Office of the Attorney-General of the Federation representative); Interviews (2 Nigeria National Counter Terrorism Centre representatives).

228 Interviews, *ibid.*

229 Interviews (2 Global Counterterrorism Forum Capacity-Building in the East Africa Region Working Group representatives); Interviews (2 Global Counterterrorism Forum Capacity-building in the West Africa Region Working Group representatives); Interview (UNODC Regional Office for East Africa representative); Interview (UNODC Regional Office for West and Central Africa representative). See also Global survey of the implementation of Security Council resolution 1373 (2001) and other relevant resolutions by Member States, *supra* note 191.

230 In the present study, human trafficking and migrant smuggling are defined in the same way as the relevant UNTOC protocols, *supra* note 44. See also L.I. Shelley, 'Illicit Trade and Terrorism', 14 Perspectives on Terrorism 7 (2020); Smith, *supra* note 11; FATF-GIABA-GABAC, Terrorist Financing in West and Central Africa, *supra* note 191, at 24.

that trafficking in persons and smuggling of migrants from Sub-Saharan Africa to Libya are profitable and resilient business models and generate funding for all of the actors involved along the entire chain of operations, including state agents. Terrorist groups in the Sahel are not directly involved in such activities; however, they benefit indirectly through the exaction of passage taxes and provision of protection services to the smugglers' convoys against payment.[231] The UNODC estimates that migrant smuggling from West to North Africa generates $760 million to $1.1 billion USD per annum, indicating a potentially lucrative revenue stream for any groups able to tax smuggling routes.[232]

The OAU Convention does not address terrorist groups who engage in or generate funding from the trafficking in persons or the smuggling of migrants. This regulatory gap is compounded by the Convention failing to capture the involvement of state agents who may enable and facilitate these criminal activities. Moreover, the trafficking in persons and the smuggling of migrants are not considered criminal behaviour in many local communities: they are merely ways of life which provide economic benefit.[233] Therefore, the Convention is ineffective in coordinating the practice of AU member states in combatting the link between terrorism and these types of criminal activity. In recent years, several AU member states have criminalized the trafficking in persons as part of the implementation of UNTOC's human trafficking protocol.[234] A total of 22 member states criminalize migrant smuggling in the implementation of

---

231 Interviews (Global Counterterrorism Forum Capacity-building in the West Africa Region Working Group representative); Interview (Global Initiative against Transnational Organized Crime representative); Interviews (2 Institute for Security Studies representatives). See also Letter dated 5 September 2018 from the Panel of Experts on Libya established pursuant to resolution 1973 (2011) addressed to the President of the Security Council, UN Doc. S/2018/812, para. 48 (2018).

232 Twenty-fifth report of the Analytical Support and Sanctions Monitoring Team submitted pursuant to resolution 2368 (2017) concerning ISIL (Da'esh), Al-Qaida and associated individuals and entities, *supra* note 167, para. 30.

233 Interview (Global Initiative against Transnational Organized Crime representative); Interview Institute for Security Studies representative). See also T. Reitano and M. Shaw, 'People's perspectives of Organized Crime in West Africa and the Sahel', Institute for Security Studies (2014).

234 E.g., Organic Law No. 2016-61 on the Prevention of Trafficking in Persons (Tunisia); Law No. 006/PR/2018 on Combatting Trafficking in Persons (Chad); Trafficking in Persons (Prohibition), Enforcement and Administration Act 2015 (Nigeria); Law No. 2012-023 on the Fight Against Trafficking in Persons and Associated Practices (Mali); Law No. 2011/024 relating to the Fight against Trafficking in Persons and Slavery (Cameroon); Ordinance No. 2010-86 of 2010 on the Fight Against Trafficking in Persons (Niger); Act No. 029-2008/AN on the Fight against Trafficking of Persons and Similar Practices (Burkina Faso).

UNTOC's migrant smuggling protocol.[235] However, domestic laws relating to human trafficking and migrant smuggling tend to be severed from terrorism and organized crime, as well as public corruption which may enable and facilitate these activities. Unlike the OAU Convention, there is no requirement in the UNTOC's protocols to establish extraterritorial criminal jurisdiction and extradite or prosecute alleged offenders. As a result, the extraterritorial ambit of domestic laws in order to combat cross-border criminal activity is rather divergent and limited. Therefore, it is unclear the extent to which such laws may be applicable to terrorist groups that facilitate, engage in or benefit from human trafficking or migrant smuggling, either domestically or transnationally. In any event, some participants suggested that enacting legislation to criminalize human trafficking and migrant smuggling enables certain AU member states, particularly those who are transit countries, to give the appearance of compliance with international treaty obligations, while masking their inability or unwillingness to cooperate in the investigation and prosecution of those who engage in or benefit from such activity, including terrorist groups.[236] For instance, as a transit country and a major hub for migrant smuggling, Niger was the first country in the Sahel to adopt legislation criminalizing this illegal activity. Yet, Nigerien authorities have made relatively few arrests and initiated even fewer prosecutions.[237]

Human trafficking and migrant smuggling are often integrated with other criminal activities, including the illicit traffic of drugs.[238] Similar to the trafficking in humans and the smuggling of migrants, the OAU Convention does not address terrorist groups who engage in or generate funds from the production,

235 L. Bird, 'Criminalization of human smuggling in Africa', ENACT Policy Brief (2020).

236 Interview (Global Initiative against Transnational Organized Crime representative); Interview Institute for Security Studies representative).

237 Interview (Global Initiative against Transnational Organized Crime representative).

238 Interview (Global Counterterrorism Forum Capacity-Building in the East Africa Region Working Group representative); Interview (Global Counterterrorism Forum Capacity-building in the West Africa Region Working Group representative); Interviews (2 Global Initiative against Transnational Organized Crime representatives); Interviews (2 Institute for Security Studies representatives); Interview (Mali Bamako Court of Appeal representative); Interview (Mali Specialized Judicial Unit to Combat Terrorism and Transnational Organized Crime representative); Interviews (2 Kenya National Counter-Terrorism Centre representatives). In the present study, 'illicit traffic' means the offences set forth in Article 3 of the 1988 UN Convention against Illicit Traffic in Narcotic Drugs and Psychotropic Substances, 1582 UNTS 95, while 'drugs' refers to narcotic drugs and psychotropic substances, whether natural or synthetic, in the 1961 Single Convention on Narcotic Drugs, as amended by the 1972 Protocol Amending the Single Convention on Narcotic Drugs, 976 UNTS 105, and the 1971 Convention on Psychotropic Substances 1019 UNTS 175.

manufacture, possession or illicit traffic of drugs. Additionally, the Convention does not capture individual terrorists or terrorist groups who convert funds generated from drugs into financial assets or moveable or immovable property such as weapons and vehicles. Such activity will not normally fulfil the constituent elements of a terrorist act. As a result, the Convention does not coordinate the practice of member states in the criminalization of relevant behaviour or cooperation in the investigation and extradition or prosecution of alleged offenders when drugs have a transnational dimension. Most AU member states have ratified the 1988 UN Convention against Illicit Traffic in Narcotic Drugs and Psychotropic Substances.[239] However, several participants suggested that there is a need for greater harmonization of domestic laws as well as law enforcement cooperation, particularly as the legislative and prosecutorial practice of many member states treat the illicit traffic of drugs and terrorism as distinct and unrelated phenomena.[240] More concerning, some participants explained that certain member states fundamentally have no interest in the criminalization of drug trafficking; and even when they do criminalize this activity, they are unwilling to investigate and extradite or prosecute alleged offenders because of the potentially large economic benefits.[241]

The extent of the link between terrorism and drugs in Africa is a source of controversy in scholarship. For instance, Lacher suggests that the notion of a 'drug-terror nexus in the Sahel is misleading'.[242] According to Lacher, some of the members within MUJAO and AQIM are involved in drug trafficking rather than direct group involvement as such.[243] Numerous other actors, facilitated by corrupt public officials, play a more important role in drug trafficking.[244] In the present study, participants confirmed that Africa is both a transit and destination hub for drugs, and that the link between terrorism and drugs manifests in three discernible dimensions.

---

239 *Ibid.*

240 Interview (Global Counterterrorism Forum Capacity-Building in the East Africa Region Working Group representative); Interview (Global Counterterrorism Forum Capacity-building in the West Africa Region Working Group representative); Interview (2 Institute for Security Studies representatives).

241 Interview (Global Counterterrorism Forum Capacity-Building in the East Africa Region Working Group representative); Interview (Global Counterterrorism Forum Capacity-building in the West Africa Region Working Group representative); Interviews (2 Global Initiative against Transnational Organized Crime representatives); Interviews (2 Institute for Security Studies representatives).

242 Lacher, *supra* note 14, at 3.

243 *Ibid.*, at 5. See also FATF-GIABA-GABAC, Terrorist Financing in West and Central Africa, *supra* note 191, at 20.

244 *Ibid.*, at 8.

The most common of these dimensions comprises terrorist groups such as AQIM, Ansar Dine, MUJAO, Boko Haram, ISWAP and Al-Shabaab benefitting indirectly from drug trafficking by forcing criminal networks to pay 'transit taxes' and 'protection fees' to pass through territory under their control and influence.[245] For instance, in 2009 a US District Court charged three Malian nationals for providing material support for terrorism. The defendants agreed with an undercover US Drug Enforcement Administration agent posing as a FARC representative to transport shipments of cocaine through West and North Africa and arrange protection from AQIM. In return for protection, the defendants agreed to provide property, currency, and monetary instruments to AQIM.[246] West Africa is a major transit region in the international cocaine trade: cocaine from South America enters carefully chosen parts of the region by boat and plane, and is then conveyed northwards towards the Mediterranean and Europe.[247] Taliban-controlled production of heroin in Afghanistan is transported to markets through various export routes, generating the Taliban an annual income of at least $400 million USD and representing the group's most significant source of income.[248] Major trade routes have opened up in Eastern and Southern Africa to facilitate the heroin trade: Taliban

245 Interview (EU Counter-Terrorism Coordinator representative); Interview (European External Action Service representative); Interview (Global Counterterrorism Forum Capacity-Building in the East Africa Region Working Group representative); Interview (Global Counterterrorism Forum Capacity-building in the West Africa Region Working Group representative); Interviews (2 Global Initiative against Transnational Organized Crime representatives); Interviews (3 Institute for Security Studies representatives); Interview (Kenya Customs and Border Control representative); Interviews (2 Kenya National Counter-Terrorism Centre representatives); Interview (Mali Specialized Judicial Unit to Combat Terrorism and Transnational Organized Crime representative); Interviews (2 Nigeria National Counter Terrorism Centre representatives); Interview (UNODC Regional Office for East Africa); Interview (UNODC Regional Office for West and Central Africa representative). See also P. Tinti, 'Drug Trafficking in Northern Mali: A Tenuous Criminal Equilibrium', *ENACT Research Paper* (2020); Assanvo et al., *supra* note 167, at 12; Reitano and Shaw, *supra* note 233, at 12; Saul, supra note 11, at 435.

246 FATF Report, TERRORIST FINANCING IN WEST AFRICA, *supra* note 191, at 26–27.

247 Interview (Global Counterterrorism Forum Capacity-building in the West Africa Region Working Group representative); Interview (Global Initiative against Transnational Organized Crime representatives); Interviews (2 Institute for Security Studies representatives); Interview (Mali Specialized Judicial Unit to Combat Terrorism and Transnational Organized Crime representative); Interviews (2 Nigeria National Counter Terrorism Centre representatives); Interview (UNODC Regional Office for West and Central Africa representative).

248 Letter dated 10 June 2019 from the Chair of the Security Council Committee established pursuant to resolution 1988 (2011) addressed to the President of the Security Council, UN Doc. S/2019/481, para. 26 (2019).

and Al Qaeda operatives transport heroin to Pakistan; from there, the heroin is shipped by criminal networks to the African continent and transported to markets in Africa and Europe.[249] The heroin is repackaged and commonly transported by individuals from ethnic, tribal and nomadic communities who have knowledge of smuggling routes and vast areas of desert.[250] Al-Shabaab and Islamic State operatives in East Africa facilitate the transportation of heroin across the Sahara by offering protection in exchange for money. And it is estimated that up to 40 percent of the heroin sold in Europe is trafficked through East Africa.[251] The illicit traffic of drugs may in some instances be facilitated by public corruption at every level of authority (ranging from high-ranking members of government, to law enforcement, customs and border enforcement and the military).[252] The extent of state involvement in drug trafficking in Africa varies from direct involvement to officials who are, at the very least, complicit and willing to 'look the other way'.[253]

The second dimension between terrorism and drugs comprises individuals and cells within some terrorist groups, rather than the groups as such, that are directly involved in the illicit traffic of drugs. For instance, some members of Islamic State in Libya finance themselves and their activities primarily by smuggling drugs from Chad, Niger and Sudan across the borders with Libya; the drugs are then transferred to armed groups in Libya who have control and influence over ports for onward travel to Europe.[254] Members of MUJAO

---

249 Interview (Global Counterterrorism Forum Capacity-Building in the East Africa Region Working Group representative); Interviews (2 Global Initiative against Transnational Organized Crime representatives); Interviews (2 Institute for Security Studies representatives); Interview (Kenya Customs and Border Control representative); Interviews (2 Kenya National Counter-Terrorism Centre representatives); Interview (South Africa Directorate for Priority Crime Investigation representative); Interview (UNODC Regional Office for East Africa). See also S. Haysom, P. Gastrow and M. Shaw, 'The Heroin Coast: A Political Economy Along the Eastern African Seaboard', ENACT Research Paper (2018).

250 Interviews, *ibid.*

251 Interviews, *ibid.*

252 Interviews, *ibid.* See also Izenman and Keatinge, *supra* note 26, at 14; House of Commons Foreign Affairs Committee, 'The UK's response to extremism and instability in North and West Africa', Seventh Report of Session 2013–14, para. 23 (it is widely acknowledged that Guinea-Bissau is a major landing point for drugs and a country permeated at almost every official level by the corrupting effect of trafficked cocaine from South America. In Mali, it is alleged that the former government had, at the very least, tolerated the presence of international drug traffickers on its soil); UNODC, 'Transnational Organized Crime in West Africa: A Threat Assessment' (2013), at 9–10.

253 Interview (Global Initiative against Transnational Organized Crime representative).

254 Interview (UNODC Regional Office for West and Central Africa representative). See also Final report of the Panel of Experts on Libya established pursuant to Security Council resolution 1973 (2011), UN Doc. S/2021/229, para. 13 (2021).

finance themselves by trafficking drugs across West Africa.[255] Boko Haram members facilitate criminal networks trafficking cocaine and heroin across Nigeria, Niger and Chad.[256] In 2015, nine (alleged) AQIM members travelling from Libya in new 4x4 vehicles and carrying weapons, ammunition and cash amounting to EUR 539,000 were arrested in Niger. The investigation revealed that they had sold drugs in Libya and used the proceeds to purchase these items.[257]

The most recent dimension of the link between terrorism and drugs is terrorist groups who are the consumers of synthetic drugs. For instance, in 2017 Italian police seized 37 million tablets of Tramadol worth $75 million in three shipping containers travelling from India and due for onward shipment to Libya.[258] The drugs had been purchased by the Islamic State in Libya and were intended for two purposes: to help finance Islamic State operations and for use by its members as a stimulant and to heighten resistance to physical stress.[259] Boko Haram fighters ingest Tramadol (including by feeding the drug to child soldiers) in order to numb their fear when undertaking terrorist attacks and engaging in organized crime activities such as KFR, robbery and the seizure of weapons from the Nigerian army.[260] Al-Shabaab are using drugs as an incentive in order to recruit new fighters and supporters from Kenya, Ethiopia, Sudan and Tanzania.[261]

4.5 *Natural Resource Exploitation*

The final major theme emerging from the interview data is the ability of some terrorist groups to generate funds or procure logistical supplies (such as food

---

255 Interview (Global Counterterrorism Forum Capacity-building in the West Africa Region Working Group representative); Interview (Institute for Security Studies representative); Interview (Mali Bamako Court of Appeal representative); Interview (Mali Specialized Judicial Unit to Combat Terrorism and Transnational Organized Crime representative).

256 Interviews (2 Nigeria National Counter Terrorism Centre representatives); Interview (UNODC Regional Office for West and Central Africa representative).

257 FATF-GIABA-GABAC, Terrorist Financing in West and Central Africa, *supra* note 191, at 19–20.

258 Interview (UNODC Regional Office for West and Central Africa representative). See also R. Santacroce, E. Bosio, V. Scioneri and M. Mignore, 'The New Drugs and the Sea: The Phenomenon of Narco-Terrorism', 51 International Journal of Drug Policy, 51 (2018) 67–68.

259 Interview, *ibid.*

260 Interview (Nigeria National Counter Terrorism Centre representative).

261 Interviews (2 Global Counterterrorism Forum Capacity-Building in the East Africa Region Working Group representatives); Interviews (2 Global Witness participants); Interviews (2 Kenya National Counter-Terrorism Centre representatives); Interview (Tanzania National Counter Terrorism Center representative).

and medicine, weapons and ammunition, vehicles and fuel and communication equipment) by the illicit exploitation, both direct and indirect, of natural resources.[262] Natural resources include deforestation, charcoal production, precious stones, metals and minerals, wildlife products and endangered species.[263] One notable example is the illegal poaching of rhinoceros and elephant. The extent of the involvement of terrorist groups in wildlife poaching is contested in scholarship due to the lack of empirical data and the difficulty in gathering relevant evidence.[264] In the present study, several participants confirmed that, for decades, the Lord's Resistance Army and the Sudanese-backed Janjaweed militia have poached rhinoceros and elephant across Central Africa for 'bushmeat' and ivory.[265] The bushmeat is sold to local communities, a trade that has long been recognized as a major threat to biodiversity in Central and West Africa.[266] Ivory operates as 'currency', which is either sold or exchanged for money, weapons and vehicles with criminal networks, armed groups and state military personnel.[267] On the other hand, Al-Shabaab is not involved directly in poaching wildlife, but, rather, imposes taxes on poachers who reside in or transit through Al-Shabaab-controlled territory and acts as an intermediary in the illicit ivory trade, utilizing its regional networks to smuggle ivory to

262 The exploitation of natural resources by non-state armed groups is not new; for instance, Al-Qaeda has been involved in the rough diamond trade in Sierra Leone and Liberia since the 1990s, Interview (Global Witness representative). In 1998, the UN Security Council imposed sanctions to prohibit the import of conflict diamonds from Angola, Sierra Leone and Liberia, and endorsed the 2002 Kimberley Process Certification Scheme and later imposed it on Liberia. The Council also banned timber exports from Liberia in 2003. GIABA Report, *supra* note 71, at 27–28.

263 See also Shelley, *supra* note 230, at 8; Saul, supra note 11, at 441; FATF-GIABA-GABAC, Terrorist Financing in West and Central Africa, *supra* note 191, at 11, 19, 23.

264 T. Maguire and C. Haenlein, 'An Illusion of Complicity: Terrorism and the Illegal Ivory Trade in East Africa', RUSI Occasional Paper (2015).

265 Interviews (2 Global Counterterrorism Forum Capacity-building in the West Africa Region Working Group representatives); Interview (Global Witness representative); Interviews (2 Institute for Security Studies representatives); Interviews (2 Kenya Wildlife Agency representatives); Interview (Tanzania Wildlife Agency representative); Interview (UNODC Regional Office for West and Central Africa representative). See also Poaching and Terrorism: A National Security Challenge, House Hearing, 114 US Congress (22 April 2015).

266 Interviews, *ibid.*

267 Interview (Global Witness representative); Interviews (2 Institute for Security Studies representatives); Interview (Kenya Wildlife Agency representative); Interview (Tanzania National Task Force Anti-Poaching representative); Interview (UNODC Regional Office for West and Central Africa representative). See also Report of the Chairperson of the Commission on Terrorism and Violent Extremism in Africa, *supra* note 20, para. 15.

Asian countries.[268] Corruption among public officials in institutions charged with the protection of wildlife and at border crossings and ports, particularly in Kenya, Tanzania and Somalia, is facilitating the ability of terrorist groups to benefit from poaching and the transportation of ivory across borders and out of continent.[269]

Another example is Al-Shabaab's exploitation of illicit logging and cross-border trade in charcoal. In addition to sugar and livestock, the taxation of charcoal exports, in violation of the Security Council ban, represents significant revenue stream for Al-Shabaab.[270] The charcoal is produced by local communities and, thereafter, is sold to Somali-based businesses which are part of transnational criminal networks that transport the charcoal to neighbouring Kenya or by sea to Kuwait, Iran, Iraq, Oman and the United Arab Emirates using falsified paperwork and front companies.[271] The charcoal is then repackaged and sold for domestic consumption or trans-shipped to neighbouring countries in the Middle East. In its 2018 report, the Monitoring Group on Somalia and Eritrea estimated Somali charcoal exports around 3 million bags or $150 million USD wholesale value.[272] Since that time, there is a lack of evidence to suggest that any major exports of charcoal from Somalia have occurred. However, the production and stockpiling of charcoal in Somalia, worth more than $40 million USD in wholesale value and export ready, is ongoing; and the transnational criminal networks involved in the trade remain active.[273] While Al-Shabaab maintains a diversified revenue base and is not financially dependent on the charcoal trade, the stockpiles represent an immediate risk as a future export would result in a substantial financial inflow to the group.[274]

The OAU Convention does not address terrorist groups that benefit from the exploitation of natural resources, including corrupt practices among public

268 Interview (Global Counterterrorism Forum Capacity-Building in the East Africa Region Working Group representative); Interview (Kenya Wildlife Agency representative).

269 Interviews, *ibid.*; Interview (Tanzania National Task Force Anti-Poaching representative).

270 SC/RES/2498 (2019), para. 23.

271 Interview (Global Counterterrorism Forum Capacity-Building in the East Africa Region Working Group representative).

272 Letter dated 2 October 2018 from the Monitoring Group on Somalia and Eritrea addressed to the Chair of the Security Council Committee pursuant to resolutions 751 (1992) and 1907 (2009) concerning Somalia and Eritrea, UN Doc. S/2018/1002 (2018).

273 Letter dated 28 September 2020 from the Panel of Experts on Somalia addressed to the Chair of the Security Council Committee pursuant to resolution 751 (1992) concerning Somalia, UN Doc. S/2020/949 (2020), para. 146.

274 Interview (Global Counterterrorism Forum Capacity-Building in the East Africa Region Working Group representative); Interviews (2 Kenya National Counter-Terrorism Centre representatives).

officials and private entities. The Convention could be indirectly applicable to terrorist groups that commit acts of violence, which amount to a terrorist act, against a segment of the population or state authorities in the exploitation of natural resources. For instance, heavily armed terrorist groups threaten or use violence against state authorities in poaching activities or the transportation of ivory.[275] Similarly, the Convention could be applicable to terrorist groups that use violence to challenge and displace state authorities and gain control of artisanal mining sites across East, West and Central Africa for the illicit mining and cross-border trade and transportation in gold, diamonds and precious metals.[276] Terrorist groups are seeking to control such sites in order to act as 'managers', 'regulators' and 'facilitators' of illegal activities through the sale of mining licences, the imposition of taxes on miners and criminal networks who serve as conduits in the illicit trade of materials, and the supply of chemicals and explosives used in the mining process.[277] Terrorist groups also take a share of the mined materials, which can be sold or exchanged for logistical equipment and subsistence.[278] For instance, AQIM and MUJAO operating in the Sahel have conducted several attacks against security and customs posts in Western Mali, which accounts for an estimated 77% of Mali's gold production, in order to gain control over mining sites in the region.[279] JNIM operatives have launched attacks against state security forces in gold mining sites in Senegal.[280] The Macina Liberation Front, which is allied with Ansar Dine, has established in the border areas between Burkina Faso, Niger, Benin and Togo, with the aim of taking over the management of numerous artisanal gold mines.[281] Terrorist

275 Interview (Global Counterterrorism Forum Capacity-Building in the East Africa Region Working Group representative).

276 Interview, *ibid.*; Interview (Global Counterterrorism Forum Capacity-building in the West Africa Region Working Group representative); Interviews (2 Global Witness representatives); Interviews (3 Institute for Security Studies representatives); Interview (Mali Specialized Judicial Unit to Combat Terrorism and Transnational Organized Crime representative); Interviews (2 Nigeria National Counter Terrorism Centre representatives); Interview (UNODC Regional Office for East Africa); Interview (UNODC Regional Office for West and Central Africa representative).

277 Interviews, *ibid.* See also Assanvo et al., *supra* note 167, at 16.

278 Interviews, *ibid.*

279 Interview (Mali Specialized Judicial Unit to Combat Terrorism and Transnational Organized Crime representative). See also UN Secretary-General Report, Situation in Mali, UN Doc. S/2021/519, para. 59 (2021).

280 Interview (Global Counterterrorism Forum Capacity-building in the West Africa Region Working Group representative); Interviews (3 Institute for Security Studies representatives).

281 Interviews, *ibid.*

groups in Burkina Faso and Niger have attacked and overwhelmed state security and defence forces from mining areas and filled the vacuum as 'security providers' and 'managers' for the mines.[282] However, the Convention would not capture corrupt activities on the part of public officials who exchange illicitly mined resources for weapons and ammunition, or the activities of public officials and legal entities that facilitate the illicit cross-border transportation, sale and laundering of such resources benefiting terrorist groups. For instance, the European Parliament has estimated that billions of USD worth of gold is smuggled out of the Sahel region every year by criminal groups. The United Arab Emirates acts as a major trading hub that receives, processes and launders African gold.[283] In turn, the revenue from gold smuggling is funding some terrorist groups in Africa who manage mining operations.[284] These groups are able to launder the money through the purchase of property and investment in licit business enterprises.[285]

Several participants suggested that the OAU Convention has not coordinated the legislative and law enforcement practice of member states in countering terrorist groups that exploit natural resources.[286] Most member states regulate wildlife, hunting and mining, but domestic laws are not harmonized, and they do not adequately criminalize these activities or provide for law enforcement cooperation. Relatedly, domestic laws are territorial in application and, thus, are inapplicable to cross-border activity. Moreover, domestic laws do not generally treat natural resource exploitation as a form of serious or organized crime or as having links with terrorism. With the exception of initiatives such as the AU Regional Task Force Against the Lord's Resistance Army, most member states are unwilling or unable to conduct law enforcement operations and cooperate with each other in countering natural resource exploitation.[287]

---

282 Interviews, *ibid.*

283 European Parliament, resolution of 16 September 2020 on EU-African security cooperation in the Sahel region, West Africa and the Horn of Africa (2020/2002(INI)).

284 Interview (Global Counterterrorism Forum Capacity-building in the West Africa Region Working Group representative); Interviews (3 Institute for Security Studies representatives).

285 Interviews, *ibid.*

286 Interviews, *ibid.*; Interview (UNODC Regional Office for West and Central Africa representative).

287 Interviews, *ibid.*

5 Conclusion

This study has empirically demonstrated some of the most significant links between terrorism and organized crime in East and West Africa and the Sahel. These categories of organized crime, which may be domestic or transnational, include the illicit sourcing, manufacture and traffic of weapons, ammunition and IED components; KFR; illegal taxation of local communities and business; the illicit traffic of people and drugs; the smuggling of migrants; and the exploitation of natural resources. These organized crime activities benefit individual terrorists and terrorist groups, both directly and indirectly, either financially, logistically, or operationally. Additionally, there is evidence to suggest that terrorist groups exploit two further types of organized crime, both of which are enablers and facilitators of organized crime: namely, public and private corruption and money laundering. This study has further empirically demonstrated that the AU's legal instruments relevant for combatting terrorism, in particular the OAU Convention, are largely inapplicable to these links. These empirical findings are significant for two principal reasons. First, the ability of terrorist groups to benefit from these categories of organized crime have long been unclear and contested in scholarship due to the lack of empirical data. Second, the AU has consistently maintained, absent any evidence, that the OAU Convention provides a sound legal basis to facilitate and promote coordinated and effective action against terrorism and its links with organized crime.

The limited relevance of the OAU Convention is because the instrument does not criminalize and combat organized crime or its links with terrorism. Since its adoption, the Convention has deliberately excluded organized crime, including public and private corruption which may enable and facilitate organized crime, from its purview; and the instrument has failed to keep pace with the evolving modi operandi of terrorist groups in this regard. Moreover, the Convention requires, as a core focus, proof of a special terrorist intent in the definition of acts of terrorism. If activities lack the necessary *terrorist* intent, it cannot be considered as terrorism under the Convention. As a result, terrorist acts within the context of the Convention are intended to be distinguished from other types of crime, including organized crime, a distinction that is accentuated by the Model Law which additionally requires terrorist acts to advance a 'political, religious or ideological cause'.[288] Notably, the special intent element of a 'political, religious or ideological cause' was drawn from

288 According to the Model Law, *supra* note 135, para. xxxix, a terrorist act must be intended 'to intimidate the public or any section of the public or compel a government or

common law jurisdictions, in particular South Africa, and is inconsistent with international treaties and UN Security Council resolutions regarding terrorism. This special intent element was originally included in South African law based on the wording of a UK Terrorism Bill.[289] In recent years, South Africa has considered the amendment of this requirement because some terrorist actors lack the requisite mental element and also due to practical implications for law enforcement and prosecutorial authorities.[290]

The rather narrow and somewhat outdated focus of the OAU Convention and the inaction of the AU in the formulation of an appropriate policy and review of the effectiveness of existing legal instruments to combat the links is not a neutral outcome: many AU member states lack the willingness and/or capacity to combat certain types of organized crime. In some circumstances, organized crime can also be beneficial to member states and individual state agents of every rank. The AU, it would appear, merely reflects the political will of its member states.[291] As has been shown, the AU and many of its member states are not even willing to share information with each other (or the present author) regarding the links between terrorism and organized crime due to a lack of trust and the desire to avoid external scrutiny. The AU Peace and Security is aware, it would appear, of the limited efficacy of the OAU Convention for combatting the links; however, the AU Commission, which reflects the views of member states, has yet to implement its decisions in this regard. Thus, there is a degree of tension and discord, it would appear, between the Peace and Security Council and the Commission. In the words of one participant, 'the AU does not know to what extent terrorist groups are involved in or benefit from organized crime, or the effectiveness of the [OAU] Convention. The AU cannot begin to solve potential problems until it is willing to understand them'.[292]

international organization to do or refrain from doing any act and to advance a political, religious or ideological cause'.

289 South African Law Commission, Review of Security Legislation (Terrorism: Section 54 of the Internal Security Act 1982) (2000).

290 The special intent requirement was ultimately retained in South African legislation: the Protection of Constitutional Democracy against Terrorist and Related Activities Amendment, Act, 2022, section 1(r) defines 'terrorist activity' as any act which committed 'directly or indirectly, in whole or in part, for the purpose of the advancement of an individual or collective political, religious, ideological or philosophical motive, objective, cause or undertaking'.

291 The Fragile States Index (FSI) shows that in 2021, out of the 25 top fragile states in the world, 18 were located in Africa (Fund For Peace, 2021). The Corruption Index shows that in 2020, out of the 25 top corrupt states in the world, 14 were located in Africa; Transparency International, Corruption Perceptions Index (2020).

292 Interview (Institute of Security Studies representative).

As this study has shown, the OAU Convention could capture certain types of organized crime benefitting terrorist groups indirectly, as long as the constituent elements of a terrorist act are fulfilled and proven, including the special intent requirement. However, most organized crime is committed independent of a terrorist act or it is difficult to prove that the alleged offender acted with a special terrorist intent. Even in circumstances where the Convention could be applicable to terrorist groups that are involved in or benefit from organized crime, the Convention is not being utilized by member states.

In this regard, the OAU Convention is ineffective in preventing and combatting the links between terrorism and organized crime. The Convention is failing to promote harmonized and coordinated practice in the domestic criminalization of terrorist acts and behaviour relevant to the links between terrorism and organized crime, a problem that is exacerbated by the broad discretion given to member states allowing for disparities in the underlying harmful conduct that may be included as terrorist acts. The multiplicity of different domestic approaches to understanding, defining and criminalizing terrorist acts, organized crime and the links between these phenomena frustrates and inhibits the operation of the law 'on the ground' in terms of law enforcement cooperation in the investigation, prosecution and extradition of suspects among the member states that are willing to combat terrorism and organized crime.[293] Some member states are cooperating to facilitate the investigation, extradition and prosecution of terrorist suspects;[294] however, they are not utilizing the OAU Convention as a legal basis.[295] While some member states are unwilling to implement the law enforcement provisions of the Convention, others evade them by using counterterrorism powers and methods that violate international human rights law. The ineffectiveness of the Convention has two broader implications for the international community. First, as the epicentre of the links between terrorism and organized crime globally, terrorist groups in Africa are resilient and their activities have a direct impact on states both inside and outside the continent. Second, UN Security Council resolutions and the Hague Good Practices relevant to combatting the links, which are based on the underlying assumption that states are willing and able to cooperate including by sharing information in this regard, are likely to be undermined.

---

293 See also J.T. Omenma, 'African Union Counterterrorism Frameworks and Implementation Trends among Member States of the East African Community', 76 India Quarterly 103 (2020).

294 E.g., *US v. Alhassane Ould Mohamed*, 148 F. Supp. 3d 232 (E.D.N.Y. 2015).

295 Interviews (3 Institute for Security Studies representatives).

In the light of these empirical findings, it is proposed that the AU Commission, as a first step, adopt a policy addressing the links. As a priority, the Commission should revise the OAU Convention including the legal definition of 'terrorist act' and the constituent element of terrorist intent to prevent its potential misuse and encourage member states to comply with their international law obligations, on the one hand, and to encompass domestic and transnational organized crime activities that benefit individual terrorists and terrorist groups, on the other. The Convention could, for example, include organized crime (both domestic and transnational) in the definition of terrorist act or introduce a separate offence of organized crime activities connected with a terrorist act. Criminal activities that benefit terrorism should be clearly and concisely defined in order to facilitate harmonization in domestic law. Additionally, criminal activities should be included as a precursor offence, in order that it is not necessary to establish the actual attempt or commission of a terrorist act and no final target needs to be specified. The Convention should capture public and private corruption as an enabler and facilitator of the links. In turn, organized crime activities would be regulated by the Convention's mandatory provisions relating to the criminalization of the relevant behaviour and extradition or prosecution of alleged offenders.

Of course, the inclusion of organized crime in the OAU Convention would greatly expand the definition of terrorist act. It is understandable that such a move would be objected to by many, not least the UN Special Rapporteur on the promotion and protection of human rights while countering terrorism, on the basis that overly broad definitions of terrorism are essential for the serious and systematic misuse and misapplication of counterterrorism law.[296] However, in Africa terrorism and organized crime are clearly entwined to such an extent that the links between them must no longer be ignored. Some member states already link counterterrorism legislation with organized crime.[297] The UNODC suggests that there needs to be greater coherence between counterterrorism and organized crime legislation.[298] Additionally, the UN Security Council has encouraged states to utilise international treaties relating to terrorism to combat the links and called upon states to adopt new laws and mechanisms allowing for greater cooperation in the investigation and prosecution of organized crime that has links with terrorism. The misuse of counterterrorism law

296 UN Special Rapporteur, *supra* note 11.

297 Interview (South Africa Directorate for Priority Crime Investigation representative); Protection of Constitutional Democracy Against Terrorist and Related Activities Act 2004 (South Africa).

298 UNSC, 74th Year, 8569th Meeting, UN Doc. S/PV.8569, at 3 (9 July 2019).

already occurs in the practice of some AU member states and needs to be prevented by the introduction of a more effective and transparent continental treaty monitoring body and closer monitoring by relevant UN entities including the Security Council's Counter-Terrorism Executive Directorate.

An alternative approach to the revision of the OAU Convention is to utilise the UNTOC. As has been shown, however, despite the AU placing weighty reliance on the UNTOC for filling potential regulatory gaps in the OAU Convention, the UNTOC regime and its three protocols do not capture some of the types of organized crime benefitting terrorist groups identified by the present study including purely domestic organized crime. The UNTOC regime certainly does not target state involvement in organized crime or public and private corruption which enable and facilitate the links between terrorism and organized crime.[299] Therefore, it may be more preferable to adopt a new criminal law instrument targeting organized crime, both domestic and transnational, which could be applied alongside the OAU Convention. The main problem with this approach is that it would further entrench the outdated assumption that terrorism and organized crime are distinct phenomena and would require appropriate interaction between the two regimes. But it may also encourage relevant state agencies (intelligence, police, prosecution, judiciary, customs and revenue, border force and military) to continue to work in operational silos. In AU member states, there is already a need to improve cooperation and coordination between different agencies within the same state.[300] In this regard, Burkina Faso and Mali have adopted legislation establishing specialized judicial units to investigate and prosecute terrorism, terrorist financing and transnational organized crime, including the illicit traffic of weapons, drugs and humans.[301] However, such laws are not facilitating inter-state cooperation.

Both of the approaches proposed above are likely to meet with considerable resistance by the AU Commission, given that many member states have shown to be unwilling to combat the links between terrorism and organized crime and, in some instances, may even benefit from them. As terrorism in Africa poses a threat to international peace and security, it may be necessary

299 See also Izenman and Keatinge, *supra* note 26, at 13, 18; Hübschle, *supra* note 8, at 92.

300 Interview (Global Counterterrorism Forum Capacity-Building in the East Africa Region Working Group representative); Interview (Global Counterterrorism Forum Capacity-building in the West Africa Region Working Group representative); Interview (UNODC Regional Office for East Africa representative); Interview (UNODC Regional Office for West and Central Africa representative).

301 Law No. 2013-016 of 21 May 2013 amending Law No. 01-080 of 20 August 2001 enacting the Code of Criminal Procedure, Arts. 610 and 610-1 (Mali).

for the UN Security Council and its Counter-Terrorism Committee to engage in high-level dialogue and consider placing some pressure on the AU and its member states. The EU also has the ability to influence the AU and its member states, based on the amount funding, equipment and training the EU provides for combatting terrorism and organized crime in Africa and through the conclusion of economic partnership agreements. Ultimately, whichever approach is preferred, national implementation requires mandatory independent and transparent monitoring, which to date has been severely lacking.

CHAPTER 6

ASEAN and Organized Criminal Terrorism

Hitoshi Nasu

1 Introduction

Due to geographical proximity and high traffic sea lanes Southeast Asia has been prone to various forms of transnational crime. Because of this shared problem, tackling transnational organized crime has been at the forefront of regional cooperation in the Association of Southeast Asian Nations (ASEAN) since 1990s. ASEAN has addressed a range of transnational organized crimes including terrorism, money laundering, the trafficking in drugs and persons, piracy, and armed robbery at sea, based on the understanding that there are significant overlaps between terrorism and other areas of transnational criminal activity.[1] ASEAN's efforts to counter terrorism are therefore embedded in its broader regional cooperation to address transnational organized crimes. Categorized as 'non-traditional security' issues,[2] these transnational organized crimes have served as a litmus test for ASEAN's success in ensuring regional security by complementing national and sub-regional efforts.

While originally addressed under the broad category of transnational crime, the threat of terrorism has emerged as a distinct agenda requiring regional cooperation after the New York terrorist attacks in September 2001 and the Bali Bombings in October 2002. Central to regional cooperation on counter-terrorism in Southeast Asia is the ASEAN Convention on Counter-Terrorism (ACCT).[3] However, the regional approach to counter-terrorism has faced challenges because ASEAN member states remain ambivalent towards

1 See generally Arabinda Acharya. *Targeting Terrorist Financing: International Cooperation and New Regimes* (Routledge, 2009); Graham Gerard Ong-Webb (ed), *Piracy, Maritime Terrorism and Securing the Malacca Straits* (ISEAS Publishing, 2006); Paul J. Smith (ed), *Terrorism and Violence in Southeast Asia: Transnational Challenges to States and Regional Stability* (M.E. Sharpe, 2004).

2 See Mely Caballero-Anthony and Pau Khan Khup Hangzo, 'Transnational Crime' in Mely Caballero-Anthony and Alistair D.B. Cook (eds), *Non-Traditional Security in Asia: Issues, Challenges and Framework for Action* (Institute of Southeast Asian Studies, 2013) 234.

3 Adopted 13 January 2007 (entered into force 27 May 2011).

 | DOI:10.1163/9789004424579_008

harmonization of national counter-terrorism measures.[4] This ambivalence derives, by and large, from the historical and political settings in which national counter-terrorism efforts are enmeshed with each country's own political agenda on national harmony and combating dissidents.

This chapter examines the applicability of ASEAN instruments on counter-terrorism to organized criminal terrorism, with a particular focus on the extent to which these instruments are capable of regulating transnational association of criminal groups with terrorism. In so doing, the chapter reveals the complexity of counter-terrorism efforts to combat organized criminal terrorism in Southeast Asia due to the political, cultural and religious diversity that has plagued regional cooperation against transnational organized crime and terrorism. To that end, after reviewing the association of organized crime with terrorism in Southeast Asia, this chapter introduces relevant ASEAN instruments and considers their applicability to organized criminal terrorism. It then critically examines the challenges to the application of these instruments in facilitating coordinated response against organized criminal terrorism. The chapter concludes with an observation that although ASEAN is well placed to address the association of organized crime and terrorism, the regional principle of non-interference poses a structural obstacle to greater harmonization and cross-border cooperation. The strong assertion of sovereignty impedes regional cooperation necessary to break the organizational link of criminals with international terrorist networks.

2 The Linkage between Organised Crime and Terrorism in Southeast Asia

A wide range of organized crimes are prevalent in Southeast Asia, where numerous mountainous terrains and scattered remote islands are used for escape routes in the trafficking of drugs, persons, forest products, wildlife, and counterfeit consumer goods. The so-called 'Golden Triangle' straddling the borders of Lao People's Democratic Republic, Myanmar, and Thailand constitutes the world's second largest opium-producing region, sustaining insurgency operations against the Myanmar government for many years.[5] In the

4 For detailed analysis, see, eg, Andrew Chau, 'Security Community and Southeast Asia: Australia, the U.S., and ASEAN's Counter-Terrorism Strategy' (2008) 48 Asian Survey 626, 637–646; Amitav Acharya and Arabinda Acharya, 'The Myth of the Second Front: Localizing the "War on Terror" in Southeast Asia' (2007) 30(4) Washington Quarterly 75, 80–85.

5 Anshuman Behera, 'Insurgency, Drugs and Small Arms in Myanmar' (2017) 41(1) Strategic Analysis 34, 41–43.

southern Philippines region of Mindanao, various insurgent movements such as Abu Sayyaf and Maute Group have taken advantage of weak governance in the Sulu-Celebes (Sulawesi) Seas in organizing and sustaining criminal activities – most famously, kidnapping for ransom operations – which have oscillated between ideologically-driven violence of terrorism and profit-driven organized crime.[6] The United Nations Office on Drugs and Crime estimates the regional value of transnational crime reaching over USD100 billion per year,[7] with its 2019 report painting an unpropitious picture about the effectiveness of law enforcement efforts against organized crime in the region.[8]

In Southeast Asia, criminal networks are operating across borders, highly organized, and well resourced. Weak border control, numerous ungoverned spaces, incongruent legal systems, and unsettled territorial and maritime disputes between states are all conducive for organized crimes to flourish.[9] The improved transport links across Southeast Asia has also benefitted criminal networks with greater mobility in the region. The rapid economic development has stimulated the demand for illicit goods and cheap labour, creating opportunities for criminal organizations to expand their networks. Southeast Asia is also vulnerable to maritime terrorism, piracy, and armed robbery at sea due to the vast maritime space that lies in the region providing strategic waterways for the majority of international shipping.[10]

---

6 Cameron Sumpter and Joseph Franco, 'Migration, Transnational Crime and Terrorism: Exploring the Nexus in Europe and Southeast Asia' (2018) 12(5) Perspectives on Terrorism 36, 42; Bilveer Singh, 'Crime-Terror Nexus in Southeast Asia: Case Study of the Abu Sayyaf Group' (2018) 10(9) Counter Terrorist Trends and Analyses 6; Rommel C. Banlaoi, 'Maritime Terrorism in Southeast Asia – The Abu Sayyaf Threat' (2005) 58(4) Naval War College Review 63.

7 UNODC Regional Office for Southeast Asia and the Pacific, 'Protecting Peace and Prosperity in Southeast Asia: Synchronizing Economic and Security Agendas' (UNODC, 2016) 3, available at https://www.unodc.org/documents/southeastasiaandpacific//Publications/2016/Protecting_peace_and_prosperity_in_SEA.pdf.

8 UNODC Regional Office for Southeast Asia and the Pacific, 'Transnational Organized Crime in Southeast Asia: Evolution, Growth and Impact' (UNODC, 2019), available at https://www.unodc.org/documents/southeastasiaandpacific/Publications/2019/SEA_TOCTA_2019_web.pdf.

9 See, eg, Matthew Abbey, 'Crime, Terror, and Porous Borders in Southeast Asia', Asia Sentinel, 31 May 2017, available at https://www.asiasentinel.com/politics/southeast-asia-crime-terror-borders/; Jeremy Douglas, 'Transnational Threats in Southeast Asia', The Diplomat, 2 November 2016, available at https://thediplomat.com/2016/11/transnational-threats-in-southeast-asia/.

10 David Letts, 'Maritime Security in South East Asia' in Donald R. Rothwell and David Letts (eds), *Law of the Sea in South East Asia: Environmental, Navigational and Security Challenges* (Routledge, 2019) 63–79.

Although clear evidence is hard to obtain,[11] the association of criminal and terrorist organizations is a real risk as the proceeds of various criminal activities and illicit money flows may be used to fund terrorist groups.[12] Kreiman and Espadafor conducted an empirical study showing that counter-terrorism has a negative impact on state capacity and legitimacy, arguably because the concentration of resources in the urban areas to combat terrorist groups creates greater room for organized criminal groups to operate more freely in remote and border areas.[13] In addition, religious ideology can mediate the crime-terror nexus; for example, the so-called Islamic State and the Jemaah Islamiyah are both known to use religious ideology to describe criminal acts as part of jihad.[14] Pre-existing ethnic or religious tensions and socio-economic conditions, such as poverty, can also create a fertile ground for violent extremism, conducive to exploitation by terrorist and criminal groups.[15] The cross-fertilisation of organized crime and terrorism demonstrated its destabilizing impact most dramatically when local militants in Lanao del Sur, led by the Maute Group, and foreign fighters affiliated with the so-called Islamic State, joined forces in launching sustained attacks, which culminated in the five-month siege of Marawi from May to October 2017.[16]

For ASEAN, this linkage is easy to recognize as terrorism has always been treated as a subset of transnational crime. The 1997 ASEAN Declaration on Transnational Crime addressed terrorism as one of the transnational crimes that had pernicious effects on regional stability and development, the maintenance

---

11 Cf Louise I. Shelley et al, 'Methods and Motives: Exploring Links between Transnational Organized Crime & International Terrorism' (US Department of Justice, 2005), available at https://www.ncjrs.gov/pdffiles1/nij/grants/211207.pdf.

12 See generally, Steven Hutchinson and Pat O'Malley, 'A Crime-Terror Nexus? Thinking on Some of the Links between Terrorism and Criminality' (2007) 30 Studies in Conflict & Terrorism 1095; Tamara Makarenko, 'The Crime-Terror Continuum: Tracing the Interplay between Transnational Organised Crime and Terrorism' (2004) 6(1) Global Crime 129.

13 Guillermo Kreiman and Mar C. Espadafor, 'Unexpected Allies: The Impact of Terrorism on Organised Crime in Sub-Saharan African and South-East Asia' (2022) 45 Studies in Conflict & Terrorism 348.

14 Rajan Basra and Peter R. Neumann, 'Crime as Jihad: Developments in the Crime-Terror Nexus in Europe' (2017) 10(9) CTC Sentinel (Combating Terrorist Center at West Point) 1.

15 See, eg, Amalina Abdul Nasir, 'IS' Determination to Stay Relevant and Visible in Malaysia' (2019) 11(7) Counter Terrorist Trends and Analyses 11, 12; Allan Ngari and Denys Reva, 'How Ethnic and Religious Discrimination Drive Violate Extremism' (Institute for Security Studies, 2017), available at https://community-democracies.org/app/uploads/2018/06/aitwr-4-1.pdf.

16 See, eg, Rohan Gunaratna, 'The Siege of Marawi: A Game Changer in Terrorism in Asia' (2017) 9(7) Counter Terrorist Trends and Analyses 1–5.

of the rule of law, and the welfare of people.[17] ASEAN Regional Forum more explicitly acknowledged terrorism 'links with transnational organised crime, such as money laundering, arms smuggling, people smuggling, and the protection of and trafficking in illicit drugs'.[18] In 2017, regional leaders gathered for the East Asia Summit recognized the potential linkage between terrorism and organized crime, noting that 'money laundering through organised criminal groups can finance terrorist activities'.[19] The same Summit in 2019 expressed concern that 'terrorists can benefit from transnational organised crime as a source of financing or logistical support, recognising that the nature and scope of the linkage between terrorism and transnational organised crime vary by context'.[20] The awareness of this linkage indicates that ASEAN is well placed to address the challenges posed by organized criminal terrorism.

3 ASEAN Legal Framework for Counter-Terrorism

Since its establishment in 1967,[21] ASEAN has evolved into a premier security institution in Southeast Asia with the mandate to maintain and enhance regional peace, security and prosperity.[22] It is specifically tasked to 'respond effectively, in accordance with the principle of comprehensive security, to all forms of threats, transnational crimes and transboundary challenges'.[23] Its activities are guided by the fundamental principles of ASEAN, such as respect for sovereignty and the principle of non-interference.[24] Of particular importance is the regional principle of non-interference,[25] which is distinguished

17 ASEAN Declaration on Transnational Crime, adopted 20 December 1997, preamble para. 2.

18 ASEAN Regional Forum (ARF) Statement on Cooperative Counter-Terrorist Action on Border Security, adopted 17 June 2003, para. 1.

19 East Asia Summit Leaders' Declaration on Anti-Money Laundering and Countering the Financing of Terrorism, adopted 14 November 2017, preamble para. 11.

20 East Asia Summit Leaders' Statement on Cooperation to Combat Transnational Crime, adopted 4 November 2019, preamble para. 10.

21 Declaration Constituting an Agreement Establishing the Association of South-East Asian Nations, adopted 8 August 1967, 1331 UNTS 235 (entered into force 8 August 1967).

22 Charter of the Association of Southeast Asian Nations, adopted 20 November 2007, 2624 UNTS 223 (entered into force 15 December 2008) art. 2(2)(b) (hereinafter ASEAN Charter); Treaty of Amity and Cooperation in Southeast Asia, adopted 24 February 1976, 1025 UNTS 319 (entered into force 15 July 1976) art. 1.

23 ASEAN Charter, art. 1(8).

24 For details, see Hitoshi Nasu et al, *The Legal Authority of ASEAN as a Security Institution* (Cambridge University Press, 2019) 26–42.

25 ASEAN Charter, arts. 2(2)(e) and 2(2)(f).

from the principle of non-intervention under general international law in that the former even prohibits otherwise lawful forms of interference that would not involve an element of coercion as required for the latter.[26] This means that regional cooperation on counter-terrorism is necessarily restricted to the extent that it constitutes an interference with the internal affairs of ASEAN member states, such as ethnic or religious tensions, political subversion, and socio-economic problems.

Building upon this normative structure ASEAN has adopted two legal instruments for regional cooperation on counter-terrorism: the ACCT and the Mutual Legal Assistance Treaty (MLAT).[27] This legal framework, albeit yet to be completed, represents a criminal justice approach to counter-terrorism, as opposed to military response to terrorist threats. The regional cooperation has incrementally developed through a series of meetings, declarations, and plans of action within ASEAN as part of a broader attempt to tackle transnational crimes prevalent in Southeast Asia.[28] The obligations set out in these instruments, therefore, are by and large reflective of the informal arrangement or the cooperative agreements that had previously been put in place bilaterally or within a small group of member states.

The ACCT aims to localize various counter-terrorism obligations under international law by providing 'the framework for regional cooperation to counter, prevent and suppress terrorism in all its forms and manifestations and to deepen cooperation among law enforcement agencies and relevant authorities of the Parties in countering terrorism'.[29] As a framework convention, the ACCT does not impose any specific obligation but rather sets legal parameters within which ASEAN member states have agreed to implement their respective obligations derived variously from the counter-terrorism conventions each

26 *Case Concerning Military and Paramilitary Activities in and against Nicaragua* (*Nicaragua v. United States*) [1986] ICJ Rep. 14, 108 para. 205. For discussion of this difference, see Hitoshi Nasu, 'Revisiting the Principle of Non-Intervention: A Structural Principle of International Law or a Political Obstacle to Regional Security in Asia?' (2013) 3 Asian Journal of International Law 25, 36–37.

27 Treaty on Mutual Legal Assistance in Criminal Matters, adopted 29 November 2004 (entered into force 28 April 2005 for Singapore, 25 October 2005 for Vietnam), 1 June 2005 for Malaysia, 15 February 2006 for Brunei Darussalam, 25 June 2007 for Lao PDR, 9 September 2008 for Indonesia, 12 December 2008 for the Philippines, 22 January 2009 for Myanmar, 8 April 2010 for Cambodia, 31 January 2013 for Thailand).

28 For details, see See Seng Tan and Hitoshi Nasu, 'ASEAN and the Development of Counter-Terrorism Law and Policy in Southeast Asia' (2016) 39 University of New South Wales Law Journal 1219, 1222–1225; Jonathan T. Chow, 'ASEAN Counterterrorism Cooperation Since 9/11' (2005) 45 Asian Survey 302.

29 ACCT, art. I.

member is a party to,[30] identifying areas of cooperation for regional efforts to address threats of terrorism.[31] It is driven by ASEAN's fundamental norms, such as respect for sovereignty and the principle of non-interference, with wide discretion granted to each member state in adopting domestic measures as may be necessary.[32]

Within this legal framework, ASEAN subsequently developed a more detailed implementation programme by adopting the 2009 ASEAN Comprehensive Plan of Action on Counter Terrorism.[33] Pursuant to this plan of action, ASEAN member states have committed themselves, inter alia, to:

- establish institutionalized mechanisms for the exchange of information and intelligence on the surveillance and tracking of suspected terrorist organisations;
- establish computerized shared databases on terrorist organizations with a view to developing a joint risk and threat assessment;
- enhance the existing regulations and procedures in the control of illicit trade of arms and explosives; and
- develop procedures, in accordance with MLAT, for cross-border investigation and prosecution of terrorist activities.[34]

As this author observed elsewhere, regional counter-terrorism cooperation facilitated under this scheme is best characterized as 'multilateral initiatives that complement respective national efforts',[35] rather than an attempt to harmonize domestic laws and procedures.

The MLAT, on the other hand, aims to achieve more effective cooperation among law enforcement agencies in the investigation and prosecution of transnational crimes.[36] The scope of its application is not limited to terrorist offences, but provides a general process whereby the States Parties are required to render 'the widest possible measure of mutual legal assistance' in the collection of evidence for criminal investigations and criminal proceedings.[37] It is also intended to complement regional cooperation on counter-terrorism

30 ACCT, arts. II, V.

31 ACCT, art. VI.

32 ACCT, arts. III–IV, IX.

33 Adopted 30 June 2009, reproduced in ASEAN Documents on Combating Transnational Crime and Terrorism (2012) 69–75.

34 Ibid, paras 10, 11, 14, 17.

35 Tan and Nasu, above n 28, 1227.

36 MLAT, preamble.

37 MLAT, art. 1.

under the ACCT by facilitating the implementation of ASEAN member states' obligations to provide legal assistance established through various international instruments, including counter-terrorism conventions.[38] Although the term 'mutual' indicates the reciprocal nature of obligations, each request for legal assistance must be assessed on its own terms by each member state pursuant to the mandatory and permissive grounds for refusal.[39] There is no legal basis for expecting that 'the granting of assistance by one State in respect of one matter imposes on the other State the obligation to do likewise when assistance is requested of it in turn'.[40] Nor is there any obligation to harmonize domestic laws and procedures among member states.

The MLAT does not apply to the request for extradition of a person, or the arrest or detention for that purpose. The Vientiane Action Programme, adopted on 29 November 2004, envisaged the conclusion of an ASEAN Extradition Treaty, alongside with the ACCT and the MLAT, within its broader objective of 'shaping and sharing regional norms'.[41] However, the negotiations for a region-wide extradition treaty has been delayed. Instead, extradition arrangements within the region have so far been made solely on a bilateral basis, where strategic and political benefits are shared and where legal systems and procedures are compatible. For example, Singapore has a bilateral extradition arrangement with Malaysia and Brunei due to the shared common law tradition. Singapore's extradition treaty with Indonesia came packaged with the Defense Cooperation Agreement and the Re-Alignment Flight information Region Adjustment Agreement, which simultatenously entered into force on 21 March 2024.

The move towards a region-wide extradition treaty has resurged when the Prime Minister of Singapore, Lee Hsien Loong, at the Opening Ceremony of the 32nd ASEAN Summit called for a renewed effort to conclude the treaty as a means to strengthen ASEAN's resilience and capacity to combat transnational crime.[42] Given the ease with which people can move across borders in Southeast Asia, the adoption of a region-wide extradition treaty is expected to help ensure that suspected terrorists who flee to other ASEAN states are returned promptly to face

38 See *ASEAN Handbook on International Legal Cooperation in Trafficking in Persons Cases* (ASEAN Secreteriat, 2010) 26.

39 MLAT, art. 3.

40 *Certain Questions of Mutual Assistance in Criminal Matters* (*Djibouti v France*) [2008] ICJ Rep 177, 221.

41 Vientiane Action Programme, 29 November 2004.

42 Remarks of PM Lee Hsien Loong at the Opening Ceremony of the 32nd ASEAN Summit, 28 April 2018, available at: https://www.mfa.gov.sg/Newsroom/Press-Statements-Transcripts-and-Photos/2018/04/20180428_Opening_Ceremony.

charges.[43] However, an effective extradition agreement requires ASEAN states to mutually recognize and, to a certain degree, harmonize their substantive criminal laws so that extradition requests can satisfy the procedural requirements such as double criminality and no double jeopardy.[44] As will be discussed below, mutual recognition and compatibility of criminal laws poses a particular challenge to the application of ASEAN counter-terrorism instruments, and more broadly the regional effort to combat transnational organized crime, in the context of organized criminal terrorism.

4 Challenges to ASEAN in Fighting Organized Criminal Terrorism

ASEAN counter-terrorism instruments have played a normative role in localizing and internalizing various obligations under relevant rules of international law in each member state.[45] Upon adoption of the ACCT, and even before its ratification, Cambodia introduced the Law on Counter-Terrorism, enacting a suite of terrorism offences addressed in various international law instruments identified by the ACCT, as well as extradition and mutual legal assistance in relation to terrorism offences.[46] In the same year, Singapore also enacted the Terrorism (Suppression of Bombings) Act, together with accession to the Terrorism Bombing Convention.[47] Vietnam issued a decree on counter-terrorism in 2007,[48] although it did not ratify the ACCT until 30 January 2011. Furthermore, Myanmar enacted the Mutual Legal Assistance in Criminal Matters Law in 2004 soon after the adoption of the MLAT, followed by Brunei Darussalam in 2005,[49] Indonesia in 2006,[50] and Vietnam in 2007,[51] whereas

43 Takashi Nakano, 'Southeast Asia Lays Groundwork for Terrorism Extradition Treaties', Nikkei Asian Review, 24 April 2018, available at https://asia.nikkei.com/Politics/International-relations/Southeast-Asia-lays-groundwork-for-terrorism-extradition-treaties.

44 See generally Ivan A. Shearer, *Extradition in International Law* (Manchester University Press, 1971).

45 With regard to ASEAN's legal authority in localising and internalising norms and rules of international law, see Hitoshi Nasu et al, above n 24.

46 Law on Counter-Terrorism 2007 (Cambodia), enacted on 20 July 2007.

47 Singapore ratified the ACCT on 31 October 2007 and acceded to the Terrorist Bombing Convention on 31 December 2007.

48 Decree No 25/2007/CT-TTg on Countering Terrorism.

49 Mutual Assistance in Criminal Matters Order 2005.

50 Law Concerning Mutual Assistance in Criminal Maters 2006.

51 Law No 08/2007/QH12 on Legal Assistance.

Malaysia, Singapore, and Thailand already had pre-existing legislation on mutual legal assistance.[52]

While ASEAN instruments have thus provided a legislative baseline, this does not necessarily mean that ASEAN has achieved greater coordination and harmonization of counter-terrorism laws among member states. Indeed, the cooperative criminal justice approach adopted by ASEAN instruments has its own limit. The remainder of this chapter dissects this limit into three specific areas of concern: (1) the diversity of counter-terrorism laws; (2) money-laundering risks for the financing of terrorism; and (3) cross-sectoral cooperation between military and law enforcement authorities on counter-terrorism.

4.1 *Diversity of Counter-Terrorism Laws*

The legal framework on counter-terrorism established through ASEAN involves little attempt to coordinate national counter-terrorism efforts beyond the minimum baseline agreed upon, with a variety of counter-terrorism measures pursued in many Southeast Asian nations. Malaysia spearheaded with various law reform efforts to strengthen law enforcement powers against the offences of terrorism in a manner closely aligned with the legal developments in other common law countries.[53] For the Philippines and Thailand, counter-terrorism forms part of their traditional counter-insurgency operations, with a broad definition of terrorism.[54] Singapore has adopted a comprehensive counter-terrorism strategy under the 'total defence' paradigm encompassing national security in military, economic, social and psychological terms with an emphasis on ethnic and religious harmony,[55] whilst employing the Internal Security

52 Mutual Assistance in Criminal Matters Act 2002 (Malaysia); Mutual Assistance in Criminal Matters Act 2000 (Singapore); Mutual Assistance in Criminal Matters Act 1992 (Thailand).

53 Penal Code (Amendment) Act 2003; Prevention of Terrorism Act 2015; Special Measures against Terrorism in Foreign Countries Act 2015. See also, Kent Roach, 'Comparative Counter-Terrorism Law Comes of Age' in Kent Roach (ed), *Comparative Counter-Terrorism Law* (Cambridge University Press 2015) 1, 25–27.

54 Human Security Act 2007 (Philippines) s. 3 (which defines terrorism as a punishable act 'sowing and creating a condition of widespread and extraordinary fear and panic among the populace, in order to coerce the government to given in to an unlawful demand'); Criminal Code 1956 (as amended in 2003) (Thailand) s. 135/1.

55 Amendments to the Maintenance of Religious Harmony Act 1990 (Singapore) have been introduced in 2019 to, among other things, create new offences on religiously motivated violence and to require religious organizations to disclose any single-time donation of 10,000 Singaporean Dollars or more from non-Singaporean citizens or residents: Bill No. 25/2019.

Act to detain and arrest terrorist suspects.[56] Indonesia, on the other hand, has been cautious with the introduction and development of counter-terrorism legislation out of public fear as it resonated with the use of draconian laws to suppress dissidents during the Suharto era.[57]

Vietnam, for a long time, maintained the official position that the existing criminal law provides a comprehensive and effective legal framework to combat terrorism,[58] but in 2015, introduced a wider range of terrorist offences by amending its Criminal Code.[59] Since then the Vietnamese government has made use of the newly expanded offences of terrorism to suppress dissidents and critics of the government.[60] In January 2019, Chau Van Kham, an Australian who fled Vietnam as a refugee in 1983, was arrested and charged for opposing the people's government, alongside two Vietnamese citizens who were reportedly affiliated with Việt Tân, an organization that has been designated as a terrorist group by the Vietnamese Ministry of Public Security.[61] Likewise, the Government of Myanmar has relied upon the Counter-Terrorism Law, since it was enacted in 2014,[62] to suppress ethnic armed groups such

56 See Senia Febrica, 'Securitizing Terrorism in Southeast Asia: Accounting for the Varying Responses of Singapore and Indonesia' (2010) 50 Asian Survey 569, 576–580.

57 See Kent Roach, *The 9/11 Effect: Comparative Counter-Terrorism* (Cambridge University Press, 2011) 145–153. The legislative amendment process was expedited in the aftermath of the East Java bombings of 2018, which led to the adoption of Law No. 5/2018 on Eradication of Criminal Acts of Terrorism.

58 Letter Dated 10 July 2007 from the Chairman of the Security Council Committee Established Pursuant to Resolution 1373 (2001) Concerning Counter-Terrorism Addressed to the President of the Security Council, UN Doc S/2007/425 (12 July 2007) annex. The offence of terrorism was originally enacted in 1999 when Vietnam's legislature did not have in mind the international dimension of terrorism and therefore it was designed to defend national security rather than preventing international terrorism: Le Thi Van Anh, 'Vietnamese Law and Assessment of the Legal System in Vietnam in Comparison to the United Nations Convention Against Terrorism' (UN Asia and Far East Institute Resource Material No. 71, 2007) 61, 64–65, available at https://www.unafei.or.jp/publications/pdf/RS_No71/No71_13PA_Anh.pdf.

59 Criminal Code 2015 (Vietnam) No. 100/2015/QH13, art. 113.

60 For detailed analysis, see UK Home Office, 'Country Policy and Information Note – Vietnam: Opposition to the State' (2023), available at https://www.gov.uk/government/publications/vietnam-country-policy-and-information-notes/country-policy-and-information-note-opposition-to-the-state-vietnam-august-2023-accessible.

61 Ben Doherty, 'Terrorist Claim against Australian Man in Vietnam "Absolutely False", His Wife Says', The Guardian, 10 November 2019, available at https://www.theguardian.com/world/2019/nov/11/terrorist-claim-against-australian-man-in-vietnam-absolutely-false-his-wife-says.

62 Law No. 23/2014.

as the Arakan Rohingya Salvation Army.[63] With the proliferation of tougher counter-terrorism laws, concerns have been expressed about the potential misuse of counter-terrorism legislation to target human rights defenders or to hinder their work and endanger their safety.[64]

The variation in national criminal laws is thus reflective of the particular historical and socio-political settings in which each state's national counter-terrorism policy has been developed. This diversity in the criminal justice approach to counter-terrorism may pose an obstacle to the effective regulation of cross-border activities relating to organized criminal terrorism.[65] This is particularly so when, in the absence of a substantive offence of terrorism having been committed, various forms of participation or involvement in the activities – criminal or otherwise – of an organized criminal group are not criminalized in neighbouring jurisdictions. For example, there is no specific offence for conspiracy or participation in organized terrorism under the criminal laws of Indonesia and Thailand,[66] whereas Malaysia has created a suite of offences to criminalize various forms of support for terrorism.[67] An inconsistent approach to organized criminal terrorism has the potential for the criminals shopping around jurisdictions in which no criminal offence is enacted or defined for planning, financing or otherwise supporting terrorism.

ASEAN counter-terrorism instruments do not currently address this specific gap in the criminalization of association between criminal organizations and terrorism, whilst identifing as one of the areas of cooperation the need to ensure that 'any person who participates in the financing, planning, preparation or perpetration of terrorist acts or in supporting terrorist acts is brought to justice'.[68] The gap in relation to the association of organized criminal groups and terrorism indicates the possibility that law enforcement and judicial authorities in each country may not afford mutual recognition as the basis for

63 Melissa Crouch, 'The Twisted Politics of Terrorism in Myanmar', The Interpreter (Lowy Institute), 12 September 2017, available at https://www.lowyinstitute.org/the-interpreter/threat-terrorism-too-convenient-myanma.

64 Human Rights Council Res. 25/18 (11 April 2014) preamble para. 12.

65 See Tom Obokata, 'The Value of International Law in Combating Transnational Organized Crime in the Asia-Pacific' (2017) 7 Asian Journal of International Law 39, 41–47.

66 Cf Criminal Code (Indonesia) ch. V (participation in punishable acts), art. 110 (conspiracy and participation in crimes against the security of the state), art. 169 (participation in an association in relation to crimes against public order); Criminal Code 1956 (Thailand) s. 140 (participation in crimes against officials), s. 294 (participation in crimes causing death), s. 299 (participation in crimes causing bodily harm).

67 Penal Code 1936 (as amended) (Malaysia) chs. VI–A and VI–B.

68 ACCT, art. VI(1)(m).

providing legal assistance and law enforcement cooperation. It could also frustrate the negotiations for a region-wide extradition treaty. In the most recent comprehensive plan of action, ASEAN has planned to establish computerized shared databases on terrorist organizations and their associations, as well as transnational criminal groups with possible links to terrorist organizations for the purpose of developing a joint risk and threat assessment.[69] However, in the absence of a common approach to organized criminal terrorism, the effectiveness of such cooperation and information sharing among law enforcement and judicial authorities may be limited.

By contrast, the ASEAN Convention Against Trafficking in Persons, Especially Women and Children, adopted eight years after the ACCT, expressly addresses the issue of organized crime, defining organized criminal group as 'a structured group of three or more persons existing for a period of time and acting in concert with the aim of committing one or more serious crimes or offences established in accordance with this Convention, in order to obtain, directly or indirectly, a financial or other material benefit'.[70] Based on this definition, the Convention requires the States Parties to criminalize the participation in an organized criminal group – separate from offences involving attempt or completion of a criminal activity – such as agreeing to commit a serious crime for financial or other material benefit, taking an active part in activities of an organized criminal group with the knowledge of the criminal aim, intention or nature of the activity, and organizing, directing, aiding, abetting, facilitating or counselling the commission of serious crime involving an organized criminal group.[71] Given the increased awareness of the linkage between organized crime and terrorism, it remains to be seen whether ASEAN moves towards legislative harmonization within the framework of the ACCT through the Senior Officials Meeting on Transnational Crime or with the adoption of future plans of action.

4.2 *Money-Laundering Risks for the Financing of Terrorism*

All ASEAN member states have, in a virtually uniform manner, enacted legislative measures to address the financing of terrorism as part of anti-money

---

69 ASEAN Comprehensive Plan of Action on Counter-Terrorism, adopted on 20 September 2017, para. 11, reproduced in *ASEAN Document Series on Transnational Crime: Terrorism and Violent Extremism; Drugs; Cybercrime; and Trafficking in Persons* (ASEAN Secretariat, 2017) 95, 103.

70 ASEAN Convention Against Trafficking in Persons, Especially Women and Children, adopted 21 November 2015 (entered into force 8 March 2017) art. 2(f).

71 Ibid, art. 6(1).

laundering policy.[72] While this is consistent with ASEAN's approach to regional cooperation against transnational crime, broader international pressure appears more likely to have pushed each state to align themselves with the international standard of financial regulation as it emerged since 2001. Security Council Resolution 1373 has been the primary vehicle for the international regulation of the financing of terrorism,[73] establishing the Counter-Terrorism Committee to monitor UN member states' compliance with various obligations imposed under relevant Security Council resolutions.

Another significant mechanism is the Financial Action Task Force (FATF), an inter-governmental task force established by the Group of Seven (G-7) in 1989, which has provided financial institutions with detailed guidelines and recommendations on the measures to be adopted to tackle money-laundering.[74] The FATF has been influential in pushing Southeast Asian states to reform their financial regulation due to the negative economic consequences that follow from resisting compliance with FATF recommendations, such as capital flight, increased borrowing costs, and isolation from international capital markets.[75] This could be reflective of greater sensitivity shared among Southeast Asian states to international investment and capital flight in the aftermath of the 1997 Asian Financial Crisis.[76] In 2012–13, Indonesia, the Philippines and Thailand responded swiftly to concerns raised by FATF by replacing their anti-money

72 See Anti-Terrorism (Financial and Other Measures) Act 2002 and Anti-Terrorism (Terrorist Financing) Regulations 2013 (Brunei Darussalam); Law on Anti-Money Laundering and Combating the Financing of Terrorism 2007 (Cambodia); Law on Prevention and Eradication of Crimes of Financing of Terrorism 2013 (Indonesia); Law on Anti-Money Laundering and Counter-Financing of Terrorism 2015 (Lao PDR); Anti-Money Laundering, Anti- Terrorism Financing and Proceeds of Unlawful Activities Act 2001 (Malaysia); Control of Money Laundering Law 2002 (Myanmar); Terrorism Financing Prevention and Suppression Act 2012 (Philippines); Terrorism (Suppression of Financing) Act 2002 (Singapore); Counter-Terrorism Financing Act 2013 (Thailand); Decree No 74/2005/ND-CP on Prevention and Combat of Money-Laundering 2005 (Vietnam).

73 Security Council Res. 1373 (28 September 2001).

74 FATF, International Standards on Combating Money Laundering and the Financing of Terrorism & Proliferation – The FATF Recommendations (2012, as amended in 2019), available at http://www.fatf-gafi.org/publications/fatfrecommendations/documents/fatf-recommendations.html; FATF, 40 Recommendations (2003), available at https://www.fatf-gafi.org/publications/fatfrecommendations/documents/the40recommendationspublishedoctober2004.html.

75 Shahar Hameiri and Lee Jones, 'Regulatory Regionalism and Anti-Money Laundering Governance in Asia' (2015) 69 Australian Journal of International Affairs 144, 153–154.

76 See Yongwook Ryu, 'The Asian Financial Crisis and ASEAN's Concept of Security' (S Rajaratnam School of International Studies Working Paper No 148, 2008) 12–15, available at https://www.rsis.edu.sg/wp-content/uploads/rsis-pubs/WP148.pdf.

laundering legislation with a new, specific counter-terrorism financing law in order to avoid possible financial penalties.[77]

Despite a heightened level of technical compliance with FATF recommendations, Indonesia remains a high risk country regarding the financing of terrorism with regulatory concerns identified in several areas, such as the limited implementation of targeted financial sanctions under the UN counter-terrorism sanctions regime and the lack of consistency in providing constructive and timely mutual legal assistance where requested.[78] The FATF removed Cambodia from the watchlist in 2015, but subsequently identified technical compliance deficiencies in multiple areas,[79] which led to the decision on 22 February 2019 adding the country back on the list due to concerns about high levels of corruption in the country's regulatory and judicial system.[80]

Notwithstanding the virtually uniform adoption of anti-money laundering measures, ASEAN member states have been experiencing challenges in tracking, freezing, and confiscating the proceeds of crime or terrorism-relating financing when funds are transferred through informal financing channels or alternative remittance systems that operate outside the formal banking system.[81]

---

77 Ben Otto, 'Indonesia Takes Aim at Financing of Terrorism', The Wall Street Journal, 13 February 2013, available at http://www.wsj.com/articles/SB10001424127887323511804578299911897063222; 'FATF Upgrades Philippines for Move against Money Laundering, Terrorist Financing', Global Times, 23 June 2012, available at http://www.globaltimes.cn/content/716615.shtml; Ministry of Foreign Affairs of the Kingdom of Thailand, 'FATF Removes Thailand from Public Statement on Money Laundering/ Financing of Terrorism' (Press Release, 1 May 2013), available at http://www.mfa.go.th/main/en/media-center/14/34910-FATF-removes-Thailand-from-Public-Statement-on-Mon.html.

78 The Asia/Pacific Group on Money Laundering, 'Anti-Money Laundering and Counter-Terrorist Financing Measures: Indonesia' (Third Round Mutual Evaluation Report, 2018), paras 203–224 and 380–410, available at http://www.fatf-gafi.org/media/fatf/documents/reports/mer-fsrb/APG-Mutual-Evaluation-Report-Indonesia.pdf.

79 The Asia/Pacific Group on Money Laundering, 'Anti-Money Laundering and Counter-Terrorist Financing Measures: Cambodia' (Mutual Evaluation Report, 2017), available at http://www.fatf-gafi.org/countries/a-c/cambodia/documents/mer-cambodia-2017.html; The Asia/Pacific Group on Money Laundering, 'First Follow-up Report: Mutual Evaluation of Cambodia' (2018), available at http://www.fatf-gafi.org/countries/a-c/cambodia/documents/fur-cambodia-2018.html.

80 'Cambodia Put on Money-Laundering Watchlist in Move That May Curtain Foreign Investment', Straits Times (Singapore), 22 February 2019, available at https://www.straitstimes.com/asia/se-asia/cambodia-to-be-put-on-money-laundering-watchlist-in-move-that-may-curtail-foreign.

81 Asian Development Bank, Enhancing the Asian Development Bank's Role in Combating Money Laundering and the Financing of Terrorism (March 2003), para 8, available at https://www.adb.org/sites/default/files/institutional-document/32109/money-laundering-terrorism.pdf.

In addition, the widespread use of modern technology, such as Internet-based payment services and crypto-currencies, has also created new opportunities for the financing of terrorism.[82] In recent years, Islamic charity groups have reportedly been exploited in collecting, channelling and using funds for terrorist purposes.[83] These challenges indicate a potential limit of the legislative scheme against money laundering, casting doubt on the extent to which the law can accommodate variation in local economic structure, cultural and religious diversity, and new technological advances in financial transaction.

4.3 *Cross-Sectoral Coordination on Counter-Terrorism*

As the global landscape of terrorism evolves, local insurgent groups have increasingly been operating beyond national borders and challenging the traditional legal boundaries based on state sovereignty between international law and domestic law. Abu Sayyaf, for example, have shifted the focus of their kidnapping for ransom operations to sailors and fishermen on the high seas, exploiting the unsettled maritime boundary between the Philippines and Malaysia (owing to the long-standing territorial dispute over Sabah), and between Malaysia and Indonesia.[84] In Malaysia, local issues such as ethnic and religious tensions have been exploited to inspire Islamic extremists from foreign countries to join local Islamic State supporters in planning the launch of terrorist attacks.[85] Following the Islamic State's loss of territorial control in Syria, the return of foreign terrorist fighters to Southeast Asia has further internationalized local insurgency, as illustrated by the siege of Marawi in May 2017. In the lead up to the siege, the Maute Group appeared to have adopted the

82 Sylvia Windya Laksmi, 'Terrorism Financing and the Risk of Internet-Based Payment Services in Indonesia' (2017) 9(2) Counter Terrorist Trends and Analyses 21–25.

83 See Sylvia Windya Laksmi, 'Nexus between Charities and Terrorist Financing in Indonesia' (2019) 11(7) Counter Terrorist Trends and Analyses 6; Australian Transaction Reports and Analysis Centre, 'Non-Profit Organizations and Terrorist Financing: Regional Risk Assessment 2017' (Commonwealth of Australia, 2017), available at https://www.austrac.gov.au/sites/default/files/2019-06/regional-NPO-risk-assessment-WEB-READY_ss.pdf.

84 Zachary Abuza, 'Why Vietnam Must Fight the Islamic State Terror Threat', The Diplomat, 3 August 2017, available at https://thediplomat.com/2017/08/why-vietnam-must-fight-the-islamic-state-terror-threat/.

85 Laura Steckman, 'The Abu-Sayyaf-ISIS Nexus: Rising Extremism and its Implications for Malaysia' (2016) 8(5) Counter Terrorist Trends and Analyses 16–21. In May 2019, Malaysian authorities arrested a group of Islamic extremists, including those from Indonesia and Rohingya Muslims, for their plan to launch a series of large-scale terrorist attacks in retaliation to the death of a local fireman Muhammad Abid Mohd Kassim: Nasir, above n 15, 12.

Islamic State-related imagery, while leveraging frustration with stalled peace process in Mindanao.[86]

With the escalation of terrorist violence, military forces have gained prominence in their counter-terrorism role.[87] Most illustrative is the involvement of the Armed Forces of the Philippines in countering the coordinated offensives launched by Islamic militants during the siege of Marawi. Singapore also offered unmanned aerial vehicles and its urban warfare training facilities to help Philippine troops fight against Islamic militants.[88] In the maritime domain, the Philippines, Indonesia and Malaysia have been conducting joint patrols by sea and air to monitor suspicious activities in Sulu and Sulewasi.[89] The tripartite defense cooperation was subsequently expanded into the Our Eyes Initiative, which was officially adopted on 19 October 2018 at the Fifth ASEAN Defence Ministers' Meeting in Singapore as a regional platform for sharing strategic intelligence on Islamic militants.[90]

While the Philippines turn their attention to countering violent extremism in the reconstruction of Marawi with reduced military involvement, Indonesia has stepped up its militaristic approach to counter-terrorism by forming the Special Operations Command tasked to perform special operations across

86 For details, see Joseph Franco, 'Philippines: Addressing Islamist Militancy After the Battle for Marawi' (International Crisis Group, 17 July 2018), available at https://www.crisisgroup.org/asia/south-east-asia/philippines/philippines-addressing-islamist-militancy-after-battle-marawi.

87 For details, see Olli Suorsa, 'The Growing Role of the Military in Counter-Terrorism in Southeast Asia' (ISEAS Yusof Ishak Institute Perspective No. 69, 2 November 2018), available at https://www.iseas.edu.sg/images/pdf/ISEAS_Perspective_2018_69@50.pdf.

88 Raul Dancel, 'Singapore Offers Drones, Urban Warfare Training Grounds, Aid to Help Philippines Fight Militants in Marawi', Straits Times, 19 July 2017, available at https://www.straitstimes.com/asia/se-asia/singapore-offers-saf-assistance-to-philippines-in-fight-against-terrorism.

89 Ian Storey, 'Trilateral Security Cooperation in the Sulu-Celebes Seas: A Work in Progress' (ISEAS Yusof Ishak Institute Perspective No. 48, 27 August 2018), available at https://www.iseas.edu.sg/images/pdf/ISEAS_Perspective_2018_48@50.pdf; Raymond Jose G. Quilop, 'Trilateral Cooperation by Indonesia, Malaysia and the Philippines: Temper Expectations', Global Asia, 26 March 2018, available at http://globalasia.org/v13no1/feature/trilateral co-operation-by-indonesia-malaysia-and-the-philippines-temper-expectations_raymund-jose-g-quilop.

90 Prashanth Parameswaran, 'What's Next for the New ASEAN "Our Eyes" Intelligence Initiative?', The Diplomat, 27 January 2018, available at https://thediplomat.com/2018/01/asean-launches-new-our-eyes-intelligence-initiative/; Tom Allard, 'Southeast Asian States Launch Intelligence Pact to Counter Islamic Threat', Business Insider, 25 January 2018, available at https://www.businessinsider.com/r-southeast-asian-states-launch-intelligence-pact-to-counter-islamist-threat-2018-1?r=US&IR=T.

Indonesia and abroad under direct presidential authority.[91] However, military response alone would be insufficient to break the link between criminal groups and terrorism. Indeed, the Manila Declaration to Counter the Rise of Radicalisation and Violent Extremism acknowledges the need to develop 'an integrated, evidence-based approach' by, among other things, promoting dialogue, strengthening good governance, human rights and the rule of law, and strengthening strategic communications.[92]

Intelligence sharing constitutes a core element in the fight against violent extremism, particularly as it finds roots in the ethnic and religious tensions or the socio-economic condition facilitating closer linkage between organized crime and terrorism. As the former Defence Minister of Indonesia Ryamizard Ryacudu has noted, a multilateral intelligence sharing platform is vital to 'detect routes taken by FTFs [Foreign Terrorist Fighters], location of their training camps, means and patterns of propaganda dissemination as well as sources and channels of their funding'.[93] The significance of intelligence sharing is further reinforced in the ASEAN Plan of Action to Prevent and Counter the Rise of Radicalisation and Violent Extremism 2018–2025, which aims to strengthen 'sharing of information and intelligence among security agencies regionally to prevent and counter radicalisation and violent extremism'.[94]

The cross-fertilization of transnational organized crime and terrorism means that there is need for cross-sectoral sharing of intelligence on criminal networks and terrorist organizations between ASEAN member states.[95] The cross-sectoral cooperation is necessary to unravel factors accounting for cooperation and resource-sharing between criminal groups and terrorist networks, rather than focusing solely on motivating factors for radicalization and joining a terrorist group.[96] However, there is a perceived risk in sharing military intelligence for the purposes of criminal investigation and prosecution due to the

91 John McBeth, 'Indonesia's Military Tightens its Anti-Terror Grip', Asia Times, 8 August 2019, available at https://www.asiatimes.com/2019/08/article/indonesias-military-tightens-its-anti-terror-grip/.

92 Manila Declaration to Counter the Rise of Radicalisation and Violent Extremism, adopted 20 September 2017, para 6.

93 Ryamizard Ryacudu, 'Terrorism in Southeast Asia: The Need for Joint Counter-Terrorism Frameworks' (2018) 10(11) Counter Terrorist Trends and Analyses 1, 2.

94 ASEAN Plan of Action to Prevent and Counter the Rise of Radicalisation and Violent Extremism, adopted at the 12th ASEAN Ministerial Meeting on Transnational Crime, 31 October 2018, para 3.7.

95 Marguerite Borelli, 'ASEAN Counter-Terrorism Weaknesses' (2017) 9(9) Counter Terrorist Trends and Analyses 14, 16.

96 Beliveer Singh, 'Terrorist Networks in Southeast Asia and Implications for Regional Security' (2018) 10(5) Counter Terrorist Trends and Analyses 8, 10.

security value of the information or the specific technique employed in the gathering of information.[97] For Southeast Asian states, the imperative interest of national security is an overriding concern, limiting the extent to which regional cooperation on counter-terrorism can move across different agencies and penetrate into the realm of national defense to break the organizational link between local criminal groups and international terrorist networks.

5 Conclusion

Having framed terrorism as part of transnational crime, ASEAN is well placed to address the association of organized crime with terrorism. However, the legal landscape for combating terrorism in ASEAN remains incomplete, with the ACCT providing only a general framework for cooperation and a region-wide extradition treaty yet to be adopted. There is sufficient room to adapt ASEAN's legal response to various forms of terrorism as they evolve, but the criminal justice approach has its own limit. This chapter has identified three areas of concern where the impact of ASEAN instruments is limited: (1) the harmonization of national counter-terrorism laws with a common approach to organized crime; (2) the adaptation of anti-money laundering measures to accommodate variation in local economic structure, cultural and religious diversity, and new technological advances in financial transaction; and (3) cross-sectoral counter-terrorism cooperation that penetrates into the realm of national defense with the risk of undermining the imperative interest of national security.

The cross-fertilization of transnational organized crime and terrorism across national borders presents a particular challenge to ASEAN. It exploits regulatory gaps that have been left open due to the ambivalent attitude among ASEAN member states towards harmonization of counter-terrorism laws, underlying ethnic and religious tensions, pre-existing socio-economic condition, and the overriding concern about the fight against insurgents, dissidents and critics of government. The regional principle of non-interference, premised upon the strong assertation of sovereignty, is designed to protect each state's authority to deal with these issues without any external interference. This necessarily poses a structural obstacle to greater harmonization and cross-border cooperation at the regional level necessary to break the organizational link between local criminal groups and international terrorist networks.

97 Sandy Gordon, 'Regionalism and Cross-Border Cooperation against Crime and Terrorism in the Asia-Pacific' (2009) 5(4) Security Challenges 75, 82.

CHAPTER 7

Terrorism and Transnational Organized Crime as Challenges to Multidimensional Security

The Response of the Organization of American States

Mirko Sossai

1 Introduction

The Organization of American States (OAS) has portrayed itself as a valuable partner of the United Nations in the fight against both terrorism and transnational organized crime (TOC): like any other regional organization, it has "a deeper understanding of the dynamics and realities of their Member States", and it is instrumental "in strengthening implementation of international obligations by promoting buy in and a sense of ownership by governments".[1] The role the OAS has played with respect to the threat posed by terrorist and criminal groups can be summarized as a twofold action: the organization has acted both as a standard-setter and as a service-provider for its 35 members. Not only did the organization perform a law-making function, through the adoption of a series of international conventions on counterterrorism and the fight against organized crime, but it has also created an institutional framework aimed at promoting cooperation and information sharing as well as implementing capacity-building programs.

It is important to situate the OAS activities aimed at countering terrorism and organized crime against the background of the overall evolution of the Inter-American system: since its creation in 1948, the organization has been characterized by the evident power asymmetry between the United States and the other Caribbean and Latin American members. This contributes to explain why the OAS has undergone a series of highs and lows:[2] after a period of decline

---

1 'Opportunities and challenges in strengthening international cooperation through the sharing of information, expertise and resources': Remarks by Alison August Treppel, Executive Secretary, Inter-American Committee Against Terrorism (CICTE), UN High-Level Conference on Counter-Terrorism, New York (28 June 2018) http://www.un.org/en/counterterrorism/hlc/statements.shtml.

2 See T. Legler, 'Beyond Reach? The Organization of American States and Effective Multilateralism' in J. Dominguez and A. Covarrubias (eds), *Routledge Handbook of Latin America in the World* (London/New York: Routledge, 2014) 311.

 | DOI:10.1163/9789004424579_009

in the Seventies and Eighties, the end of the cold war seemed to inaugurate a period of dynamism and multilateral cooperation.[3] After 2001, notwithstanding the threat of global terror significantly shifted the US attention outside the American hemisphere, the narrative of the war on terror spread its effects on the continent, constituting the lens through which many situations of violence and armed conflict were perceived.[4]

In the post 9/11 world, OAS member States defined security in multidimensional terms at the special conference which took place in Mexico City in 2003: the Declaration on Security in the Americas stressed the importance of improving coordination and technical cooperation to address new threats, including 'terrorism, transnational organized crime, the global drug problem, corruption, asset laundering, illicit trafficking in weapons, and the connections among them'. This led to the development of a new normative framework and to the creation of new institutional mechanisms within the organization.

The chapter will assess the specific contribution of the OAS in combating terrorism and organized crime: in addition to the international cooperation in criminal matters, by way of the harmonization of the domestic legal orders, the regional initiatives have been characterized by an emphasis on the measures of prevention. It is not by chance that in the last decade the OAS has understood the nexus between international terrorism and organized crime not so much in terms of interactions and synergies between terrorist and criminal groups, but in terms of a parallelism with respect to the vulnerabilities that are exploited by both.[5] Therefore, this chapter will focus on three major themes: criminal cooperation and information sharing; money laundering; and the illicit trafficking of firearms and other items.

3 See B. Horwitz, *The Transformation of the Organization of American States: A Multilateral Framework for Regional Governance* (London: Anthem Press, 2010) 31; H. Caminos, 'The Role of the Organization of American States in the Promotion of Democratic Governance' (1998) 273 *Recueil des Cours* 107.

4 See O. Palma, 'The Changing Meaning of 'Terrorism' in Colombia: A Matter of Discourse' in M. J. Boyle (ed), *Non-Western Responses to Terrorism* (Manchester: Manchester University Press, 2020) 246.

5 'Enhancing Synergies Between the United Nations and Regional and Subregional Organizations to Address the Nexus between Terrorism and Transnational Organized Crime': Remarks by Alison August Treppel, Executive Secretary of The Inter-American Committee Against Terrorism (CICTE), UN Security Council (9 April 2018).

2 Terrorism and Transnational Organized Crime as 'Non-traditional' Threats to Hemispheric Security

In comparison with other areas of the world, the threat of terrorism in Latin America and the Caribbean has been described to remain generally low.[6] In the first decade of the twenty-first century, the qualification as terrorist acts was mainly applied to the activities of the armed groups operating in Colombia and Peru. Nonetheless, since early 1990s, concern was expressed with respect to the risk that Muslim fundamentalism could penetrate in Latin America, particularly after the two bombings against the Israeli Embassy and the Argentine-Israeli Mutual Association (AMIA) in Buenos Aires.[7] In more recent years, the US warned that the Islamic State in Iraq and the Levant (ISIL, also known as Da'esh) could find logistical and financial support in South America and the Caribbean, including the issue of individuals from the region leaving to fight with the Islamic State.[8] In addition, the risk of recruitment to terrorism and radicalization to violent extremism conducive to terrorism, the growing volume and accessibility of terrorist propaganda, and the potential exploitation of the banking system and informal economies of many States to fund terrorist networks remain matters of concern.[9]

The terrorist attacks of 9/11 had a profound impact on the ways violence has been addressed and security governed in the American continent. In September 2001, the OAS Foreign Affairs Ministers, acting as an organ of consultation under the Inter-American Treaty of Reciprocal Assistance (the 'Rio Treaty'),[10] classified the terrorist attacks against the US as 'attacks against all

6 M.P Sullivan and J.S. Beittel, *Latin America: Terrorism Issues* (Washington, DC: Congressional Research Service, 2016) i.

7 See A. H. Levine and N. Zaretsky (eds), *Landscapes of Memory and Impunity: the Aftermath of the AMIA Bombing in Jewish Argentina* (Leiden/Boston: Brill, 2015).

8 See *Latin America and the Caribbean: Key Issues and Actions in the 114th Congress* (Washington, DC: Congressional Research Service, 2017) 22. See 'Joint Communique of the Third Hemispheric Ministerial Conference to Combat Terrorism' (20 January 2020) https://www.gov.br/mre/en/contact-us/press-area/press-releases/third-hemispheric-ministerial-conference-to-combat-terrorism-joint-communique, in which the Participating Governments "[a]ffirmed that the terrorist organizations ISIS/Daesh and Al-Qaida and their affiliated organizations constitute a threat to collective security, to the security of citizens inside and outside their territories, and to all persons within their jurisdictions" and "[e]xpressed their concern about Hezbollah networks' activities in some areas of the Western Hemisphere".

9 M. Müller, 'Enter 9/11: Latin America and the Global War on Terror' (2020) 52 *Journal of Latin American Studies*, 545.

10 The Inter-American Treaty of Reciprocal Assistance, adopted 9 February 1947, 21 UNTS 77 (entered into force 12 March 1948).

American states',[11] in accordance with Article 3 of the Rio Treaty, which refers to the right to collective self-defence pursuant to Article 51 of the UN Charter. The terrorist attacks against the World Trade Center and the Pentagon consolidated a shift in the perception of situations of violence in the Western hemisphere: as a paradigmatic example, particularly under the presidency of Alvaro Uribe Vélez, Colombia succeeded in considering the internal armed conflict with the guerrilla groups as part of the global 'war on terror'.[12]

It remains that for the OAS member States, "the security challenges posed by transnational organized criminal activity take greater precedent than the threat of an act of terrorism"[13] in Latin America and the Caribbean. The OAS has on several occasions emphasized the multidimensional character of the TOC, particularly when associated to new criminal trends, including *inter alia* "the smuggling and trafficking of persons, drugs, weapons, and currency; the smuggling of illegal products and substances, including but not limited to medications, biological specimens, flora and fauna; the trade and smuggling of counterfeit and pirated goods; crimes against cultural heritage, including but not limited to the illicit traffic of cultural property; the counterfeiting of currency and security documents; financial crimes; and the illegal use of virtual currencies; etc."[14] Undoubtedly, drug trafficking has been deemed to represent the manifestation *par excellence* of organized crime in the region: recent

11 OAS Meeting of Consultation of Ministers Foreign Affairs, 'Terrorist Threat to the Americas' OEA/Ser.F/II.24, RC.24/RES.1/01 (21 September 2001). See S. Ratner, '*Ius ad bellum* and *ius in bello* after September 11' (2002) 96 *American Journal of International Law* 905, 909; J.-M. Arrighi, 'The Prohibition of the Use of Force and Non-Intervention: Ambition and Practice in the OAS Region' in M. Weller (ed), *The Oxford Handbook of the Use of Force in International Law* (Oxford: OUP, 2015) 507, 522.

12 See C. Von der Groeben, 'The Conflict in Colombia and the Relationship between Humanitarian Law and Human Rights Law in Practice: Analysis of the New Operational Law of the Colombian Armed Forces' (2011) 16 *Journal of Conflict & Security Law* 141; M. Sossai, 'The Internal Conflict in Colombia and the Fight against Terrorism: UN Security Council Resolution 1465 (2003) and Further Developments' (2005) 3 *Journal of International Criminal Justice* 253.

13 'The Nexus between International Terrorism and Organized Crime': Remarks by Maria Fernanda Sarmiento, Program officer of the Inter-American Committee against Terrorism (CICTE), Secretariat for Multidimensional Security, Organization of American States (26 April 2019); see L. E. Nagle, 'The Challenges of Fighting Global Organized Crime in Latin America' (2003) 26 *Fordham International Law Journal* 1648, 1661.

14 OAS General Assembly, 'Advancing Hemispheric Security: A Multidimensional Approach', Doc. AG/RES. 2950 (L-O/20) (21 October 2020).

studies have elucidated the main peculiarities of the 'systemic drug violence'[15] which has affected the urban areas of countries like Mexico and Colombia.

As reported by the *Global Study on Homicide*, released by the United Nations Office on Drugs and Crime (UNODC) in 2019, "in the Americas membership of organized crime groups and gangs is largely responsible for the high homicide rates in that region".[16] Similarly, the United Nations Development Programme (UNDP) found in its reports on Latin America that: "[transnational organized crime] operates in a complex context of local crime and violence that occurs both in private settings and the public spheres. The interwoven nature of these threats explains the deterioration of security in the region and the emergence of a spiral of violence in some cities and regions of Latin America."[17] A World Bank study on violence in seven Central American countries identified three primary causes: drug trafficking, youth violence, and the availability of firearms.[18] As observed by the Inter-American Commission on human rights (IACHR), "the countries of the region have some of the highest rates of crime and violence in the world and their young population has been the most affected, both as victims and as perpetrators. For the first time in decades the population of Latin America lists crime as a major concern, even greater than unemployment."[19]

In recent years, an impressive amount of literature has sought to analyze a plethora of armed groups, which are present in almost every country of the region, with the employment of a vast array of names to refer to them: *gangs, clicas, combos, posses, bandas, oficinas, pandillas, maras, factions, quadrilhas,*

---

15 See A. Durán-Martínez, *The Politics of Drug Violence: Criminals, Cops, and Politicians in Colombia and Mexico* (Oxford: OUP 2018) 42; B. Lessing, *Making Peace in Drug Wars: Crackdowns and Cartels in Latin America* (Cambridge: CUP 2018); M. Dugato, M. De Simoni and E. U. Savona, *Measuring OC in Latin America: a methodology for developing and validating scores and composite indicators for measuring OC at national and subnational level* (July 2014) https://www.transcrime.it/wp-content/uploads/2014/06/Measuring-OC-June-2014.pdf.

16 UNODC, *Global Study on Homicide 2019: Executive Summary* (July 2019) https://www.unodc.org/documents/data-and-analysis/gsh/Booklet1.pdf.

17 UNDP, *Citizen Security with a Human Face: Evidence and Proposals for Latin America*, Regional Human Development Report for Latin America 2013–2014 (November 2013) IX.

18 Banco Mundial, *Crimen y Violencia en Centroamérica: Un Desafío para el Desarrollo* (Washington DC: World Bank, 2011) 23; see Gino Costa, 'Citizen Security and Transnational Organized Crime in the Americas' (2012) 9 *SUR – International Journal on Human Rights* 16 (2012) 127.

19 IACHR, *Report on Citizen Security and Human Rights*, OEA/Ser.L/V/II. Doc. 57 (31 December 2009).

comandos, militias, cartels, syndicates, movements, families, and traffickers.[20] The debate on similarities and differences between the various types of armed groups and whether they might all fall within the category of TOC is not without consequences with respect to the qualification of their behavior and the specific policies which could be used against them.

3 Multidimensional Security Required a New Institutional Framework

Terrorism and TOC were identified by the 2003 Declaration on Security in the Americas, as belonging to the first group of the "new threats, concerns, and other challenges of a diverse nature", together with "the global drug problem, corruption, asset laundering, illicit trafficking in weapons, and the connections among them".[21] Not only did the Declaration emphasized the importance of mutual cooperation and effective implementation of the existing obligations under the relevant universal and regional conventions, but it also focused on certain institutional issues: as part of the commitment to revitalize the organs, institutions, and mechanisms of the inter-American system, the OAS member States recommended to strengthen the capacity of the General Secretariat to better serve the member States and the political bodies of the Organization on matters of hemispheric security". It is important to evaluate the impact of the 2003 Declaration on the institutional infrastructure: the OAS General Secretariat was substantially restructured, giving way for the creation of a Secretariat for Multidimensional Security (SMS) in 2005, with the mandate of addressing traditional as well as non-traditional threats.[22] One of the purposes of the change in the institutional architecture was to assemble the existing bodies dealing with terrorism and organized crime, and a new Department of Public Security under one administrative roof:[23] at present,

---

20 See J. Albarracín and N. Barnes, 'Criminal Violence in Latin America' (2020) 55 *Latin American Research Review* 397.

21 'Declaration on Security in the Americas' OEA/Ser.K/XXXVIII CES/DEC.1/03 rev. 1 (28 October 2003).

22 See J.-M. Arrighi 'L'Organisation des États américains et le droit international' (2011) 355 *Recueil des cours* 235, 355.

23 See e.g. OAS General Assembly, 'Modernization and Reorganization of the General Secretariat in Accordance with the Strategic Vision for the Organization and for Strengthening the Inter-American System' AG/RES. 2876 (XLV-O/15) (15 June 2015); see M. Herz, *The Organization of American States (OAS): Global Governance away from the Media* (London/New York: Routledge, 2011).

the dependencies of the SMS include the executive secretariat of the Inter-American Drug Abuse Control Commission (CICAD), the secretariat of the Inter-American Committee against Terrorism (CICTE), the department on Public Security (whose mandate includes anti-trafficking in persons) and the department against Transnational Organized Crime (DTOC).

The OAS had begun to take action against non-traditional security issues well before 2000: CICAD and CICTE were a product of the last two decades of the twentieth century. Already in the eighties, it clearly emerged that the OAS should have played a role in developing a regional policy strategy to tackle the drug problem, given the regional nature of the threat – at that time, known as the 'cocaine epidemic' and its impact on peace, security and development of the member States.[24] In 1986 the OAS General Assembly had established the Inter-American Drug Abuse Control Commission (CICAD) as the main Western Hemisphere's policy forum to deal with the "illicit use and production of narcotic drugs and psychotropic substances and traffic therein".[25] Initially established with the main goal of assisting governments lacking an antidrug strategy in adopting one,[26] the range of activities of the CICAD – that is composed of the competent national authorities of the thirty-five OAS member states – evolved over the last twenty-five years, in application of the various strategies and plans of action adopted by the OAS institutions. A similar mandate to "to develop cooperation"[27] characterized the establishment by the OAS General Assembly in 1999 of the the Inter-American Committee against Terrorism (CICTE) as a result of the five-year diplomatic effort, which started with the 1994 First Summit of the Americas.[28] The CICTE was meant to be a forum for discussion and decision-making in order "to prevent, combat, and

24 See S. Herencia Carrasco, '¿Una organización regional para un problema regional? El papel de la organización de los estados americanos en la articulación de un enfoque regional sobre las drogas' in K. Ambos, E. Malarino, and M.-C. Fuchs (eds), *Drogas ilícitas y narcotráfico: nuevos desarrollos en América Latina* (Bogotà: Temis, 2017) 91.

25 See OAS General Assembly, 'Inter-American Program of Action of Rio de Janeiro against the Illicit Use and Production of Narcotic Drugs and Psychotropic Substances and Traffic Therein' AG/RES. 814 (XVI-0/86) (15 November 1986).

26 See C. Granada, 'The OAS and Transnational Organized Crime in the Americas' in M. Berdal and M. Serrano (eds), *Transnational Organized Crime and International Security: Business as Usual?* (Boulder, CO: Lynne Rienner, 2002) 1.

27 OAS General Assembly, 'Hemispheric Cooperation to Prevent, Combat, and Eliminate Terrorism' AG/RES. 1650 (XXIX-O/99) (7 June 1999).

28 'Summit of the Americas Plan of Action' (Miami, 9–11 December 1994) http://www.summit-americas.org/i_summit/i_summit_poa_en.pdf. See see M. Scalabrino, 'Fighting against International Terrorism: The Latin American Response' in A. Bianchi (ed), *Enforcing International Law Norms Against Terrorism* (Oxford: Hart, 2004) 163.

eliminate terrorist acts and activities". In two decades, the CICTE engaged in a variety of programs including border controls, critical infrastructure protection, international cooperation and partnership, legislative assistance and combating terrorism financing.[29]

Finally, not only did the adoption of the Hemispheric Plan of Action against Transnational Organized Crime[30] in 2006 mark the commitment of the OAS member States for the full implementation of the 2000 United Nations Convention against Transnational Organized Crime,[31] but also reinforced a comprehensive regional vision for preventing and confronting organized crime, by delineating a series of specific actions and the contribution of working groups and other consultative bodies.[32] The emphasis on providing technical assistance to member States in countering TOC in all its different manifestations eventually led to the creation by the Secretary General of the Department against Transnational Organized Crime (DTOC) in 2016, with a broad mandate which includes money laundering, illicit drug trafficking, the related contraband, the trafficking of firearms, ammunition, explosives and related materials; the traffic of cultural goods, trafficking in persons, the illicit traffic of migrants by land, sea and air; and cybercrime.

4 Cooperation on Criminal Matters and Information Sharing

Undoubtedly, a good part of the regional legal regime consists of 'suppression conventions',[33] which oblige States Parties to criminalize certain conducts and to cooperate in the prosecution of these offences, under the principle *aut*

29 Remarks by Alison August Treppel, Executive Secretary of the Inter-American Committee against Terrorism (CICTE) of the Organization of American States during the Virtual Open Briefing of the Counter-Terrorism Committee on "The threat of terrorism in Latin America and the Caribbean" (14 December 2020); for an overall assessment, see E. Rosand, A. Millar, and J. Ipe, *Implementing the UN Global Counter-Terrorism Strategy in the Latin America and Caribbean Region* (Center on Global Counterterrorism Cooperation, 2008).

30 OAS Permanent Council, 'Emispheric Plan of Action against Transnational Organized Crime' OEA/Ser.G CP/RES. 908 (1567/06) (26 October 2006).

31 United Nations Convention against Transnational Organized Crime, adopted 15 December 2000, 2225 UNTS 209 (entered into force 29 Septeber 2003).

32 See M. B. Lloyd, *Transnational Crimes in the Americas: Law, Policy and Institutions* (London/New York: Anthem, 2018).

33 For this notion, see N. Boister, *An Introduction to Transnational Criminal Law* (2nd ed, Oxford: OUP 2018) 20; R. Clark, 'Treaty Crimes' in W. Schabas (ed), *The Cambridge Companion to International Criminal Law* (Cambridge: CUP, 2016) 2014.

dedere aut judicare.[34] One of the first attempts to establish a OAS response to terrorist activities was the adoption in 1971 of the Convention to Prevent and Punish Acts of Terrorism Taking the Form of Crimes against Persons and Related Extortion that are of International Significance,[35] as a reaction to the multiple episodes of kidnapping of diplomats by revolutionary groups to obtain political concessions from governments.[36]

Paradigmatic in this framework is the content of the 2002 Inter-American Convention against Terrorism, which was one of the first treaties to be drafted after 9/11. Its final text reflected the pragmatic approach proposed by the US and Canada at the time of negotiations:[37] in consideration of the difficulties in identifying the specific features of 'terrorism' as a legal concept, the 2002 Convention avoided to offer a comprehensive definition of the crime; rather, it relied on the list of offences as established in the pre-existing sectoral conventions concluded under the auspices of the UN. Its Article 2 stresses that the main purpose of the convention remained that of promoting the ratification of the international instruments and their effective implementation at domestic level.

The task of creating incentives for States to raise their own standards seems to characterize as well the fight against organized crime: the two main trajectories of the work of the OAS have been the adoption of multilateral conventions – including the the 1996 Inter-American Convention against corruption (IACAC)[38] and the Inter-American Convention against the Illicit Manufacturing of and Trafficking in Firearms, Ammunition, Explosives and Related Materials (CIFTA)[39] – and the development of model laws and regulations concerning

---

34 On the obligation to extradite or prosecute, see 'The obligation to extradite or prosecute (*aut dedere aut judicare*): Final Report of the International Law Commission' in *Yearbook of the International Law Commission 2014*, vol. II, Part Two, 92; moreover, see M. Bassiouni and E. M. Wise, *Aut Dedere Aut Judicare: The Duty to Extradite or Prosecute in International Law* (Dordrecht/Boston/London: Martinus Nijhoff, 1995) 207.

35 OAS Convention to Prevent and Punish Acts of Terrorism Taking the Form of Crimes against Persons and Related Extortion that are of International Significance, adopted 2 February 1971, 194 UNTS 1438 (entered into force 16 October 1973).

36 R. Brach, 'The Inter-American Convention on the Kidnapping of Diplomats' (1971) 10 *Columbia Journal of Transnational Law* 392.

37 E. Lagos and T. D. Rudy, 'Preventing, Punishing, and Eliminating Terrorism in the Western Hemisphere: A post-9/11 Inter-American Treaty' (2002–2003) 26 *Fordham International Law Journal* 401, 423.

38 Inter-American Convention against Corruption, adopted 29 March 1996, 35 ILM 724 (entry into force 6 March 1997).

39 Inter-American Convention against the Illicit Manufacturing of and Trafficking in Firearms, Ammunition, Explosives and Related Materials, adopted 14 November 1997, 37 ILM 143 (entry into force 1 July 1998).

different manifestations of organized crime: laundering offenses connected to illicit drug trafficking and other serious offense;[40] the control of chemical substances used in the illicit production of narcotic drugs and psychotropic substances;[41] illicit enrichment and transnational bribery;[42] the control of the international movement of firearms, their parts, and components.[43] It is important to stress the combination and the interplay of hard law and soft law instruments[44] as part of a codification and institutionalization process at regional level, aimed at promoting the implementation in the domestic legal orders of the relevant conventions adopted at national level.[45]

Several studies have stressed the symbiotic relationship between organized crime, drug trafficking and corruption in the Americas: as observed by the IACHR, "in some countries of the region, corruption and impunity have enabled criminal organizations to develop and establish parallel power structures."[46] The OAS was the first organization to adopt an anti-corruption convention in 1996.[47] Subsequently, it was followed by other regional and

---

40 CICAD, 'Model Regulations Concerning Laundering Offenses Connected to Illicit Drug Trafficking and Other Serious Offense' (1992, as finally amended in 2011), http://www.cicad.oas.org/lavado_activos/eng/Model_regula_eng12_02/REGLAMENTO%20LAVADO%20-%20ENG.pdf.

41 CICAD, Model Regulations for the control of Chemical Substances Used in the Illicit Production of Narcotic Drugs and Psychotropic Substances (1999), http://www.cicad.oas.org/reduccion_oferta/resources/chems/Model%20Regulations-Approved%20CICAD%2066-Final.pdf.

42 Comité Jurídico Interamericano, 'Legislación Modelo sobre Enriquecimiento Ilícito y Soborno Transnacional', http://www.oas.org/juridico/spanish/legmodel.htm.

43 CICAD, 'Model Regulations for the Control of the International Movement of Firearms, their Parts and Components and Ammunition' (1997) http://www.cicad.oas.org/Desarrollo_Juridico/esp/Reglamentos/ReglamentoModelo/RegModeloIdiomas/ReglArmseng.doc.

44 The notion of soft law is employed in this context as covering all those social rules generated by States or other subjects of international law which are not legally binding but are nevertheless capable of producing certain legal effects: see inter al. D. Thürer, 'Soft Law' in R. Wolfrum (ed) *Max Planck Encyclopedia of Public International Law* (Oxford: OUP, 2012) vol. IX, 269; P.-M. Dupuy, 'Soft Law and the International Law of the Environment' (1991) 12 *Michigan Journal of International Law* 420; C. Chinkin, 'The Challenge of Soft Law: Development and Change in International Law' (1989) 38 *International and Comparative Law Quarterly* 850.

45 See C. Mougnok, 'The Codification of Inter-American Drug Law' (2018) 56 *Canadian Yearbook of International Law* 258.

46 IACHR, *Report on Citizen Security and Human Rights* (n 19) para 33; Id., *Report on Corruption and Human Rights in the Americas* (2019) para 99; OAS Secretary General, *El Problema de las Drogas en las Américas* (2013) 57.

47 On the origins of the international efforts against corruption see C. Rose, 'The Origins of International Anti-Corruption Law: The Failed Negotiation of an International

international instruments: notably, the Organization for Economic Co-operation and Development (OECD) in 1997[48] and the UN in 2003.[49] Not only does the preamble of the OAS Convention make a link between corruption and narcotrafficking, but it also focuses on the stability of democratic institutions and society's moral fiber rather than merely on economic considerations, reminiscent of the former dictatorial regimes in Latin America.[50] The purposes of the Convention are both "[t]o promote and strengthen the development [...] of the mechanisms needed to prevent, detect, punish and eradicate corruption" as well as to facilitate and regulate cooperation among the parties.

The importance of the IACAC – which follows the model of the suppression conventions with respect to the duty to criminalize and the identification of the jurisdictional links, but with an emphasis on preventive measures – lies in its quasi-universal ratification as well as in its scope of application, that has been described as broader in comparison with other regional instruments, particularly the 1997 OECD anti-bribery convention:[51] it requires State to establish as criminal offences domestic and transnational bribery – the former both active and passive – of public officials, fraudulent concealment and use of proceeds, and several forms of complicity. Moreover, the convention also criminalizes 'illicit enrichment', i.e. a significant increase in the assets of a public official which he or she cannot reasonably explain, and calls on States parties to consider additional offences, as part of the 'progressive development'. At first, the IACAC had no implementation mechanism. However, since 2001, the First Conference of States Parties established the Mechanism for Follow-Up of Implementation of the Inter-American Convention against Corruption ('MESICIC'), a peer review system administered by a committee of party-appointed experts.[52] Significantly, the mechanism has developed a series of model laws, including those on assets and interests declarations and

---

Agreement on Illicit Payments' in N. Boister, S. Gless, and F. Jeßberger (eds), *Histories of Transnational Criminal Law* (Oxford: OUP, 2021) 187.

48 OECD Convention on Combating Bribery of Foreign Public Officials in International Business Transactions, adopted 17 December 1997, 37 ILM 1 (entry into force 15 February 1999).

49 United Nations Convention against Corruption, adopted 31 October 2003, 2349 UNTS 41 (entry into force 14 December 2005).

50 See J. Wouters, C. Ryngaert, and A. S. Cloots, 'The International Legal Framework Against Corruption: Achievements and Challenges' (2013) 14 *Melbourne Journal of International Law* 205.

51 See K. W. Abbott, 'Corruption, Fight against', in *Max Planck Encyclopedia of Public International Law* (n 44) vol. II, 813.

52 See G. D. Altamirano 'The Impact of the Inter-American Convention against Corruption' (2006–07) 38 *University of Miami Inter-American Law Review* 487.

whistleblower protection, and offered legislative guidelines containing the basic elements that, according to the review carried out by the Committee and recommendations formulated, States should take into account when drafting laws on matters to which the Convention refers to.

In recent years, the connection between anti-corruption and human rights protection has been emphasized within the Inter-American system: States have a duty to adopt effective measures for investigating and punishing acts of corruption. As one of the factors that turn corruption into a structural phenomenon is impunity for those who perpetrate it, "States must adopt legislative measures to prohibit acts of corruption, establish proportionate punishments for it, and, above all, adjust oversight and punishment systems".[53] On a wider perspective concerning the relationship between organized crime and human rights, both the Inter-American Commission and Court have nonetheless made clear that the repressive policies should not amount to violation of fundamental guarantees: concern has been expressed with regard to the risk of misapplication of anti-terrorism legislation in various American countries – including the possibility of using antiterrorist laws against indigenous peoples and, even, human rights defenders – because of the vague or imprecise character of the criminal offences.[54]

Regional criminal cooperation should not be simply understood in terms of criminalizing certain conduct, establishing jurisdiction over it, and prosecuting or extraditing suspected offenders. The relevant regional conventions – along with the multilateral treaties adopted at the UN level – make explicit reference to mutual legal and technical assistance: in this regard, the 1992 Inter-American Convention on Mutual Assistance in Criminal Matters

53 *Report on Corruption and Human Rights in the Americas* (n 46) para 268; see J. Reyes, 'State Capture through Corruption: Can Human Rights Help?' (2019) 113 *AJIL Unbound* 331; S. Wirken and H. Bosdriesz, 'Privatisation and Increasing Complexity of Mass Violence in Mexico and Central America: Exploring Appropriate International Responses' in H. Van der Wilt and C. Paulussen (eds), *Legal Responses to Transnational and International Crimes: Towards an Integrative Approach* (Cheltenham: Edward Elgar Publishing, 2017) 245.

54 In 2014, the Inter-American Court on Human Rights concluded that Chile violated the American Convention on Human Rights ('Pact of San José, Costa Rica', signed 22 November 1969, 1144 UNTS 143) for having applied its Counter-terrorism Act against leaders and activists of the Mapuche indigenous people, in relation to offenses committed in the context of the social protest. The Court found that use of stereotypes and prejudices on the reasoning of the judgments against the indigenous authorities, constituted a violation of the principle of equality and non-discrimination and the right to equal protection of the law, recognized in Article 24: *Norín Catrimán et al v Chile* (2014) IACtHR (Ser C) No 279 [228].

offers a definition of assistance in this realm as including, among other things, "taking of testimony or statements from persons ... searches or seizures; transmittal of documents, reports, information, and evidence". In 1997, for the purpose of enhancing "legal and judicial cooperation in the Americas", the OAS General Assembly recommended the holding of a meeting of ministers of justice, or of ministers or attorneys general of the Americas:[55] since then, REMJA represented the hemispheric political and technical forum on justice and international legal cooperation, with a broad mandate.[56] Already the 2003 Declaration on Security in the Americas stressed that REMJA "and other meetings of criminal justice authorities are important and effective fora for promoting and strengthening mutual understanding, confidence, dialogue, and cooperation in developing criminal justice policies and responses to address new threats to security."[57] At the fifth meeting, which took place in 2004, the Ministers of Justice placed particular emphasis on the cooperation in countering TOC and terrorism.[58] The subsequent Hemispheric Plan of Action against TOC contains detailed actions on training, international cooperation and assistance, as well as information-sharing, including the enhancement of "real-time operational information, among national institutions with similar competence; maximizing the use of technology, particularly databases or other technical mechanisms such as secure information systems; and using, inter alia, INTERPOL and the OAS Network for Mutual Legal Assistance in Criminal Matters and Extradition."[59] The same goal of enhancing inter-State cooperation on information-sharing has characterized the Inter-American Network on Counter-Terrorism, a project launched in 2019 and aimed at facilitating

55 OAS General Assembly, 'Meeting of Ministers of Justice' AG/RES. 1482 (XXVII-O/97) (5 June 1997).

56 See 'Document on the REMJA Process /"Document of Washington")' OEA/Ser.K/XXXIV.7.1 OTHER, REMJA-VII/doc.6/08 rev.3, (16 October 2015); on REMJA processes: see D. P. Warner, 'Law Enforcement Cooperation in the Organization of American States: A Focus on REMJA' (2015) 37 *University of Miami Inter-American Law Review* 387; B. Zagaris,'OAS Progresses with Work of the Ministers of Justice or Attorneys General of the Americas' (2005) 76 *Revue internationale de droit penal* 119.

57 Declaration on Security in the Americas (n).

58 'Conclusions and Recommendations of REMJA-V' OEA/Ser.K/XXXIV.5, REMJA-V/doc.7/04 rev. 4 (30 April 2004).

59 OAS Permanent Council, 'Hemispheric Plan of Action against Transnational Organized Crime' OEA/Ser.G, CP/RES. 908 (1567/06) (26 October 2006).

communication of operational information among counter-terrorism points of contact designated by each member state.[60]

5 The OAS Action against Money Laundering and the Financing of Terrorism

Several reports have consistently shown that money laundering is indeed the common feature of the most serious challenges in the Americas: violent crime, drug trafficking, economic inequality and public corruption.[61] It has been estimated that, only in Mexico, drug cartels and other criminal groups laundered 50 billion dollars in 2019.[62] The CICTE stressed that money laundering and the financing of terrorism affect the development of the region's countries in various ways, as it increases crime and corruption, it weakens financial institutions, with the consequence of discouraging foreign investment; it negatively affects the macroeconomic development by diverting resources from more productive economic activities, and may also produce destabilizing impacts in neighboring countries. As a result of globalization, the negative effects of these activities impact on global integrity and financial stability.[63]

At the Lima Summit of the Americas in 2018, the Heads of State and of Government stressed the importance of strengthening domestic capacities to confront and respond to the different manifestations of TOC, including money laundering, as well as the need to promote "the broadest possible cooperation among judicial, police, and prosecutorial authorities, financial intelligence units, and administrative authorities in investigations and procedures related

---

60 OAS, 'OAS to Develop Inter-American Network on Counterterrorism to Facilitate Immediate Exchange of Information on Terrorist Threats' press release No. E-077/19 (3 October 2019).

61 United Nations Office on Drugs and Crime (UNODC), *World Drug Report 2017: Part 5, The Drug Problem and Organized Crime, Illicit Financial Flows, Corruption and Terrorism* (New York: United Nations, 2017); GAFILAT, *Report of Regional Threats on Money Laundering* (2017), https://gafilat.org/index.php/es/biblioteca-virtual/gafilat/documentos-de-interes-17/traducciones/1261-gafilat-regional-threat-assessment-2017-update/file.

62 See F. Gutiérrez, 'Tiran bloqueos de recursos a la UIF; descongeló $10,500 millones en el 2019' *El Economista* (22 January 2020) https://www.eleconomista.com.mx/sectorfinanciero/Tiran-bloqueos-de-recursos-a-la-UIF-descongelo-10500-millones-en-el-2019-20200122-0094.html.

63 CICTE, *Technical Assessment-Comparative Analysis of Typologies and Patterns of Money Laundering and Terrorism Financing in Three Free Trade Zones in Latin America* (2018) http://www.oas.org/en/sms/cicte/Documents/reports/Technical-AssessmentComparative-Analysis.pdf, 61.

to offenses of corruption, money laundering, and transnational bribery and corruption."[64] Significantly, in December 2020, OAS member states approved the new OAS Hemispheric Drug Strategy and its corresponding five-year Plan of Action 2021–2025: both documents stressed the importance of reinforcing the legislative and institutional frameworks in the areas of prevention, detection, investigation, prosecution, and control of money laundering derived from drug trafficking.[65]

Since the late eighties of the last century, the CICAD has played a pivotal role within the OAS in raising member States' capacity: in 1990 a Group of Experts for the Control of Money Laundering (GELAVEX) was created within the CICAD, as the technical forum in which country experts debate, analyze and recommend actions on asset laundering and the financing of terrorism.[66] GELAVEX currently comprises two working subgroups, namely, on International Cooperation and Confiscation; and on Coordination between Financial Intelligence Units (FIUS) and Criminal Investigation Organizations (OIC). A major development occurred in 1992, when the Commission first adopted its Anti-Money Laundering Model Regulations, which were subsequently amended several times to reflect developments in the international standards, particularly the FATF Recommendations on anti-money laundering and combating the financing of terrorism (AML/CFT).[67]

Political acts adopted within the framework of the OAS, including General Assembly resolutions[68] and the CICTE Declaration of San Carlos of 2006, have consistently underlined '[t]he need for member states to implement the 40 plus nine recommendations of the FATF on money laundering and financing of terrorism.'[69] The OAS, through the CICTE and the CICAD, has observer status in the Financial Action Task Force of Latin America (GAFILAT), a regional

64 VIII Summit of the Americas, 'Lima Commitment: Democratic Governance against Corruption' (14 April 2018) https://viiicumbreperu.summit-americas.org/us/lima-commitment-democratic-governance-against-corruption/.

65 CICAD, 'Hemispheric Drug Strategy 2020' (9–11 December 2020); Id., 'Hemispheric Plan of Action on Drugs 2021–2025' OEA/Ser.L/XIV.2.68, CICAD/doc.2533/20 (10 December 2020).

66 See S. Morán Blanco, *Lucha contra el narcotráfico en América Latina-Caribe: la labor de la Organización de Estados Americanos (OEA)* (Valencia: Tirant lo Blanch, 2021) 345.

67 FATF, 'International Standards on Combating Money Laundering and the Financing of Terrorism & Proliferation' (The FATF Recommendations) (February 2012 – updated October 2020).

68 See, OAS General Assembly, 'Support for the Work of the Inter-American Committee against Terrorism' AG/RES. 2459 (XXXIX-O/09), (4 June 2009).

69 CICTE, Declaration of San Carlos, 'Hemispheric Cooperation for Comprehensive Action to Fight Terrorism' (24 March 2006).

organization gathering 17 members, with the mandate of promoting capacity-building and cooperation in the implementation of the FATF standards.[70]

From a legal perspective, one of the most important issues is the relationship between the obligations under the 2002 Inter-American Convention and the FATF Recommendations. Under Article 4(2) of the Convention, the recommendations are referred to as 'guidelines' for the implementation of its financial control measures. The choice of the term 'guidelines' suggests not only that the recommendations can change over time, but that the provision does not intend to render the soft law instrument legally binding. But it remains that the OAS – through its formal and informal law-making initiatives[71] – has contributed to reinforce the normative dynamics between the FATF standards and legally binding instruments, including the counter-terrorism decisions of the UN Security Council, such as res. 1373 (2001) and res. 1540 (2004).[72]

Since their establishment, both FATF and GAFILAT have focused not only on standard-setting and on identifying the current threats, but also on ensuring full compliance with the Recommendations: this takes place through 'mutual evaluations', a peer-review process to assess the overall level of technical compliance and effectiveness in each country. In other terms, the assessment involves two distinct, albeit inter-related, components: on the one hand, whether the necessary laws and regulations are in force and effect, and whether institutional framework is in place; on the other, whether the AML/CFT system is working, and the extent to which the country is achieving the defined set of outcomes.[73] The mutual evaluations reports on Latin America

70 The Financial Action Task Force of Latin America was created as GAFISUD in December 2000 by means of a memorandum of understanding by representatives of the governments of nine South American countries. The change of name from GAFISUD to GAFILAT was decided in 2014, to reflect the expansion of its membership to include all Latin American countries.

71 See J. Pauwelyn, 'Informal International Lawmaking: Framing the Concept and Research Questions' in J. Pauwelyn, R. Wessel, and J. Wouters (ed), *Informal International Lawmaking* (Oxford: OUP, 2012) 13, 15, who describes informality in terms of *output* as follows: "international cooperation may be informal in the sense that it does not lead to a formal treaty or any other traditional source of international law, but rather to a guideline, standard, declaration, or even more informal policy coordination or exchange"; in addition, see R. Wessel, 'Informal International Law-Making as a New Form of World Legislation?' (2011) 8 *International Organizations Law Review* 253.

72 See A. Rodiles, *Coalitions of the Willing and International Law: The Interplay between Formality and Informality* (Cambridge: CUP 2018), particularly Chapters 5 and 6.

73 FATF, 'Methodology for assessing with the FATF Recommendations and the effectiveness of AML/CFT systems' (February 2013); 'Procedures for the FATF Fourth Round of AML/CFT Mutual Evaluations' (January 2021). See C. Rose, *International Anti-corruption Norms: Their Creation and Influence on Domestic Legal Systems* (Oxford: OUP 2015) 182–183.

and Caribbean have shown a mixed picture: whereas some members possess a 'mature regime',[74] the legal framework in force in other countries continue to suffer from 'deficiencies that limit the general system effectiveness'.[75] Still, the recent FATF reports show progress among OAS members in implementing the recommended actions: whereas in 2010–11, several of them were included in the list of jurisdictions with strategic AML/CFT deficiencies, the situation has significantly improved one decade later.[76] A UN report confirms that most States in the appear to have amended their terrorism-financing laws in the period 2015–2017.[77]

Finally, the OAS has placed emphasis on the cooperation between international and regional organizations in combating the financing of terrorism: a paradigmatic example of that has been the creation of MECOOR in 2010, a partnership between CICTE, the Anti-Money Laundering Unit of the CICAD, the Latin America Financial Action Task Force (GAFILAT), the UN Counter-Terrorism Committee Executive Directorate and the Terrorism Prevention Branch of UNODC, aimed at delivering legislative assistance and capacity building to enhance coordination and strengthen counter-terrorism efforts in the Hemisphere.

6 The Action to Eradicate the Illicit Trafficking of Small Weapons

According to a 2019 study, countries in the Americas reported 173,000 victims of intentional homicide: 37 per cent of the global total in a region that accounts for only 13 per cent of the world's population.[78] This contributes to explain why States from Latin America and the Caribbean have long been keen

74 See e.g. FATF and GAFILAT, 'Anti-Money Laundering and Counter-Terrorist Financing Measures – Mexico, Fourth Round Mutual Evaluation Report', January 2018, 3; see V. M. Garay Garzón, 'México: su lucha contra el lavado de activos y su impacto laboral' (2019) 69 *Revista de la Facultad de Derecho de México* 107.

75 See e.g. GAFILAT, 'Mutual Evaluation Report of the Republic of Nicaragua', October 2017, 6.

76 See FATF, Annual Report 2019–2020 (Paris: FATF/OECD, 2020) 37, www.fatf-gafi.org/publications/fatfgeneral/documents/annual-report-2019-2020.html.

77 UN, 'Joint report of the Counter-Terrorism Committee Executive Directorate and the Analytical Support and Sanctions Monitoring Team pursuant to resolutions 1526 (2004) and 2253 (2015) concerning Islamic State in Iraq and the Levant (ISIL) (Da'esh), Al-Qaida and the Taliban and associated individuals and entities on actions taken by Member States to disrupt terrorist financing, prepared pursuant to paragraph 37 of Security Council resolution 2462 (2019)', S/2020/493 (3 June 2020) 15.

78 See UNODC, *Global Study on Homicide 2019* (Vienna: UN, 2019) 13.

supporters of regional and universal instruments in the field of arms transfer and small arms and light weapons (SALW) controls, including the 2001 United Nations Programme of Action.[79] Moreover, they played a crucial role during the negotiations towards the Arms Trade Treaty,[80] which has received a high level of political support within the region.[81]

A combination between informal efforts and formal sources characterizes the fight against the illicit trafficking of firearms in the region. Once again, the OAS was the forerunner in adopting a legally binding instrument: the 1997 Convention (CIFTA). The explicit mention to ammunition, explosives, and other related materials, in addition to firearms, distinguishes it from other instruments on this topic. The successful negotiations towards the CIFTA were the result of the US-Mexico counter-narcotics cooperation, thanks to the diplomatic initiative of President Zedillo. A signing ceremony was held in Washington DC in November 1997: on that occasion, President Clinton affirmed that the OAS members were "speaking with one voice, acting with one conviction and leading toward one goal: to stem the illegal flow of guns, ammunition and explosives in our hemisphere."[82] The Convention has been signed by all the OAS members and ratified by 31 of them, with the notable exceptions of Canada, Jamaica, and United States.

In addition to the typical obligation to criminalize as well as the principle *aut dedere aut judicare*, the Convention contains provisions on the marking of firearms, confiscation or forfeiture, and maintaining records for tracing. Of particular importance are Article IX, which requires members to establish an effective system of import, export and international transit licensing, and Articles XIII–XV on cooperation and exchange of information and experience.[83] Since

79 UN, 'Programme of Action to Prevent, Combat and Eradicate the Illicit Trade in Small Arms and Light Weapons in All Its Aspects', A/CONF.192/15 (20 July 2001).

80 Arms Trade Treaty, adopted 2 April 2013, 3013 UNTS (entry into force 24 December 2014).

81 See M. Bromley and A. Malaret, 'ATT-Related Activities in Latin America and The Caribbean: Identifying Gaps and Improving Coordination', SIPRI Background Paper (February 2017).

82 W. Clinton, 'Remarks at the Signing Ceremony for the Organization of American States Hemispheric Arms Trafficking Convention' (14 November 1997), in *Public Papers of the Presidents of the United States: William J. Clinton, 1997 (July 1 to December 31, 1997)* (Washington DC: National Archives and Records Administration, Office of the Federal Register, 1999) 1560.

83 See M. Schroeder, *Small Arms, Terrorism and the OAS Firearms Convention*, Federation of American Scientists (FAS) Occasional Paper no. 1 (March 2004); K. L. Carlson, 'Fighting Firearms with Fire in the OAS: A Critical Evaluation of the Inter-American Convention Against the Manufacturing of and Trafficking in Firearms, Ammunition, and Other Related Materials' (2010) 25 *American University International Law Review* 611–648.

its adoption, the CIFTA has been complemented by a series of 'model regulations' to assist parties in the implementation of almost every area covered by its provisions, including transfer controls, brokering controls, and marking. These developments have been decided within the framework of the Conferences of States Parties, that are periodically convened for the purpose of examining the functioning and application of the Convention. The Conference usually adopts a final text, that, as such, is not binding from a strictly legal perspective.[84] In any case, since final documents are the product of a specific 'cooperative context', they reflect state practice and may be invoked for the interpretation of the Convention, as provided by Article 31 of the 1969 Vienna Convention on the Law of Treaties.

Moreover, the OAS has supported the parties in the implementation of the CIFTA, by designing and implementing various programs and strategies aimed at strengthening capacity of State Parties: the more recent project, called 'Countering Illicit Proliferation and Trafficking of SALW',[85] was funded by the European Union in 2018.[86]

7 Conclusions: The Emerging Threats and the OAS Response

In its res. 2482 (2019), the UN Security Council recognized the role of regional organizations *vis-à-vis* the links between terrorism and organized crime: in deepening the assessment of threats in their respective regions, in strengthening the capacities of Member States, in facilitating technical assistance and information sharing, and in contributing to national ownership and disseminating awareness. The Inter-American system has been strengthened in the past twenty-five years to favor cooperation in the fight against TOC and terrorism. After 9/11, the crime-terror nexus has been mainly conceptualized as a merger of the 'wars' on terror and drugs into a 'war on organized crime': this reflected the belief that the methods and the tools for investigating the origins

84 See e.g. Fourth Conference of the States Parties to the CIFTA, 'Course of Action 2018–2022 for the Operation and Implementation of the CIFTA', OEA/Ser.L/XXII.4.4, CIFTA/CEP-IV/doc.7/18 rev. 4 (5 April 2018).

85 See OAS General Assembly, 'Advancing Hemispheric Security: A Multidimensional Approach', AG/RES. 2945 (XLIX-O/19) (28 June 2019).

86 EU, Council Decision (CFSP) 2018/2010 of 17 December 2018 in support of countering illicit proliferation and trafficking of small arms, light weapons (SALW) and ammunition and their impact in Latin America and the Caribbean in the framework of the EU Strategy against Illicit Firearms, Small Arms & Light Weapons and their Ammunition 'Securing Arms, Protecting Citizens', in OJ L 322 (18 December 2018) 27.

of the illegal funds, to be used to finance terrorism, would be effective for suppressing drug-trafficking, and vice versa.[87]

The OAS has reacted to the challenges posed by the new threats of terrorism and TOC by setting up a regional security governance based on a series of formal and informal international instruments: such action has contributed not only to the harmonization of domestic legislations and the enhancing of cooperation on criminal matters, but also to a more holistic approach on transnational crime.[88] Institutionally, this has led to internal reform with respect to the administrative structure of the organization and the increasing participation of OAS to the net of international organs and bodies having a specific mandate on counter-terrorism and TOC.

Undoubtedly, the contemporary manifestations of terrorism and TOC represent a challenge to the existing regional security regime. The most recent counter-terrorism practice of both the OAS General Assembly and the CICTE significantly reflects the shift in focus to the topic of violent extremism at universal level: the OAS member States have expressed their commitment to implement UN Security Council Resolution 2178 (2014) and 2396 (2017), by developing *inter alia* systems to collect biometric data, as well as "watchlists or databases of known and suspected terrorists, including foreign terrorist fighters."[89] Indeed, the region is not immune to the threat posed by returning foreign terrorist fighters (FTFs): in 2018, it was reported that more than 200 FTFs from States of the Caribbean Community (CARICOM) had travelled to Iraq and the Syrian Arab Republic.[90] Moreover, in recent years, the issue of the protection of critical infrastructure has been mainly understood in terms of the emerging threat of cyber-crime: the OAS General Assembly recommended *inter alia* to consider acceding to the Convention on Cybercrime of the Council of Europe (Budapest Convention),[91] whereas the CICTE adopted four regional

87 See P. Williams, 'Terrorist Financing and Organized Crime: Nexus, Appropriation, or Transformation?' in T. J. Biersteker and S. E. Eckert (eds), *Countering the Financing of Terrorism* (London/New York: Routledge, 2018) 133.

88 See P. Hauck and S. Peterke, 'Transnational Organized Crime', in R. Geiss and N. Melzer (eds), *Oxford Handbook of the International Law of Global Security* (Oxford: OUP, 2021) 213, 227.

89 CICTE, 'Declaration: Strengthening Hemispheric Efforts to Address and Counter Violent Extremism That Is Conducive to Terrorism', OEA/Ser.L/X.2.18, CICTE/DEC.1/18, 4 May 2018.

90 The CARICOM Counter-Terrorism Strategy (26–27 February 2018) https://caricomimpacs.org/wp-content/uploads/2020/11/CARICOM-COUNTER-TERRORISM-STRATEGY-Final.pdf.

91 OAS General Assembly, 'Advancing Hemispheric Security' (n 85) para 67.

confidence-building measures (CBMs) to promote cooperation and trust in cyberspace.[92]

Finally, it is to be observed that the so-called 'securitization' of the discourse on terrorism and TOC has become itself a challenge in the Americas.[93] Both the Inter-American Commission and Court of Human Rights have expressed concern, for instance, with respect to the misuse of counter-terrorism laws and other laws relating to national security, given the risk that the adoption of broad definitions of terrorism may lead to deliberate misrepresentations of the term, for example, to respond to demands of indigenous peoples, as well as of human rights defenders. Since 2002, the IACHR has stressed States' obligation to fully respect human rights in the fight against terrorism: "the very object and purpose of anti-terrorist initiatives in a democratic society is to protect democratic institutions, human rights and the rule of law, not to undermine them."[94]

---

92 CICTE, 'Resolution: Regional Confidence-Building Measures (CBMs) to Promote Cooperation and Trust in Cyberspace, OEA/Ser.L/X.2.19, CICTE/RES. 1/19 (24 May 2019).

93 See H. Carrapiço, Transnational Organized Crime as a Security Concept' in F. Allum and S. Gilmour (eds), *Routledge Handbook of Transnational Organized Crime* (London/New York: Routledge, 2011) 19, 31.

94 IACHR, 'Report on Terrorism and Human Rights', OEA/SER.L/V/II.116, Doc. 5 rev. 1, corr. (22 October 2002) para 15.

Index

www.ingramcontent.com/pod-product-compliance
Lightning Source LLC
LaVergne TN
LVHW020635300926
849161LV00004B/718

* 9 7 8 9 0 0 4 4 2 4 5 6 2 *